The
$\mathscr{H}$APPY $\mathscr{S}$TRIPPER

The
*H*APPY *S*TRIPPER

PLEASURES AND POLITICS
OF THE NEW BURLESQUE

Jacki Willson

I.B. TAURIS
LONDON · NEW YORK

Published in 2008 by I.B.Tauris & Co Ltd
6 Salem Road, London W2 4BU
175 Fifth Avenue, New York NY 10010
www.ibtauris.com

In the United States of America and Canada
distributed by Palgrave Macmillan, a division of St. Martin's Press
175 Fifth Avenue, New York NY 10010

ISBN: 978 1 84511 318 6

A full CIP record for this book is available from the British Library
A full CIP record is available from the Library of Congress

Library of Congress Catalog Card Number: available

Typeset in Chaparral Pro by Sara Millington, Editorial and Design Services
Printed and bound in the Czech Republic by FINIDR, s.r.o.

Supported by  Arts & Humanities
Research Council

The AHRC funds postgraduate training and research in the arts and
humanities, from archaeology and English literature to design and
dance. The quality and range of research supported not only provides
social and cultural benefits but also contributes to the economic success
of the UK. For further information on the AHRC, please see our website
www.ahrc.ac.uk.

Acknowledgements

I thank my editor Susan Lawson for her enthusiasm, rigour and insights, as well as Dr Marsha Meskimmon for her advice, suggestions and wholehearted encouragement.

I need also to express my warm thanks to the contemporary artistes and artists – Ursula Martinez, Jenny Saville and Immodesty Blaize and her efficient assistant Minnie – who kindly allowed me to include the striking and appropriate images in this book. Thanks also to the Arts and Humanities Research Council for their support.

Most of all I must lovingly thank George and Mathilde for their support and patience throughout this project.

Contents

List of Illustrations viii

Introduction: Show Off 1

EMPOWERING, DISEMPOWERING, OVERPOWERING   1

FEMINISM AND POST(-)FEMINISM   8

1. Burlesque 17

WHAT IS BURLESQUE?   17

Crossing into the mainstream   17

Democratic excesses   25

'STARS' AND 'QUEENS'   33

The unruly woman   33

Menacing vamp   40

2. Body as Spectacle 49

THE NUDE   49

Pornography and erotica   49

Histories of female performance   56

THE FEMALE BODY IN PERFORMANCE   63

Carolee Schneemann   63

Hannah Wilke   70

Contents

3. The 'Leg Business' 79

MONEY 79
The man's world of business 79
Ruthless tycoons 87

SEX 95
The unholy trinity (strippers, hookers and porn stars) 95
The courtesan 101

4. Powers of Seduction 111

PAINTED LADIES 111
Artifice 111
Glamour 119

VEILING AND NAKEDNESS 126
Democracy 126
Freedom 133

5. Guerrilla Theatre 143

THE FREAK 143
Subversive submission 143
The freak show 150

KNOWINGNESS 157
Gossip 157
Networking 165

Conclusion: Showdown 173

FEMINIST FLUIDITY 173
Virus 180

Notes 189

Bibliography 211

Index 224

Illustrations

Lydia Thompson as the 'Girl of the Period' (J. Gurney Studios, c.1868). Courtesy of Billy Rose Theatre Collection, The New York Library for the Performing Arts, Astor Lenox, and Tilden Foundations.   16

Plan, 1993, by Jenny Saville. Oil on canvas. 108 × 84 in. Courtesy of the artist and Gagosian Gallery.   48

Gypsy Rose Lee. Courtesy of Culver Pictures.   78

West End bill poster advertising *Immodesty Blaize and Walter's Burlesque*, 2005. Courtesy of Immodesty Blaize, © Immodesty Blaize.   110

Ursula Martinez in *Show Off*, 2001. Courtesy of Ursula Martinez.   142

Introduction: Show Off

EMPOWERING, DISEMPOWERING, OVERPOWERING

*I*n 2001 I went to see a performance artist called Ursula Martinez. The performance – *Show Off* – began with Ursula, clothed sexily in a black dress and stilettos, seductively stripping to music. For three long minutes I sat in a mixed audience and watched, feeling a mixture of pleasure, anger and embarrassment. Winking and smiling, she took off every scrap of clothing and then disappeared behind the curtain. She then reappeared to tell us that that was it, the show was over, and we were now going to have a question-and-answer session. I left the theatre with many, many questions.

That experience was the catalyst for this book.

After the performance the striptease continued to bother me. Why did it bother me? This woman was comfortable with her body, and sexy in her confidence and charisma. Funny. Gutsy. Intelligent. Controlled. Why, therefore, did it continue to bother me? For a start I had voluntarily paid to enter the theatre, so with that payment came an element of trust. I assumed that what I would be seeing would be art. That same exchange of money created a very different situation when I was confronted with striptease, however. I was then thrust into another relationship: that of a voyeur, a sex show client – that of illegitimacy, of side streets, stale smoke, exploitation and cheap thrills.

How did stripping differ in my perceptions when it was advertised as art and housed within an art establishment, rather than a sleazy joint where I imagined men in shifty raincoats filling the room with unrequited lust, dirty secrets and shame? My pleasure and anger came from suddenly feeling immersed in this tense, intense interplay between legitimacy and illegitimacy, danger and safety, pleasure and anger, liberation and vulnerability. I felt exposed and trapped, resentful of being lured there yet completely relishing the experience – shrinking into my seat yet urging Martinez on.

Did she also feel these polarized emotions? As a feminist, were you meant to be feeling offended and uncomfortable with this action? Or were you meant to be cheering her on in affectionate post-feminist support and camaraderie? Was the fact of her being a lesbian (a fact I discovered after the strip) supposed to alter any sense of uneasiness on my part – was it fine to strip as long as you were gay and doing it with a sense of irony?

Post-feminists and antifeminists seem to be saying that it's fine to strip nowadays; we can do what we want, when we want. Where does that leave strippers as artistes? Have we got to the point in feminist progression where these women should now be viewed as empowered workers rather than disempowered, exploited and somehow damaged victims? Should we differentiate at all between a fully sentient performance by an artist like Martinez and a seemingly politically naive performance by an artiste such as, for instance, Dita Von Teese? Taking that further, what about that bad egg the prostitute – is she now our contemporary 'all-woman' heroine?

Does any of this matter anymore? Some young women now feel that these issues are old hat, tired, wearing thin and long overdue for retirement. Does this undermine my own feminist ideals and 1980s 'Alexis Carrington' teenage years? For those not of my generation, *Dynasty*'s acerbic but sexy Alexis Carrington, played by the indomitable Joan Collins, was iconic for her sex appeal, power-dressing, biting intelligence and viciously witty repartee. She represented what many young girls aspired to in terms of strength, assertiveness, intelligence, wit, success and – yes – sexiness. She was far more than just 'sex' and 'body', and she did not have to take her clothes off to gain the upper hand.

What can best be described as an 'anti-objectification militancy' cemented cultural discourse in the 1980s. This discourse was theoretically in tune with British feminist film theorist Laura Mulvey's seminal essay 'Visual pleasure and narrative cinema' (1975),[1] which critiqued mainstream cinematic representations of women – the 'to-be-looked-at-ness' of the female body screened for the male gaze and male pleasure. Feminists, indeed many young women, rallied to eradicate passively sexualized imagery of the female body. These opinions became politically correct and mainstream. Within this context many women pushed for the wholesale banning of 'page three' topless photography, berating this 'art' form as regressive and demeaning to women. Even Britain's institutionalized 'bad' boy James Bond was whipped into shape for his one and only monogamous film *Living Daylights* in 1987.

So why is this 'old-style' feminism now seen to be dated, even a tad ridiculous? The feminism of the 1970s and 1980s leaves many of today's educated young women cold. It has nothing to offer their generation. It is irrelevant. They *want* to be seen as, and *want* to look at, sex objects. In fact, the new 'empowering' model for female sexual agency now seems to be the burlesque stripper. This 'low' burlesque artiste crossed over to 'high' theatres and 'respectable' audiences in the late 1990s, creating what can only be described as a burlesque boom that is only now tailing off. Female artists, such as Ursula Martinez (UK) and Julie Atlas Muz (USA), who are conscious of the implications and history of feminism within performance, see it as a legitimate and pleasurable subject for their art, and artistes like Dita Von Teese and Catherine D'Lish (USA) and Miss Immodesty Blaize (UK) have moved into the 'high' world of fashion and celebrity as influential and desirable icons.

However, what exactly is a burlesque stripper? How does she (if at all) differ from the non-burlesque variety? Stripping of any variety has become mainstream with Jo King's London School of Striptease, the first erotic dance school in Europe, now teaching erotic pole or lap dancing to female students with ages that range from 18 to 76 years old. King founded this school because she wanted women to feel positive about themselves and their bodies. The burlesque phenomenon is connected to this craze for striptease and pole/lap dancing in its affirmation of women's sexual expression. However, unlike pure stripping, burlesque has a sting. It is witty, parodic, erotic 'tongue-in-chic'[2] irony. The burlesque performer looks back, smiles and questions her audience, as well as her own performance, a performance that is comic, outlandish and saucy – a highly camp, mostly vintage spectacle. Burlesque is the 'low' invading the 'high'. It cheekily and brashly moves into the mainstream, adopting its forms – theatre, cabaret, performance art, comedy, circus, modern dance – but without taking any one of these too seriously.

This book does not act as a survey of traditional burlesque or of the contemporary burlesque movement. Michelle Baldwin's *Burlesque {and the New Bump-n-Grind}* (2004) provides very good source material for a chronology and a description of burlesque artistes and acts, and Katharina Bosse's series of photographs in *New Burlesque* (2003) excellently demonstrates the 'wide pallet of glamour'[3] that exists on the burlesque circuit. This book will explore the phenomenon and reference many of its artistes, but for the sake of depth it will focus on the pivotally renowned mainstream artistes: Lydia Thompson (1860/70s), Gypsy Rose Lee (1920/1930s) and Dita Von Teese (1990/2000s). The key question for this book is to ask what this potent re-emergence of burlesque reveals about our contemporary post-feminist condition.

I would like to explore this question fully in the context of a rich feminist history of thinkers and artists, and in relation to the contemporary backdrop of intelligent young (or youngish) women who in the main no longer ascribe to old-school feminism. We are

constantly bombarded with news coverage concerning women's disavowal of feminism (as a word and a concept). A poll conducted by
Womankind Worldwide (an international women's rights organiza-
tion) for the International Women's Day in March 2006 revealed that
71 per cent of UK women declared that they definitely were not feminists.[4] Arifa Akbar writing for the *Independent* argues that the results
of the poll point to a generation of post-feminists who feel that the
term 'feminism' 'carries too much stigma'.[5]

This indifference to 'feminism' can also be seen in the art world.
The artist Tracey Emin, not necessarily 'young' but still a very public
figure and admired by many young women, stated, 'When I was doing
an interview for the Maidstone College, wearing high heels and a low-
cut top and looking like everything else but a feminist, they asked me:
"What do you think about feminism?" I answered them: "I don't".'[6]

This nonchalance informs many women inspired by and contrib-
uting to the present boom in burlesque. It appears acceptable, com-
mendable or even commonplace for many young women to want
to feel the empowerment, excitement and danger that comes from
openly going to see a risqué female performance or the sexual dominating sense of power, control and desire that comes from revealing
their bodies as objects. Are they becoming the aggressors? The ex-
ploiters? The profiteers? The public display of the female body is still a
hotly debated issue (even if some say generational) and an unresolved
point of contention. The actions of a burlesque stripper (as artist or
artiste), or even the actions of a sexily half-dressed young woman 'out
on the town', are still steeped in feminist history – whether or not
this is acknowledged, reflected upon, brushed off or just bracketed
and justified by the all-embracing term 'post-feminist'. Where does
this leave us? With the long, rich legacy of feminist ideas and ideals
seemingly bearing no relation to the present situation – relegated to
a historical middle class; a white, frigid insignificance rather than a
sexual and social panacea. Where do young women now stand who
seek to find a context for their desire to be both the sexy (even down
and dirty) object of the gaze *and* the empowered subject who gazes?

The huge success of burlesque seems to hinge on this perceived chasm that divides the old from the new, the low from the high, feminist from antifeminist, pleasure from empowerment. What kind of post-feminism presents itself? The burlesque body excessively and exquisitely becomes the site for these very issues of gender, sexuality, economics, power, politics, agency and class. In Robert C. Allen's important text on burlesque, *Horrible Prettiness* (1991), he discusses the reaction provoked in the USA by the burlesque phenomenon of the late 1860s. It was, he argues, a struggle over women's sexuality played out through the burlesque performer's body and the debates over the length of her skirt. Their bodies 'bore the burden of signification'.[7] Middle-class society (including the women's rights activists) was legitimizing a certain kind of femininity, the bourgeois concept of ideal 'pure' womanhood, of motherhood and wifehood, whilst rejecting what was deemed impure. Debates were loaded with sexual, race, gender and class implications. The female burlesque performer's body as spectacle became the site for this social struggle over legitimacy; to borrow the title of a book by Colette, a struggle over the pure and the impure.[8] Female sexuality became inextricably linked with morality, national identity, culture, class and economics.

By focusing on the burlesque phenomenon of the 1860s/70s and the 1920s/30s in the USA, what becomes apparent is a persistent, repetitive desire on the part of some women in these periods to want to (or to have to) reassert a sexual, eroticized depiction of their individual womanhood, re-appropriating what had been labelled 'low', 'cheap' and 'disreputable'. In each period, as we shall see, women were becoming more visible in the workplace, more financially self-reliant and more conscious of their own image and the power of their bodies as spectacle. The patterns of resistance against an oppressive concept of 'pure', 'true' and 'respectable' femininity represented itself most ardently in the reaction of the young working-class women (the new arrivals and the home-grown) in both eras, who were being enthused both by middle-class activism and by their newly acquired sense of public power.

This chasm between what was seen as an 'orthodox' sexless feminism or 'correct' femininity and a post-feminism or 'antifeminism' of sexualized dissent permeates feminist history and remains a major sticking point.

For many women growing up in the 1980s, such as myself, stripping or scantily-clad young women created tension. You wanted to be sexy – but in a suit. Your threat, your sexual potency, came from your acquisition of power in the workplace. For me, the title of this book correlates directly with Betty Friedan's landmark pre-feminist text *The Feminine Mystique* (1982 [1963]). In the chapter titled 'The happy housewife' Friedan describes a 'happy' housewife who smiled, and smiled, but secretly pined for 'something more' than housework and childcare to fill a yawning gap in her life.[9] This social arrangement (reproduction) was there to suit the machinations of the economy (production) and not women's need 'to grow and fulfil their potentialities as human beings, a need which is not solely defined by their sexual role'.[10] My title therefore plays on this idea, questioning whether the burlesque stripper *is* happy or whether the overtly 'sexualized' woman is actually pining for something more.

Feminist resistance against female sexualized display is vehemently grounded in the desire of women to be accepted as thinking individuals and not, as Griselda Pollock stated in 1981, 'explicitly as cunt'.[11] For me what continues to disturb greatly are the clearly defined gender and sex roles that still characterize the present-day selling tactics of our consumer culture. In magazines such as *Mizz*, *Sugar* or *Bliss* articles praise women who are 'pretty' and humiliate women who are caught not being 'pretty'. Men deal with the serious 'suited' matter of running the country, the economy and business, and women need to worry about getting fat, dressing well and avoiding wrinkles and cellulite at all costs. The desirability of this cellulite-free and wrinkle-free body is stereotypically sexualized rather than sexual. It is imposed upon a woman (to increase sales and profit) rather than coming from within her.

To slip back into a 'feminist', 'prudish' and 'rigid' way of seeing the world, as some would have it, it makes you wonder how far we have gone. Who really holds the reins of power?

7

... And this brings me back to burlesque.

In the 1860s and 1870s, images of burlesque performers such as Lydia Thompson and Pauline Markham revealed to women a liberated model for female agency that far exceeded the acceptable model of suppressed sexuality depicted by the canonical nude. Historically the burlesque performer used her sexual allure to lampoon this passively 'contained' model of female sexuality and desire that positioned her as talentless, 'low', working class, crude, brash, feminine, passive and sexualized. Her sexual allure therefore undermined this hierarchy in terms of sexuality, gender roles, skill, social decorum and class. It was not just the sexual allure of her body that was seen to be alarming, however, but more provocatively the performer's ability to look back at, smile and speak to her audience directly. This gesture held (and holds) empowering potential.

Does this mean, therefore, that the burlesque performer offers up the potential and possibility for women to intervene as 'knowing', empowered participants in wider sexual, social and economic relationships and systems? Or are there certain forms of burlesque that open up transgressive potential whilst other forms are seemingly naive and regressive, strengthening institutions and values that should be questioned? Is the contemporary burlesque performer a 'happy stripper'?

FEMINISM AND POST(-)FEMINISM

Thus far I have bandied about the term 'post-feminism' loosely without defining exactly what it means. Post-feminism ... postfeminism... Should the meaning change depending on whether or not we hyphenate? There are two evident readings, directions or slants on post-feminism. The hyphen is used as a matter of taste, however, and does not signal any particular meaning intentionally. More sense would be apparent therefore if this hyphen was used purposefully and not just as a semantic accident.

One meaning, let us refer to this as post-feminism, is that of a movement forward from the second wave for the next generation of women, expanding to incorporate class, race, sexuality, religion and ethnicity. This generation uphold the same core ideals of equal rights, opportunities, respect and moving beyond exploitation. What was referred to as the 'third wave of Feminism' exacted this position in the 1990s. 'Girl power' embraced contradiction and accepted that there was no pure 'correct' way to be a feminist. A young woman could wear a tutu and bovver boots, be 'girlie' and sexy *and* be a feminist.

Third-wave feminists set up a polarity, however, a tension between what came before – the Matriarchs – and the exciting, brave new 'young' world. The third-wave feminist permitted sexist banter as longer as it was said ironically; this humour was seen to be another backlash against the humourless foremothers. This intergenerational tension somehow still managed to push forward a 'correct' way of being a feminist, however. Post-feminism, to complicate things further, correlates with postmodernism in its consideration of many identities and different narratives as opposed to one master narrative, one fixed patriarchal–matriarchal way of viewing the world. The use of the hyphen here, therefore, implies both a link and a division.

For the second form, postfeminism, there is no linking hyphen, for the postfeminist generation disregard and disrespect the work achieved by second wave feminism; it means nothing to them, it is old hat … an irrelevance. 'Postfeminism' therefore is a term that strongly signals the attitudes and ideas of a new generation of young women who completely disassociate themselves from the goals of the second wave and the feminism that followed in the subsequent decades. The prefix 'post' thus points to a condition that has happened 'after' with no connection with what happened 'before', and is therefore seen by many second wave feminists and scholars as a 'betrayal of a history of feminist struggle'.[12] Faludi, in her book *Backlash: The Undeclared War Against Women* (1991), argues that postfeminism was the hostile media-fuelled backlash against the gains made by feminism. By calling it an anachronism, tired and passé, feminism would be undermined, negated and discounted. Women did not care. Because of this reaction, postfeminism was also aligned therefore with a relapse to a pre-feminist perspective.

This is obviously a crude simplification. Both terms are all-encompassing, and both terms pride themselves on their intangibility, their lack of succinctness, their openness, their fuzziness. At a Women's History Network conference in September 2005,[13] I spoke to young female scholars about the fuzzy term and what it meant to them. The responses ranged from looking at me incomprehensibly to pure puzzlement. What was gauged was its insufficiency in pinning down women's contemporary experience. One perceptive choice of term was the alternative of 'meta-feminism', a feminism that is self-reflective. Nevertheless we remained in that stalemate with an academic and media-driven language that needs to label to understand but in doing so misses or dismisses actual lived experience. It seems that in the process of stretching the term to accommodate all women it now seems to say nothing much to anybody.

We must also realize the extreme limitations of trying to understand the diversity of contemporary female experience from within a group of predominantly white, educated, middle-class women. This point is not being used to criticise or devalue these women's experiences; it is being used to point to a recurring weakness in feminist history. This 'weakness' showed itself clearly in the showdown between the leading US media 'stars' of the early 1990s like Camille Paglia, Rene Denfeld, Katie Roiphe and Naomi Wolf.[14] These writers urged women to take or grab power and pleasure whilst neglecting to speak about a feminist critique of class, race, capitalist power or unrestrained individualism. From a historical perspective these writers continued the 'feminist' train of thought in that they were all privileged, young white women who, as bell hooks argues, 'strive to create a narrative of feminism ... that recenters the experience of materially privileged white females in ways that deny race and class difference'.[15]

With regard to the current backlash to 'feminism', a spokeswoman for Womankind Worldwide argues that there are many different kinds of feminists who may well have very different ideas of what 'true empowerment' means:

> The dangers with it as an all-encompassing term is that it could mean one group of feminists from the West could end up telling women from other cultures what 'true empowerment' is when, in actual fact, this is debatable.[16]

What does 'true empowerment' mean to the many young women in the West who reject the 'empowerment' fought for by old-style feminists? New burlesque performer Bella Beretta from the Gun Street Girls comments:

> Women in the audience left our show thinking, 'Wow, she can be flippant, she can be rude, she can be really sexy, she can be big – I want to be like that.' I hate the word *empowered*, but I think that's what they felt.[17]

In this context the word 'empowerment' is linked to the word 'feminism' in that it belongs to an historical and political context that appears chasms away from contemporary young women's experience and desires to re-image how they look and feel. It is a term that is hated but begrudgingly applied to describe this narrated experience.

This tension, this distrust, however explicit in these struggles between feminisms, between difference, between correctness and incorrectness, between the pure and impure, return us to the heart of that seemingly insignificant hyphen that can be used to divide 'post' from 'feminism'. This bracketed hyphen is ripe with what is and has been the most vibrant, ambivalent and provocatively divisive debate in feminist discourse – the female body and its representation and pleasure. Burlesque sits at this point of contradiction, struggle and resistance, at that dichotomous interception between feminism and postfeminism. It becomes the hyphen that binds them together, kicking and screaming, in the dangerously pleasurable, 'low' 'Nude Woman'.[18]

This is not a book about stripping per se. There is already a good quantity of well-researched, thought-provoking studies in this area, including those by Judith Lynne Hanna, Katherine Liepe-Levinson and Rachel Shteir.[19] What can be drawn from these studies is many women's contemporary unease with any rigid positioning vis-à-vis the body, the gaze, sexuality and pleasure. This research sits on slippery terrain that does not permit reductive and simplistic presentations of strippers or stripping. Their argument is neither wholly about empowerment nor wholly about exploitation, but somehow holds both positions. This is where this book begins its premise. It explores contemporary considerations of feminism as they present themselves through art, performance, class, the female body, sexuality, gender, politics and economics, but ultimately through a more open, less polarized, more complex perspective.

I will begin in Chapter 1 by describing and exploring the phenomenon of burlesque. As well as the most recent manifestation at the turn of the millennium, this chapter will draw clear parallels with two other key eras, eras that moved from the 1860s to the 1870s and from the 1920s into the 1930s. These were eras of extremes: eras that moved out of war, into the excesses of economic boom and then into the fallout of economic bust. They were also eras of bingeing and repression in terms of alcohol, debt and inflation, of suppression, depression and hedonism. The peak of burlesque's emergence into middle-class theatres took place in the exact years when depression was also in its lowest trough. When the mainstream economic system was at its weakest, burlesque's excesses, anarchy, bawdy humour and insubordinate spirit mimicked the hedonism of the boom, accentuating the question of who was permitted access to capital, power and legitimacy.

As burlesque's figurehead the female performers (the soubrettes) sexualized and lampooned these historical moments by making power more transparent. Their transgressive 'horrible prettiness' threatened because it subversively refused categorization and categorically refused to compromise, kowtow or conform. This performer expressed the seductive powers of femininity in terms of flesh, beauty and artifice, and masculinity in terms of public freedoms – political and legal, earning a living and the power of speech. This chapter will explore the social phenomenon of burlesque as it coalesced at two localized historical points in the USA, in order to draw together more insightful conclusions about its contemporary, more global manifestations.

Chapter 2 will then situate this burlesque phenomenon within a wider feminist context. I will refer to two key performance artists, Carolee Schneemann and Hannah Wilke, in order to begin to understand why and how this recent eruption of burlesque into contemporary culture points to a particular strand of feminist thought that threads its way alongside and counter to traditional feminist politics. Traditional feminists, and by 'traditional' I mean those predominantly middle-class women's rights activists of the movement that took root in the late nineteenth century, insisted that women had to secure their power in the public domain by virtue of their mind and not their prettiness. Wilke and Schneemann were reacting against what was seen as this 'fascist' streak within feminism and a patriarchal blind spot in art history that denied the possibility of female pleasure and agency. However, by using the very same image that was deeply entrenched in the patriarchal, capitalist system as commodity and pornographic object they teetered on dangerously ambivalent ground. They were either seen as antifeminist, or castigated for their social and moral irresponsibility. The ideas of key feminist thinkers (Dworkin, Vance, Paglia and Wolf) will be interwoven in this chapter in order to demonstrate a deeply polarized polemic that has permeated feminist debate.

Chapters 3 and 4 will explore how the burlesque performer used her 'femininity' to penetrate, exploit and make transparent the power dynamics at play within the patriarchal capitalist system that sought to subjugate and eradicate women's erotic pleasure and their economic, social, political and cultural power as citizens. In the first instance I will examine the subject of money and exchange in relation to the female performer of burlesque. Burlesque was described as a 'leg business'. Its performers were astute businesswomen who realized the power of publicity. They hired their own press agents and exploited their sensational sexy acts to the full in absolute awareness of burlesque's own exploitation of a desperate situation. The girls were cheap and the punters were in need of distraction from war, poverty and broken families.

The second part of Chapter 3 will look at that unholy trinity of the porn star, stripper and hooker. Prostitution gives young working-class women economic benefits but, like the son who is encouraged to become a boxer, this route is rarely one of choice but of necessity. The late nineteenth-century courtesan (nouveau riche prostitute) may have represented this potential for 'upward mobility' and success, admired by women and feared by men, for she was economically, sexually, emotionally and intellectually central and powerful. Does the power that comes with stripping (or even prostitution) allow women to control, benefit and make transparent that historical, potentially oppressive relationship between men and women?

Chapter 4 expands further this question. Where does the actual power reside – and indeed, what constitutes 'power'? Why is it currently 'fashionable' in the Western world to be seen as a sex object? The burlesque boom is predominantly made up of US, UK and some Australian and European artistes and clubs, festivals and conventions.[20] Why is this the case? The dominant Western viewpoint, in the post-9/11 political climate, sees the permission to reveal flesh as a visual sign of democracy in the West, as opposed to the Islamic hijab that is, by contrast, viewed as a symbol of oppression. Is the revelation of flesh ultimately a source of power or are girls and young women colluding in something that gives superficial 'empowerment' in relation to sexual prowess without any possibility of obtaining any real transformative power or political worth?

This chapter explores the West's interpretation of veiling as a symbol of oppression and how the freedom to wear scantily-clad clothing has become a modern sign of democracy at work. Why is flesh and the ability to titillate and seduce seen as empowering to women? What kind of power is this? This chapter examines in more detail women's desire to construct their identities and, on the flip side of this, the point where this unstable sense of self is made to feel insecure.

Chapter 5, the final chapter, exposes and expresses this ambivalent stance through the knowing address of the burlesque performer. Her contradictory presence as a thinking spectacle works within and against stereotypes: criticizing, commenting and pleasurably regaining control over her sexuality and image. Could this articulation of a stance that seems to both take pleasure from and collude with the sexual objectification of women dissolve women's status as victims? Does burlesque need politically self-conscious performers like Britain's queen of burlesque Immodesty Blaize or Australia's Lola the Vamp, for it to be both sexy and subversive?

What this book sets out to achieve is to present young women with a context and a voice within which to situate themselves as feminists who desire both to look and be seen. What does burlesque tell us now about their feminist condition? The desire for pleasure as well as agency has always been awkwardly couched within feminist discourse. Artists expressed this ambivalence, expressed this suppression, this perceived 'fascism' and these divisive hierarchical power relations in their art and through their bodies. The intentions of this book are twofold: first, to present young women with a context, and second, to draw a bridge between antagonistic foes by positively articulating polarization, dissonance and ambivalence that intercept and fold imperceptibly into the phenomenon of burlesque.

Does the re-emergence of burlesque begin to articulate another feminism or postfeminism that supersedes traditional feminist ideology? Is this yet another wave? It is a delicious metaphor. Waves lap onto the mainland, making seemingly imperceptible changes that nevertheless over time make quite major changes to the geography of that shore. They advance and they regress. They always leave the beach with a few washed-up unwanted items, however.

There is no quick-fix sensationalist answer. I seek not to find another glib media-fired reductionist '-ism', a fourth wave or an ingenious all-embracing term. The question I seek to explore is whether by appropriating an objectified image, by being the sex object, this new feminism can shift the frame and allow women to engage as powerful participants from within the system. Art has to engage the body so that we can be transformed by the body[21] and not just the mind; it needs to disturb, to create polarized tension in order to challenge us and change us in an almost invasive, involuntary as well as pleasurable way. It needs to be dangerously pleasurable. This book seeks to explore these issues intelligently and plainly without, as Andrea Dworkin would have said it, too much 'academic horse-shit'.[22]

Lydia Thompson as the 'Girl of the Period'
(J. Gurney Studios, *c.*1868).

1.

Burlesque

WHAT IS BURLESQUE?

Crossing into the mainstream

We are in the thick of a new wave of burlesque. This formidable display of flesh seductively draws us back to a time of the eroticized pin-up. It propels us back into that era of hard glamour where such cinematic characters as Marlene Dietrich or Elizabeth Taylor reigned supreme. This provocative sexuality bubbles breathlessly from the fashion pages of glossy magazines and lures us from pop music videos and film. Does this forthright display of sexualized women take us right back to a prefeminist 1950s state, or does it communicate something much more pressing about our present post(-)feminist condition? Young women are embracing and indulging in the 'feel good' pleasures that come from this voluptuous posing and performing of 'femininity'. Not only does this display seem to acquiesce with the dominant values of surface, profit and 'vacuous' gratuitous imagery but it also profoundly departs from the 'speed' and 'slog' of everyday toil. It basks in the deliciousness of living in both a sexual and sexualized body. In order to understand the pleasures and politics of this new burlesque movement it is essential first to investigate thoroughly the phenomenon of burlesque as a historical form and as a platform for its Stars and Queens.

Modern American burlesque was launched in the late nineteenth century by the British Blondes who took New York by storm in 1868 with their chaotic and nebulous combination of dancing, singing, minstrelsy, witty repartee, political commentary, parodies of plays and scant clothing – described as the 'leg business'. At their peak in 1873 they completely cut out any reference to English plays and concentrated instead purely on frenzied can-can kicking, more revealing costumes and political witty interjections. By the 1930s the sexualized spectacle of the female performer became the catalyst for more sensation and scandal with the advent of the striptease perfected by 'star' strippers such as Gypsy Rose Lee, who then moved into mainstream legitimate theatres. A 'burlesque revival' began in 1994 with striptease artistes like Dita Von Teese headlining in strip clubs all over the USA.

Burlesque's anarchic and nonsensical concoction of forms and its figurehead sexualized, witty female performer had clear political intent. It fulfilled a necessary transgressive function, which was to undermine hierarchy in terms of authority, gender, form, skill, theatrical distance, social decorum and class. It was a testing ground that pushed and crossed boundaries aesthetically, culturally and politically. However pushing back and through limits set up a continual struggle between legality–legitimacy and illegality–illegitimacy. Burlesque teetered close to the edge of the law and consequently became an endless balancing act between pleasing censors and entertaining audiences. If burlesque can be read as sitting precariously in this in-between position then the periods in Northern American history between 1868 (the Blondes' debut in the USA) leading up to the depression of 1873 and the early 1930s, from which this chapter draws, are extremely appropriate choices for examination.

These crucial periods (the precursory and declining years) saw burlesque at its most potent: they were burlesque booms. As well as being viewed as a 'cultural phenomenon' in the 1860/70s,[1] and in its 'heyday' in the 1930s,[2] burlesque was also being rebuffed by anti-burlesque campaigners (ministers, suffragettes, literary figures and legislators) as a 'disease'. Clear parallels can be drawn between both eras to account for these extreme polar reactions. Both eras were periods of depression, repression and suppression, with a population reeling from war and anxious about national, social and personal security. Ultimately they were also times of hedonism: the boom and bust of capitalism's unbridled free market. Depressed by war (the American Civil War, 1861–5) and repressed by the bifurcation and 'bourgeoisification'[3] of the theatre and the outlawing of alcohol (which effectively closed down the honky tonk and created the subterranean culture of the speakeasy in the late 1920s), audiences were ready for something fresh, appealing and raw – and, in the case of the 1930s, cheap!

Explicit parallels can be drawn with contemporary North American history, which presents similar patterns. The terrorist events of 9/11 created a deep-seated sense of insecurity and suspicion of the 'other', in particular the Arab or Muslim 'other', and with it came a tightening up of national borders and individual citizenship. My argument makes clear comparisons between the present boom in burlesque and the other key burlesque boom periods that have been interpreted as similarly unsettling times.[4]

During the earlier key burlesque boom periods migrants and immigrants were coming to live and work in the city, bringing with them different cultural, political and theological values. The harshness of material existence also exerted its rigours on family life. Facing challenges to his role as the sole provider, the father/husband was also forced to concede some of his control over the household, sparking re-negotiating debates over gender and sexual roles. Industrial growth, overproduction and depression (the Long Depression, from 1873 to mid-1890s, and the Great Depression, 1929–36) created a transitory, dispossessed, disillusioned urban population. As with the contemporary era, there was a creeping cynicism with regard to governance.

Burlesque expressed this sense of chaos, instability and the *mélange* of a newly structuring, harsh, unsettled yet exciting urban environment. It needed to entertain and please a wide ethnic, cultural and racial mix without homogenizing. It did this by poking fun at all, like a court jester; a great leveller at a time when difference and hierarchy could so clearly have been a source of acute tension. This present moment in history also echoes this instability in terms of race, ethnicity and culture, with the evident tension in relation to terrorist attacks against the USA on 11 September 2001 and against Britain on 7 July 2005 – and also with race and immigration dominating pre-election campaigning in both countries (the run up to the 6 May 2005 elections in the UK and re-election campaign of George Bush in November 2004 in the USA). Burlesque, it seems, takes off at particularly tense and potentially eruptive pressure points in history when hierarchy, borders and boundaries oscillate and reshuffle.

The first 'wave' of burlesque was steeped in excess. It gluttonously consumed the city's energy and values – its speed and vitality as well as its harshness – communicating viscerally, theatrically and verbally the social and personal impact of industrialization. It insubordinately mimicked the greed and opportunism of the mainstream business economic boom whilst refusing to accept the limits of appropriateness imposed on the body and the mind by that very system. The effects of this insubordination became more fascinating and more subversive when burlesque 'crossed over' successfully to the middle-class audience. When the British Blondes hit the headlines in 1868 in their daring, shocking costumes the performances were at first welcomed excitedly, as they added fruitiness to an otherwise dull, predictable and passive theatre experience. As realization sunk in of their fast-growing popularity and their effect, however, what at first was seen as a refreshing distraction was soon perceived to be a glaring cause for concern.

The Blondes' streetwise coarse language and explicit, exuberant spectacle of female sexuality put class, gender and sexuality firmly at the centre of the social agenda. This was not pure titillation, went the cry; it was polluting, it was immoral. The focal point for this furore was the female figure of the burlesque 'Queen' (Lydia Thompson or Pauline Markham of the British Blondes) or 'Star' (Mae West, Gypsy Rose Lee, Ann Corio). Their unruly burlesque body contravened or exceeded what was appropriate for female behaviour with their 'horrible prettiness', so consequently they were punished either by arrest or caricatured humiliation. With 'star' strippers like Gypsy Rose Lee, it was not purely about the 'strip' or about the 'script'. It was not just the sexual allure of their bodies that was seen to be alarming but, more provocatively, the performer's ability to address their audience directly. In 1931 Gypsy Rose Lee formulated a parody patter, 'The Psychology of the Stripteaser', which she relayed to the audience whilst stripping:

> Have you the faintest idea about
> the private thoughts of a strip teaser?
> Well the things that go on in a strip-teaser's mind,
> Would give you no end of surprise...
> For example,
> When I raise my skirt with slyness and dexterity,
> I'm mentally computing just how much I'll give to charity...[5]

In a sense though, the exact words that Gypsy Rose Lee said during her performances are irrelevant. Much of her legacy is constructed around her reputation for cleverness and wit as the 'intellectual stripper',[6] being recognized as the 'perfect compromise between sex and brains',[7] 'most admired in the business by the highbrows and intellectuals of the city'[8] and as the 'teaser with a wink... sophisticate, author... superior in intelligence'.[9] It was her public image that counted, how she came across in the newspapers, in her publicity, by word-of-mouth, in the audience's memory and in her own accounts and public appearances. John Steinbeck wrote on the back cover of her memoirs, *Gypsy*, 'I found it quite irresistible. It's quite a performance. I bet some of it is even true, and if it wasn't, it is now.'[10] What Gypsy really said and really did does not seem to matter, but what does matter is how she was perceived and how she profited from and built upon this perception.

Lydia Thompson's reputation for direct retort was equally moulded and exacerbated by the media gossip, reviews and public hearsay and conjecture of her time. The infamous horsewhipping of the editor of the *Chicago Times* in February 1870, which purportedly ended in a court showdown and fine, was enough to arouse the public's attention and draw in huge crowds. Headlines relished the event: 'WHEN LYDIA LAID ON THE LASH... Chicago's Editor had Attacked the "Blondes" and Received a Severe Castigation'.[11] Allegedly, on the very same night the episode was recounted during her performance, with humorous ad-libbing. At the end Thompson addressed the audience, thanked them for their support and stated that although she had breached the law:

> The persistent and personally vindictive assault in the *Times* upon my reputation left me only one mode of redress... They were women whom he attacked. It was by women he was castigated... We did what the law would not do for us.[12]

The story changes in every account. Bernard Sobel claims in his account that Lydia Thompson admitted that it did not even happen: 'there had never been a horsewhipping; Mr. Story had not attacked her morals.'[13] Whether true or not the story caused a stir, its impact resonating with the audience both inside and outside the theatre. The dissonance and excess of burlesque therefore spilled out of the confines of the theatre and played out in the law courts, newspapers, streets and homes.

It was this cross-fertilization between the outside and the inside, fact and fiction, the public and the private, initiated and channelled through the independent, scathing, uncontrollable and witty address of the female burlesque performer that was considered so dangerous to the status quo. She was expressing and challenging (verbally and physically) certain values and behaviour that were anathema to what was expected of women in society. Ramona Curry in her essay on Mae West states that it was the technique of the address that signalled a star's presence; the characters that West played were seen as mouthpieces through which her own values and morality were voiced. So when West's character stated in *Goin' to Town* (1935): 'You're all right to play around with, but as a husband, you'd get in my hair!' audience members immediately took this to be West's own flippant attitude towards marriage and men, and a conspiratorial bond was created. The words were read 'extracinematically as well as diegetically',[14] which politicized by publicizing private, taboo thoughts. It gave women permission to laugh and permission to think beyond the accepted. Worst of all, from the point of view of her critics, Mae West as an influential icon was acting as a positive, glamorous example (probably the reason why she was so heavily censored), giving such transgressive behaviour and thoughts credence. Her address united and encouraged other women through subversive humour and wit.

Female performers of burlesque, the soubrettes, with their strong, politicized, charismatic and independent public personae, embodied the more visible and insubordinate female presence. They also embodied the potential threat that women held as future workers and family members. The fact is that women had only formed part of the workforce because of an economic demand during the downswing, and burlesque performers were only getting the work because men reeling from the depression sought cheap, sexy entertainment – but it also left an opening for women to begin to define their newly forming identities as well as their newly politicized female pleasure in resistance. Within their address was the possibility, even if it did not materialize, of permanent transformation at home and in the workplace. Lydia Thompson and the Blondes violated gender norms with their topsy-turvy bold speech and male clothing that revealed their female contours.

The demand for this spectacle of late-1860s Thompsonian burlesque was launched in the USA quite 'by accident'[15] when its direct predecessor The Black Crook, an all-women ballet troupe, performed at Niblo's Garden on Broadway in 1866. This 'mass display of ladies' legs on stage'[16] was only given theatrical space to help out the managers, who had a London ballet troupe and scenery but no theatre, after the Academy of Music on Fourteenth Street burned down. This parade appealed to bored theatre-goers and played to full houses as revivals over 25 years.

The great success of Adah Isaacs Menken, 'The Naked Lady', also created the phenomenal demand for more risqué entertainment. In 1861 Menken starred in a production adapted from Byron's *Mazeppa* when she rode onto stage on horseback, as if naked, in a flesh-coloured bodysuit. However, these performers did not directly address the audience. What was seen to be more dangerous about the British Blondes as a cultural phenomenon was not just that these women were parodying and sexualizing their historical moment but, more dangerously, that they were directly communicating with and politicizing an audience, beyond the confines of the mainstream theatre.

Why is burlesque a cultural phenomenon once again? Indeed, there has been a recent surge in books on burlesque and striptease.[17] Pushing burlesque even further into the mainstream, in 2006, the Undisputed Queen of British Burlesque, Miss Immodesty Blaize (whose signature trademark is an 8ft sparkling rocking horse), launched the Dior rouge lipstick range. In June 2007 she won the coveted Miss Exotic World title in Las Vegas. (Immodesty is now seen to be *the* performer who brought British burlesque out of the underground, having danced in Goldfrapp's music video for the single 'Train' in 2003.) Indeed in the UK burlesque has now even reached the West End, with the production *Immodesty Blaize and Walter's Burlesque*. What does this re-emergence of the female burlesque star say about our contemporary post(-)feminist condition?

In order to understand how this figurehead of burlesque impacts on our present cultural situation it is first necessary to plot in greater depth the economic, political, social and cultural function, and impact of burlesque as a form of entertainment and as a business.

Democratic excesses

The peak of burlesque's emergence into middle-class theatres occurred exactly in the years when depression was in its deepest trough. The key periods of 1868–73 and the late 1920s and early 1930s marked the years of boom and bust that moved the USA in and out of the nadir of the Long Depression in 1873 and the Great Depression in 1933. Scholars do not offer a uniform explanation for these depressions. Nevertheless, connections can be made. The transition costs and economic shifts associated with moving into the Second Industrial Revolution (1870–1914) with all its technological advances (steel, chemicals, iron), and its bad loans and over-speculation in railroads and manufacturing possibly could have attributed to the decline that took place between 1873 and the mid-1890s. Similarly the Great Depression, the deepest, most catastrophic depression in US history, followed on from the 'over-investment' and over-speculation of the Roaring Twenties, creating a financial bubble that finally and dramatically crashed on what is now referred to as Black Thursday.

Equally the long dot.com boom of the 1990s, the longest period of growth in the twentieth century, led to what is now seen as the lowest point for profits in the USA for four decades. In 2001 corporate bankruptcies were at the same massive level as in the recession of the 1930s. The effects of these booms and busts were felt internationally, the most recent downturn beginning with the East Asian financial crisis that started in Thailand in July 1997 and spread to the entire global economy, affecting stock markets and currencies. Like both the Long and Great Depressions this economic slump has been attributed to over-speculation, bad investment, credit, and the economic shifts and transition costs of the technological revolution. It is also interesting to note that all three of these periods were peaks in wealth inequality. In the immediate aftermath of the

US Civil War in 1865 the top 1 per cent of households owned one-quarter of the nation's wealth. In 1929 the richest 1 per cent in the USA owned 45 per cent of the national wealth, although this was reduced dramatically following the Wall Street Crash.[18] And in recent history, it was discovered in 2001 that in the USA and the UK the top 5 per cent had 50 times the level of financial assets of the median household.[19]

Irving Zeidman, author of *The American Burlesque Show* (1967), states: 'Burlesque thrives on depression.'[20] Burlesque thrives when the mainstream economic system collapses and tries to recover. Burlesque flourishes when the economic bubbles sink and burst. Murray N. Rothbard in *America's Great Depression* comments that, 'the depression is the 'recovery' process... the necessary and beneficial return of the economy to normal after the distortions imposed by the boom'.[21] He describes this recovery process as a period of 'consumer retribution'. Entrepreneurial demand shifts as the economy returns to the most efficient way of satisfying 'voluntarily expressed'[22] consumer demands. Prices come down as consumers and businesses try to rein in spending. Burlesque can therefore be seen to be fulfilling a consumer need – it is cheap, sexy, fast, funny entertainment, and the democratic consequence of a laissez-faire deregulated system. It is consumer-determined. It can be said therefore that burlesque solely mimicked, burlesqued and embraced the very capitalist excesses enjoyed by the bourgeois and ruling classes during the boom; that it therefore turned the world upside down, like carnival.

Burlesque cannot be explained away so simply, however. What burlesque did – and this is the key to burlesque as a social phenomenon – was to break down rigid boundaries that had become untenable. It was about excess, about exceeding the conventions, expectations, legitimacy, decency and regulated divisions that had been erected to protect those who were in control and to legitimize their access to power and capital. Rather than inverting polarities, however, burlesque exceeded and pushed through these polarized limits. It embraced both low and high culture irreverently, combining the two in a chaotic, disrespectful and nonsensical melting pot. The British Blondes used skeletal plots of classical tales such as *Ixion*, *The Forty Thieves* and *Sinbad* in order to hang topical allusions, double entendres, outrageous punning, rhymed pentameter and a fast and furious display of popular song and dance (such as the can-can).

Their bastardization of the Greek myth of Ixion put Lydia Thompson in the lead role of Ixion, the king of Thessaly who lost all of his money by betting and could no longer afford to pay the dowry for his new wife. He kills his father-in-law, which compels Ixion's wife to revolt against him. After calling on Jupiter (Ada Harland) for protection, Jupiter asks Ixion to come and live with the gods on Mount Olympus. However, when Ixion then goes on to flirt with Venus and his wife Juno, Jupiter commands that as punishment he should be tied to a giant, fiery celestial wheel. In the rewriting of this tale, the wheel becomes the steering wheel of a ship.

By putting herself behind the wheel, Thompson turns the tables – 'Ixion's *welfare*, that's Ixion's *weal*'[23] [the archaic word for prosperity or well-being] – to boldly assert another order, with riches, success and prosperity in her hands. Robert C. Allen states that this play acts to 'dig' at the elite's rising divorce figures and also that Thompson's portrayal of Ixion is an allusion to '"the wickedest man in the world", a notorious rake and con man who had recently launched a lucrative second career as a lecturer on the evils of his past'.[24] The female performer was a powerfully effective and affective tour de force, for she resolutely crystallized all of the ruling powers' fears with regard to the 'liberated' modern woman. Thompson's sexual and gender identity not only questioned how women were ranked and restricted in society but also tangentially questioned the 'naturalization' of white bourgeois power with its 'legitimate' access to the 'perks' of power, money and status.

It was this 'equal' access to money and privilege, this breaking down of the boundaries that were there to exclude and to protect, that was so unsettling for the ruling powers. In 1877 Sir Eskine

K. May warned about 'democratic excesses'.[25] A balance needed to be drawn whereby the common people (democracy) had sufficient enough stake in the system in order to 'guarantee the bourgeois social order and avoid the risk of its overthrow'.[26] Drawing a tenuous balance between order and disorder thus entailed a degree of compromise. In order for the ruling (and at this stage, the growing) middle classes to continue maintaining power economically, politically and socially, the system had to expand to include (even if only as lip service) the common people.

In the late nineteenth century, metropolitan industrial capitalism was forcing many changes on the city. One of the major threats to the established distribution of wealth and power was the new arrivals, via the phenomenon of immigration, and their contribution to the enormous rush of change and invention. The first major influx of immigrants happened between 1844 and the Civil War in 1860. These immigrants were mainly Irish and German, with the second wave between 1899 and 1924 predominantly Eastern and Southern European, such as the Slavs, Poles and Italians who were escaping extreme poverty, as well as Jews who had been driven out by Russian pogroms. Many post-Civil War old-stock Anglo-Saxon Americans felt alienated and threatened by the sprawling metropolis and the immigrants, whom they saw as deflating wages and bringing in unwanted behaviour and cultural values that were in conflict with their Victorian values and ideals. Victorian Americans generally believed in order, hard work and sobriety.

This ordered behaviour was rooted in the early days of colonization when 'those people who worked almost incessantly survived and those who played did not'.[27] On the whole the immigrants were seen to value the pleasures of life that came from the warmth of friends and family to those of hard work and the ideology of success. Ethnic stereotypes were swiftly built up, and the immigrant groups were perceived to behave in particular ways. The Irish, Slavs and Germans loved to drink; Jew, Italians and Poles had a long tradition of dancing; the Germans liked to play cards; Jews and Catholics (who constituted the majority of immigrants) were generally more liberal in their attitudes to sex. As 'birds of passage',[28] the new arrivals harboured an overall suspicion of authority and a blanket refusal to 'Americanize',[29] preferring instead the close-knit groups of the family, saloon or tavern.

The irreconcilable differences and tensions that emerged between the old and new stock fused with explosive energy in the honky tonk. Honky tonks, originating in places such as Oklahoma and Texas, were bawdy disreputable variety shows with attached gambling houses and bars. They would also have had a private box or 'third tier' where the female performers would go to privately 'entertain' members of the audience in between numbers. Many of the female burlesque performers were said to have come from this harsh environment where you had to be incisively quick-witted to survive. Up until the New York Astor Place Theatre Riot of 1849 there had been no hard-and-fast class divisions between theatres, with all theatres attracting mixed clientele. After 1849 theatres became divided along class lines, however, with certain theatres locating to more respectable areas in order to cater for families, women and more 'gentile' clients. There was definitely no third tier and no alcohol. Honky tonk saloons were gradually closed down until they were outlawed in April 1862 and driven underground.

As the predecessor to burlesque this drinking saloon diffused the threat of the other by being pleasing to and expressive of this wide plethora of identities, this 'ethno-cultural fragmentation'.[30] At an extreme level the threat of the other was finding outlets in the voice and actions of the Klu Klux Klan, created in the 1860s and reconfigured again in the 1920s heyday of heavy industrialized and urban growth in the production cities of the North East and Midwest. In the honky tonks, the girls, alcohol and bawdy humour that poked fun at all tempered the threat of the 'other', and distracted from their shared hardships and anxieties. The honky tonk mediated the pleasures that came from the buzz and excitement of earning a wage within an ever-expanding industrialized capitalist city as well as providing an escape from its cramped tenements and grinding repetitive factories. (Hobsbawm states that it was in the 1860s that the word 'capitalism'[31] entered political and economic vocabulary.) When the middle-class economic defences were weakened by depression, honky tonk haemorrhaged through the bourgeois walls of respectability creating the phenomenon that is termed burlesque. Burlesque was seen as a disease of tastelessness. It was in fact a fluid, formless testing ground of a transitional system ripe with potential.

Burlesque's success with middle-class audiences could indeed have been a necessary backlash, providing release from a society that had become untenably bland, clinical, cold and rigidly divisive. By the 1860s the onset of metropolitan industrial capitalism in cities such as New York, Detroit, Boston, Indiana and Illinois drastically reduced the chances of many journeymen (craftsmen who moved around to find work) owning their own business. Many of these workers, skilled and unskilled, native born and immigrant, black and white, had to move into cramped tenement housing. What this change in economic status also brought in its stead was a reliance on a growing bourgeoisie – the middle class – who now owned the factories and was seeking to assure its own standing by insisting on hierarchy and the 'bourgeoisification' of forms and behaviour. This not only sharply defined how the middle-classes should behave but also, more importantly, delineated what they should be spurning.

It is important to point out though that the USA in the late nineteenth century was predominantly Protestant, and this perhaps gives us another perspective on this era of industrial capitalism. Max Weber argues in *The Protestant Ethic and the Spirit of Capitalism* (1904/5) that there was more than 'pure egocentric motives'[32] involved in the seemingly self-driven desire to earn money and succeed. The biblical quotation – 'Seest thou a man diligent in his business? He shall stand before kings'[33] – was used to compel sons to follow in their father's footsteps. The duty of a calling, the proficiency in a profession, 'was intended to lead him in the path of righteousness'. Weber also comments that, 'the earning of more and more money, combined with the strict avoidance of all spontaneous enjoyment of life, is above all completely devoid of any eudaemonistic, not to say hedonistic, admixture'.[34] Emotional bonds and fleshly pleasures are therefore repressed in a bid to fulfil one's duty to God.

Christine Stansell argues that young women had a very different position within this system. Economies that were built around family businesses would have been unquestionably patriarchal. One could argue, therefore, that the transition of work from the home to the factory would have given many young working-class women (both American-born and the new arrivals) an opportunity for more freedom because they were now able to earn their own money. Charlotte Perkins Gilman in her book *Women and Economics* (1898) gives one a more solid picture of what economic dependency amounted to for women in the late Victorian era. Gilman argues that as long as women remained dependent on men they would remain 'chattel'. They would not develop their characters but would just rely on maintaining their attractiveness because this was their 'purchasability'.[35] It was not the 'sex-relation' that was incompatible with human progress but the 'sexuo-economic relation', which makes both sexes individualist and both sexes therefore weaker.[36]

However, the young women who were going out to earn their money found themselves sandwiched between many inconsistencies. They wanted to work hard for a living, yet they also wanted to enjoy the fruits of their labour: late nineteenth-century Calvinist asceticism was framed within an enticing city made up of many new tastes, sounds and sensations. They wanted to embrace opportunities in this 'land of the free' and yet they were faced with many class, gender and sexual restrictions. Any attempts to move up the social ladder would have been seen as impertinent and any display of riches seen as the frivolous, greedy antics of the nouveau riche. Many young working women wanted to re-image and refashion themselves in the public arena as vivacious, independent and sexual. Yet they were also faced with a middle-class women's rights movement that was setting expectations for correctness and decorum. Female burlesque performers, as well as the few male burlesque comics, came from this background and this inconsistent context.

In the 1930s Gypsy Rose Lee was reacting against these continuing discrepancies in her act. Her act 'A Stripteaser's Education' (1936)[37] is a fine example of burlesque's attempts to lampoon the aristocracy and the middle classes, whilst also daring to hint at the sexuality bubbling under the surface of even the most refined 'lady'. A potent combination of sexy stripping and intelligence had given this working-class girl the opportunity to live a life of riches and socialize with the intellectual elite. In this act she dresses up as 'The Gibson Girl' who was seen to personify the feminine, innocent aristocratic 'ideal': youthful features, tall, slim, hour-glass figured, tightly corseted and wasp-waisted with hair piled up on the top of the head in a 'chignon'. This image endured until after the First World War when this overtly elegant and 'feminine' style went out of fashion with many young women, who now preferred the more sober masculine suits by such designers as Coco Chanel.

Perhaps as a backlash to the feminist rhetoric of the 1920s, Gypsy was articulating a different perspective on 'empowerment'. She could be at once working class and privileged, 'feminist' and 'feminine', political and sexy. As part of her patter, she explains in rhyme that while she is revealing part of her shoulder to the audience, she is not thinking about their reaction:

> I am thinking of my country house
> And the jolly fun in shooting grouse
> And the frantic music changes, then off to my cue
> But I only think of all the things I really ought to do.
> Wire Leslie Howard, Cable Noel Coward
> Go to Bergdorf's for my fitting, buy the yarn for my mother's
>   knitting
> Put preserves up by the jar, and make arrangements for my church
>   bazaar.[38]

By using humour intelligently and cheekily, she diffuses any real antagonism. She 'gets away with' her parody of the elite as well as daring to be amongst them. Like Mae West, Gypsy Rose Lee never renounced her working-class roots.

At particularly unstable points in history, unsettling modes of thinking becomes highly combustible. All of the periods under discussion are transitional historical periods, periods of down time when the system stands pregnant with hope, when new ways of thinking and acting become possible. Its contemporary emergence could be interpreted similarly, with a growing middle-class malaise, distrust, and cynicism with regard to government decisions as well as governmental panic with regard to the sex industry, binge drinking, teenage promiscuity and credit card nonchalance. Obviously, there have been similar panics in the past, the 1950s panic over teenagers, rock and roll and sex being one pertinent instance. Interestingly the 1940s/50s 'look' feeds into the contemporary burlesque 'retro' style. In fact one of the obvious differences between the new burlesque movement and 1860s/70s and 1920/30s burlesque is that this current phenomenon came out of and continues to feeds into 'alternative' groups such as the psychobillies, rockabillies, punks and those interested in Moulin Rouge-style Victoriana such as the goths and the gothic lolitas as well as subcultural groups where, for example, tattoos and piercing are on the whole acceptable.

Burlesque collapses the distance between audience and performer, between classes and between forms erected to affirm and protect middle- and ruling-class identity through the powerful presence of the female performer. Her unruliness set up a new way of thinking by way of politicized banter and the performer's 'knowing' smile.

'STARS' AND 'QUEENS'

The unruly woman

Our contemporary queen or 'grande dame' of burlesque is Dita Von Teese. 'The girl you don't admit to your mother or wife to having heard of' is now mainstream. Burlesque's unruly woman has moved slickly into the 'high' world of fashion and 'A'-list celebrity and is now seen fraternizing in the pages of *Elle* with the likes of Jean Paul Gaultier, Galliano, Valentino and Christian Lacroix. Pop stars like Christina Aguilera (with 'Lady Marmalade') and Gwen Stefani (who had a guest appearance with the Pussycat Doll Revue, a burlesque-style cabaret act) 'do' burlesque. As for the cinema, the deliciously ravishing *Moulin Rouge* and the Charlies' Angels sequel *Full Throttle* pay homage to burlesque's glitter, costume and sexiness. A scene in *Full Throttle* (2003) recreates Von Teese's now infamous act in which Cameron Diaz 'performs' in a Martini glass bath with requisite giant olive sponge. At this moment in time Von Teese seems to be the 'it' girl who can do no wrong. However, a question that must be posed is, what happens to Von Teese's critique of the system (which is, after all, what differentiates burlesque from pure striptease) if she is now comfortably part of it?

Von Teese's inspiration comes from the glamorous 'stars' of the 1930s, the likes of Gypsy Rose Lee, Lili St Cyr and Sally Rand; it is their 'spirit' she seeks to emulate, but with more gloss. In interview she speaks about the couture gowns, the millions of dollars worth of diamonds, her 1939 Chrysler and 1965 Jaguar S-Type, her burlesque memorabilia, the nylons and the pincurls – in sum her 'look' and her unique style. These glamorous vintage poses have appeared in fashion stories for UK's *Tatler*, *W* magazine, *Vogue*, *Playboy*, UK's *Elle* and her pin-up-style cookbook, amongst many others. Is the Von Teese Internet empire testimony to the fact that she has been wholeheartedly appropriated into the mainstream ... bland stream ... sanitized, middle-of-the-road stream? Is the 'spirit' that she seeks to emulate solely based on the vintage 'look', the glamour – the creation of an iconic pin-up style?

Burlesque artistes like Gypsy Rose Lee and Lydia Thompson transgressed conventional standards and mores concerning sexuality and gender. They subverted the system, challenged traditional middle-class respectability and pushed boundaries. As fleshed out earlier, this was the essence of burlesque: its chaotic, threatening, anarchic potential, embodied and communicated through its figure-head female 'queen' or 'star'. Has the bite therefore been taken out of burlesque? Hell-bent on celebrity, money and fame, the female performer seems to have become a pure money-spinning spectacle. Performers like Dita Von Teese and Kitten DeVille now seem to be celebrating and luxuriating in their sense of achievement, their winning of the feminist battle, their sexual and personal freedom. Is Dita Von Teese the pinnacle of our achievement and our inspiration – a sexy, powerful, famous, networking new burlesque queen of the contemporary era?

Performance stills and photographic poses of Von Teese's opulent and decadent 'burlesque' seem like a luscious, technicolored pastiche of burlesque performers' sexy seduction and tease. Her photographic poses include one shot of Dita riding a carousel horse: she has a pale, translucent complexion, perfectly pencilled beauty mark and formidable powder-white breasts jutting out of an erotic, boned corset. This image stands out from all the bland images of 'sexy' girls that the media relentlessly churn out every day, vacuously staring out at us, pert and pouting, from newspapers, magazines, billboards, television and films. There is a hyper-visual sensual appeal about Von Teese's images; she seems to take slightly too much pleasure from the sexualized display. This imagery somehow embraces and exceeds the socially sanctioned need for sexual images of women, expected and demanded by our aggressively global commodity market.

Von Teese began her career as a fetish pin-up. She says that her fetish inspiration came from 'fetish goddess' Marchesa Luisa Casati, who is said to have worn live snakes around her neck, white peacock feathers dripping in fleshly slaughtered blood as a crown and eccentric elegant dresses. Von Teese describes Casati as her kindred spirit; she also entered the world 'a shy plain Jane and rediscovered herself through costume':[39]

> In the end, of course, they say she had no interior. Who cares? It was her stated goal to be a work of art, a painting, a thrilling show for the masses ... How can I admire so frivolous a life, you wonder? How can

35

I *not*? Casati's entire identity lay in the creation of fantasy. She made Europe more colourful. She sought immortality and she got it. What more can a fetish goddess ask for?[40]

Von Teese's comments leave me with two important questions that need to be addressed in this book. First, is pure spectacle, a sexually potent performance by the 'low' artiste, not enough in itself to shake up and question, to challenge and shock regarding gender and sexual conventions? And second, do you have to be informed by political or feminist debates to be transgressive?

When I went to see performance artist Ursula Martinez perform her burlesque show, her striptease left me reeling: I had thought I was safely in an art theatre. Her nakedness, her smile and her wink empowered and disturbed. I felt angry and indignant that she had displayed her body and made a public spectacle of her nakedness. I also admired her panache, her nerve and her freedom as she strutted about, parading and revelling in her sexual pleasure and sexualized display. She was confident in her power, with her sexuality and with her body. Stripping down to just her stilettos and her red lipstick was gutsy – you had to give it to her, the girl had balls! On the other hand, it was 2001 – come on, did we still feel that this was the only way to get attention? As observed by Camille Paglia, 'Feminists are currently adither over woman's status as sex object, but let them rave on in their little mental cells.'[41] It felt like this display went against everything I believed in. It felt dangerous and morally transgressive.

It was transgressive in that the 'low' had seeped into the 'high', challenging my 'respectability', my assumptions, my judgment, my fears. Had the feminism that I felt I stood for become 'respectable', and therefore, in some ways, even bourgeois? Here was a female artist stripping. Here was a naked female body looking me in the eye. Here was a naked sexual subject audaciously smiling and winking at her audience. The potent combination of comedy, a powerful sexual presence, striptease, nudity and the gaze is unsettling and unnerving. By 'making a spectacle' out of herself, Martinez joins a long tradition of unruly women who dare to be disruptive. Laughing at my assumptions, refusing to conform to expectations, transgressing the 'norm', overspilling and violating my sense of self, this transgressive female performer upsets and cajoles my 'comfort' zone, tests my boundaries. Performing and parodying an unruly sexy femininity with flamboyancy and panache, she plays potently with spectatorial power and pleasure.

By use of humour and pleasure, Martinez uses the spectacle of her femininity in order to make us question our own cultural assumptions about gender, about sex, about sexuality and about class. We later find out, matter-of-factly, that she is a lesbian. Why had I presumed that she would be heterosexual? Why was I aggrieved about her explicit display of her nakedness and her excess of pleasure? Why also was I angry when my expectations and my desire for anonymous theatrical distance were violated by the directness of her gaze, smile, wink and sexual charisma? Suddenly I was in the spotlight; I was naked; I was implicated as the desiring subject and the vulnerable object. Through being a sexualized, feminized subject Martinez was challenging through spectacle the very visual construction of her gendered self.

By playing out the power and pleasures of 'femininity' this performer created an intense topsy-turvy situation where I felt shameful and desiring, empowered and vulnerable. This challenging, disorderly provocation is typical of the 'unruly woman' who disrupts convention and turns the world (its power, values and ways of thinking and behaving) upside down. By confounding the usual responses, reactions and experiences she creates a two-way process where power is not confined but rebounds and pulsates between bodies and between subjects. By looking the spectator in the eye and smiling she is mocking, teasing and challenging the spectator as well as pleasurably and actively affirming, 'making a spectacle'[42] out of her desiring/desirable sexual self. She wants to be looked at, passively and vulnerably to succumb to the spectator's visual power and pleasure, but with this Mulvey 'to-be-looked-at-ness' is married a powerful, questioning humorous smile and wink, which thwarts and pulverizes the totality of my anonymous and aloof control. The subversion of the piece rests on this combination of satire and sexiness.

The tradition of the unruly woman might theoretically be rooted in Natalie Zemon Davis' concept of the 'woman on top', identified in her book *Society and Culture in Early Modern France* (1975). Davis argues that sexual inversion has deeper social and political ramifications because of its disobedience of what belongs 'below' and what belongs 'above'.[43] However, the unruly woman becomes utterly unmanageable when she as a subject becomes the author of her desire, of her own spectacle. Kathleen Rowe argues that: 'men have traditionally understood the need to secure their power not only by looking but by being seen – or rather, by fashioning, as author, a spectacle of themselves'.[44] By controlling her own spectacle as sexualized, feminized and 'low', and as an immigrant or foreign 'other', the burlesque performer powerfully makes transparent deeper power imbalances, instabilities and anxieties at play in society at large. Burlesque is disturbing precisely because it is a medium through which this sexual, smiling subject can seduce and weaken middle-class defences and, by her siren-like allure, unleash all manner of ills on the safe, contained and purely hierarchical arena of patriarchal white bourgeois power and control.

This, for Allen, was the quintessential transgressive power of the burlesque performer – the performer became 'too hot to handle' when she fused 'sexual allure and inversive feminine insubordination'.[45] This 'red hot' union was consummated explosively by Lydia Thompson in 1868, described by a critic of the time, William Dean Howells in *Atlantic Monthly* 1869, as 'horrible prettiness'[46] (the apt title of Robert C. Allen's 1991 book about burlesque). Although the Blondes were becoming an overnight sensation in Paris, London and New York, critics found them monstrously unnatural. Their desirable femininity incongruously jarred with their aggressively 'masculine' behaviour. They smoked, were loud, bawdy, independent and crude yet seductively drew in men and women like bees to a honey pot.

They expressed a hybrid gender that repulsed and attracted, conventionally posing in both masculine and feminine dress with an excess of artifice that played up and hinted at a voracious sexual appetite. Critic Richard Grant White stated: 'Its system is a defiance of system',[47] and according to William Dean Howells, 'The mission of the burlesque is to throw ridicule on gods and men – to satirize everybody and everything; to surround with laughter and contempt all that has been reverenced and respected.'[48]

Allen argues that as the burlesque performer lost her capacity to vocalize, she lost her transgressive potential. She became pure spectacle. When the two qualities became divided they became easier to manipulate. The burlesque performer's behaviour was transgressive in the late nineteenth century. However, when many women, particularly working class and often poor and oppressed young women, go out 'on the town' in their bra tops, drinking alcopops and smoking, this outrageous behaviour seems to lose its subversive power. Germaine Greer's cautionary discussion in *The Whole Woman* (1999) should be noted here. In the book she comments that:

> The propaganda machine that is now aimed at our daughters is more powerful than any form of indoctrination that has ever existed before... To deny a woman's sexuality is certainly to oppress her but to portray her as nothing but a sexual being is equally to oppress her.[49]

Greer has been aligned with the many feminist critics who have poured scorn on the contemporary postfeminist imaging and marketing of women as pure sexualized spectacle. For Greer the marketing of 'girl power' elicits no real power, it is all about appearance, style and the accoutrements of sexualized femininity, as sexual 'freedom' is big business. In the swing from desexualized to overly sexualized femininity (in the 1990s) the pressures and control remained consistent and young girls are still seen to have no real power (political, legislative or social) in the public realm.

So how is the contemporary turn-of-the-millennium new burlesque stripper anything more than pure exploitation of sexualized femininity? What about the unruliness, the inversive insubordination? There is a stark difference between being a *sexual* (coming from within) and a *sexualized* (imposed from the outside and therefore passive) subject. Contemporary burlesque's return to the glamour and awe-inspiring sexuality of Mae West or Sophie Tucker seems therefore to be a rejection and a voluptuous disavowal of the immature sexuality of 1990s girlie feminism, as well as a definitive push towards character, charisma and a pointedly threatening sexual allure.

Menacing vamp

The furore over the burlesque performer clearly demonstrated a fear of her unbridled sexuality. She was viewed as a loose canon. Dorothy Rowe's description of how women were depicted during the Weimar period in Germany from 1896 to 1930 could equally apply to the periods of burlesque that I am discussing. Rowe argues that the 'sexually voracious and devouring female' became the key symbol of the city's decadent modernity.[50] The city and female sexuality came to be 'situated as the two most powerful agents in the destruction of masculine subjective identity already traumatized by war'.[51] To some degree therefore it can be taken as read that the women's movement was not perceived to be uncontrollably threatening. This movement was both middle class and sexually contained so therefore operated within safer, even if somewhat troublesome, parameters. The greatest fear came from changes in how femininity was being interpreted by the young. More liberated sexual attitudes and behaviour, especially amongst working-class females, were now seen to be influencing middle-class young ladies and threatening to upset and undermine the fabric of family life and values.

In the late nineteenth century, young women of all classes were looking for new sexual/social role models in order to create and express new modes of femininity that negotiated a space in-between the only polarized roles available, typified in the archetypal mother–whore dichotomy. The 'stars' and 'queens' of burlesque were perhaps the first female performers to realize the influential power of the mass media as a tool for pulling in the crowds and promoting transgressive modes of 'femininity' that seduced and tantalized precisely because they broke existing moulds. These sexual, de-contained identities gradually became more digestible and attractive to 'respectable' middle-class women when they were filtered though the glamour, celebrity, style and modernity of the now accepted iconic face of the female burlesque 'star' or 'queen'. We can draw obvious parallels of course with our contemporary 'queen' of burlesque, Dita Von Teese, who has become similarly accepted as a stylish and sexy icon.

With the dawning of the cult of celebrity, more sexual, risqué images of 'stars' like Adah Menkin and then Lydia Thompson were being placed in personal albums alongside and 'often on the same pages as photographs of family and friends'.[52] It was this assimilation into the middle-class home that compounded bourgeois male fears that these outrageous performers were encouraging new, aggressively sexual modes of behaviour and thinking. The challenge to the romantic ideal of natural femininity was already being questioned by the new elitist fashion, the 'Grecian bend'. This tightly corseted 's'-shaped dress that emphasized the hips, buttocks and bust was what Lois Banner has called the 'the most erotic style of the century'.[53] The British Blondes exploded onto the New York cultural scene at precisely the same moment as this dress style. Thompson wore this fashion in her performances of both *Ixion* and *Sinbad*.

It was the fact that the very feminized, sexualized and 'low' spectacle that had been removed from 'respectable' society had now moved right back into the heart and under the skin of the newly sanitized and controlled environment of 'high' theatre that made the phenomenon of burlesque so much more effective, radical and hard hitting. Issues of class, gender and sexuality, issues that could potentially create social unrest and disrupt the bourgeois patriarchal social order, were causing a stir once again. This time the ripples were not coming from the illegitimate edge but emanating, shockingly, from the very centre of bourgeois cultural life.

In the late nineteenth century, the 1930s and the present era, there has been and still is a real need to regulate female sexuality, whether that be through marriage and motherhood or by way of religion, public policy and legislation. In all three of these eras the clearest example of this clash between the private and the public is in the abortion debates that took place in both Western Europe and Northern America. At a women's history conference in 2005 the theme of abortion was still sensitive enough to break up a very enjoyable evening. There was the assumption that as feminists and as women we were 'naturally' all pro-abortion, as pro-abortionists were pro-women. There was also the assumption that if you were not pro-abortion, or should I say pro-choice, then you were obscenely right wing and lacking in liberal sensitivity. No one ever questions whether in fact submitting women to what is effectively a traumatic operation is not in some ways actually brutal, especially when in most cases contraception could prevent the need for it.

This is clearly meant to be a divided camp of bitter opponents. There is no other issue that marries (although perhaps dysfunctionally) the private and the public domain as fundamentally and provocatively as the subject of abortion. It is extremely and painfully personal and any interference, policy-making and even opinion on the matter is bound to impinge emotionally and cause offence. It is an emotional landmine site and therefore taboo. Any discussion will ultimately end in tears.

This issue tugs hard from a private and a public standpoint; it is a tug of war between woman's wishes, ethics and public policy. If I can state the obvious boldly, that the female organ is a source for both pleasure and life, it becomes evident that there is going to be conflict. It has always been in the interest of patriarchy and capitalism, economically, demographically and socially, to contain and control the female body as a source of pleasure, domestic work and as commodity. During the 1930s depression in the USA, the immature sexuality of Shirley Temple and not the mature sexuality of Mae West was forwarded as exemplary.[54] The sexuality modelled by West was seen to be the cause for the onset of the depression as uncontained female sexuality equated to a total loss and breakdown in patriarchal social order.

Young women are the cause of much anxiety and panic, since they are in that intermediary time of experimentation between growing up and settling down, when they are brimming over with energy, enthusiasm and sexual prowess and are ripe with sexy dreams. A balance is seen to be drawn, allowing for this youthful freedom in society: they are given just enough space to be able to attract a mate – and no more.

From the late 1860s female castration or clitoridectomy was used in the USA to curb sexual unruliness in those middle-class young women who 'transgressed' conventional bourgeois sexual behaviour, whilst working-class women were looked upon as criminal or mentally defective.[55] By the turn of the century, a new category of female offender was created, the 'sex delinquent', who criminalized sexual offences from prostitution to premarital and extramarital sex. Andrea Stuart claims that age of consent legislation replaced prostitution as the great concern of American suffragettes. Designed to protect young girls from predatory males it in fact, argues Stuart, criminalized 'an entire group of sexually active young women'.[56]

Nevertheless, if this question is applied to the present day, young women are still under intense pressure to be sexual, especially with role models such as Christina Aguilera. It is therefore very difficult to differentiate between those teenage girls who genuinely are sexual and want to be sexually active, and those teenage girls who *say* that they want sex because they think they are supposed to. One wonders if young girls therefore ought to be more protected from predatory males.

In the current climate the 'social problem' and therefore the 'social stigma' has moved on from unmarried mothers to teenage mothers (predominantly from lower-income and working-class families). This group of young mothers was described in a conference paper for the British Society for Population Studies as the ones who now suffer 'social death'.[57] Young girls are constantly berated (working class) or guided (middle class) about STDs, teenage pregnancy, promiscuity, binge-drinking and smoking. Women are too sexual or not sexual enough; too young to have children or too old to have children. It is also interesting how frequently the media warn us about the perils of binge-drinking, excessive exercise, or the stress on women's fertility. There are endless constraints (both sense and nonsense) put upon women's pleasure and procreation.

Glamorous, tantalizing images of the first wave of burlesque 'stars' and 'queens' wholeheartedly upset the applecart of convention. They were clearly staging and amplifying modern trends and aroused fears of the dawning of a menacing tribe of sexually aware, young modern women. Elizabeth Lynn Linton in her popular and influential 'Girl of the Period' essay of 1868 bitterly attacked the appearance of a self-consciously sexual, manipulative woman who was appearing at that time in Britain. She claimed these girls were worryingly imitating the styles of celebrities as well as the flirtatiously open and bold manner and behaviour of the *demi-monde*. This led young women 'to slang, bold talk and fastness … the love of pleasure and indifference to duty … to uselessness at home, dissatisfaction with the monotony of ordinary life, and horror of all useful work'.[58] In a review of this essay Henry James saw in many American women a similar attitude: 'Accustomed to walk alone in the streets of a great city, and to be looked at by all sorts of people, she has acquired an unshrinking directness of gaze. She is the least bit *hard*.'[59]

City life was offering up to young women whimsical and pleasurable distractions. For young women who were in that 'home-to-home' spatial and emotional transitory period of their life, the city offered up an exciting time of experimentation. Even though life, behaviour and roles were very much mapped out for the majority of young women, work, street life, shops and cafés introduced them to other avenues and walks of life, different kinds of femininity and ways of dressing and behaving. Young working-class girls in the 1860s, the Bowery Girls or 'Gals' (the young workingwomen of the Bowery, which was a broad avenue running down the east side of Manhattan), and the 'Tough Girls' of the turn of the twentieth century (a subculture of young working-class teenagers who were confrontational and sexual in their attitude and styles), were destined to be shop girls or factory workers (including Mae West) and modelled their garish[60] fashions on the prostitute's attire, whose clothes hugged all contours and unveiled the face, leaving the eyes free to wander. This was a bold gesture, for at that point in time this searching, direct gaze was still firmly associated with the *fille publique* or 'common prostitute'.

In tune with contemporary debate, Lydia Thompson created a series of images based on her stage personae that reflected this contemporary 'awarishness'. She both satirized and confidently asserted this self-consciously sexual manner and style. In her 'Girl of the Period' *carte de visite* (promotional postcard pin-up) the burlesque star mocked her own reputation as an 'awarish' modern girl. In this image she gazes, smiling at the viewer like a dominatrix school ma'am, riding crop in hand, wearing an ostentatious stuffed squirrel hat and monocle. The image is humorously ridiculous as well as threatening in its vampish sincerity. A thin line is being negotiated and regulated between sexual willingness, and thus availability, and a more distant self-reflexive sexual 'awarishness', opening up a huge grey expanse of muddy, veiled intentions and confused meanings. It is uneasy territory. With the blurring of roles between lady and hussy also came a blurring of clarity and an evident opportunity or excuse for misreading.

The need to express oneself as feminine and sexual has been condemned historically and silenced, and still forms a forbidden space that is shut out from both our society and our cultural imagination. This sensuous *joie de vivre* has been supplanted and flattened by a dominant, masculinized profit-making perspective on sexiness – whether that be pert and pretty passivity or illegal, dirty whorishness – which simply empties representation of the female sexual agent and uses this 'sexiness' to fuel fantasy. The articulation of this sensual pleasure, this particular self–knowledge, has been therefore pushed into invisibility or out of existence, either by a 'masculinist' culture that has hijacked it for its own aims, or, understandably, by feminists who have sought to disassociate themselves from any sexual display in order to be taken seriously. Burlesque is an overwhelming need that identifies a yawning cultural gap, a lack, a sensual negation.

The contemporary burlesque performer does not necessarily depart from masculine ideas of sexiness but embraces and appropriates the many sexualized clichéd codes and stereotypes embedded in our visual culture. Some of the many identities reinterpreted by the new burlesque performers in the USA and the UK include the pin-up (Dita Von Teese); the Moulin Rouge performer (Candy Whiplash); the showgirl (Bebe Bijoux); the slutty bad girl (Dagger Lee); the classic rock chick (Miss Malone); and the courtesan (Gwendoline Lamour). New burlesque's use of parody with its smiling, winking imitation of stereotypes and 'male' fantasies is perhaps burlesque showing its audience that it *knows* that it does not yet know any new forms. Could there be a sexy 'look' that we can't even picture yet, because we can only see the standard versions passed down to us that are based on *male* fantasies? Is this what the female performers have been trying to push towards in their excessive 'playing' and pushing of existing limited erotic boundaries (and in the mean time perhaps gaining a bit too much pleasure, having a bit too much fun!)?

Before we can delve further into what this contemporary boom in burlesque explicitly relays to us about our feminist or post(-)feminist condition, we first need to identify the strands within feminism and within feminist performance. This will clearly then provide us with a platform for understanding burlesque, not as an isolated cultural binge but as a cultural form that has a definite purpose and intent. The next chapter will begin to thrash out and disentangle a space of pleasure and displeasure that straddles both the need to desire and to be desired as an (often) heterosexually active woman and the need to be heard and imaged as an independent subject. I will now probe more deeply into this space of pleasure and displeasure by first looking at the tradition of the nude and its dismissal of and blindness to female sexual agency.

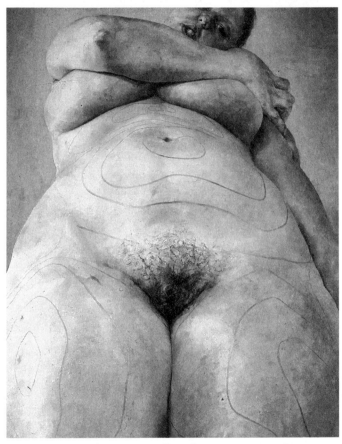

Plan, 1993, by Jenny Saville. Oil on canvas. 108 × 84 in.

2.
Body as Spectacle

THE NUDE

Pornography and erotica

In *The Nude: A Study of Ideal Art* (1956), Kenneth Clark differentiates between a naked and nude body. For Clark, 'nakedness' means 'to be deprived of our clothes' and implies some form of 'huddled and defenceless' embarrassment. To be 'nude' on the other hand implies a 'balanced, prosperous and confident body: the body re-formed'.[1] Clark argues that when we see a naked body we do not feel empathy but disillusionment and dismay. Artists therefore do not want to imitate this naked body; they strive to demonstrate their skill and mastery in refining it into an ideal form. Our bodies therefore always feel unsatisfactory when compared with the bodies imaged in art. They always look imperfect.

Clark insists that in order for art to be excellent it has to arouse erotic feelings in the spectator. If it does not do this it indicates 'bad art and false morals'.[2] 'Good' art – artistic and cultural excellence – is therefore defined by and controlled by the male artist's heterosexual desiring gaze.

Lynda Nead in *The Female Nude* (1992) argues that the 'principal goal of the female nude has been the containment and regulation of the female sexual body'.[3] With reference to Kenneth Clark's concept of 'The Naked' and 'The Nude', she argues that the nude was the elevated ideal body transformed by aesthetics and culture, and the naked body was the inferior raw matter prior to this transformation. Representing female sexuality and the body by way of the female nude allowed the male artist to control this uncontrollable body, to make it clean, smooth, silent and aesthetically pleasing. Nakedness, women's erotic expression as sexual subjects, stood 'outside of cultural representation',[4] for it was either contained by the nude, veiled by convention and stigma, or condemned as immoral and assigned to a promiscuous, whorish working-class other. The concept of nakedness was therefore connecting the female body with class, monetary exchange, shame and sexual deviancy.

By finely tuning an ideal depiction of woman and serving it up as 'high' art, male artists were putting forward as respectable and morally correct a particular set of values and beliefs: a particular way of living and thinking that was shot through with class, race, gender and sexual implications. They were also of course setting up simultaneously a polarized tension between defined class-based opposites: between the respectable and the disreputable, art and non-art, the cultural and the crass, the elite and the popular, learned and ignorant, cheap and valued, quality and disposable, immoral and moral, good and bad, masculine and feminine, artist and artiste.

In 1989 Tory MP Norman Tebbit defended the *Sun*'s topless 'Page Three girls'. When attacked by Clare Short as part of an anti-pornography campaign, he asserted that Page Three was a working-class alternative to the high art 'nudes' on display in national galleries.[5] This example highlights two glaring points. First, why is it the case that eroticism when under the auspices of the ruling class is seen as legitimate, thoughtful and cultured whilst erotic representations that cater for the working class are often considered pornographic? One representation is seen as cheap, its cultural conception directly linking to its worth in monetary and cultural value – it can be bought for

30p and then thrown away. The other costs thousands or even millions of pounds and is hung in a permanent, guarded position in a stately home or national gallery. One is to be looked at furtively in a rustle of embarrassment, the other to be gazed upon reflectively with privileged appreciation and knowledge. There is also the obvious difference that Page Three displays photographs and nudes are represented in paintings, therefore the photographs are perceived as more 'immediate'. However, if pornography is the raw objectification of power and desire then why is the entire tradition of the nude exempt?

'High' art is intended to intellectually arouse. This is what gives it that moral edge. It is thoughtfully created by way of paint to engage the viewer's cerebral and spiritual faculties. The immediacy of a journalistic glamour shot on the other hand acts only to provoke temporary physical titillation. Yet Angela Carter incisively cuts through this moral high ground when she describes this high art nude tradition as 'the pornography of the elite'.[6] Both depict naked, young nubile women – there to be looked at, posed and paid for by a male authorial presence – as receptacles for male identity and desire. They are used to sexualize their historical moment and a particular way of seeing the world, whether that be a white-teethed, smiling 'Scorcher' proudly jutting out her breasts to the camera – 'Southport's Sophie Howard is crazy about cricket'[7] – or the succulent body of a lady languidly sojourning on a lawn, picnic grove or chaise longue. Both disregard the model.

This brings me to my second point. What about the model? What about her sexuality bubbling away under the gaze of the viewer? What did she think? What about her desires, motivations and feelings?[8] As Lisa Tickner describes in her essay on female sexuality and women artists: 'Living in a female body is different from looking at it. Even the Venus of Urbino menstruated, as women know and men forget.'[9] It is an ideal body that is relentlessly depicted with no reference to real pubic female genitalia; this is rendered, according to Amelia Jones in 'Interpreting feminist bodies', as 'ob-scene' and therefore outside of the 'scene' of art.[10] The canonical nude's (official 'high' art, pre-1960s feminist intervention) principle goal was to objectify perfectly the purity of female beauty, even if this meant painting over female desire.

This prompts me to a question that has permeated and continues to permeate Western feminist debate. Is there a way in which imagery can celebrate rather than objectify female sexuality? In order to explore this we need to move right back to a key, foundational feminist text: Mary Wollstonecraft's *A Vindication of the Rights of Woman* (1792). In this polemic we see the foundations of a problematic that clearly still nags and bothers to this day. The problem that is earnestly forwarded is that of the seductive 'illegimate' power of female appearance – a woman's sex appeal. Wollstonecraft chides men for keeping women in a childish, undeveloped state whereby the only sense of power they can obtain comes through 'the arbitrary power of beauty'. If women continue to degrade themselves in this way, she argues, 'they will prove that they have less mind than man'.[11]

Simone de Beauvoir, another key feminist thinker, continued this strain of thought a century and a half later in *The Second Sex* (1949). This work asserts that if all women think about, talk about, and act on is their beauty and their physical appeal, they then have no time to develop their personalities, their intellect and their spiritual qualities. Sex appeal did not bring about real power for women at an economic, political or cultural level. This same argument was again used some 40 years later to critique 1990s 'girl power'. The 'Pencil Case Syndrome' was a derogatory turn of phrase used for young women and girls of school age (perhaps the reason for the reference to the pencil case) whose fashion accessories seemed to take priority over any politicized collectivity. They were sexy, young and trendy – but with no political clout.

Early feminists realized that in order to be accepted as strong, independent and rational subjects they had to transform and remould a fixed, persistent perception that existed of woman as pure object. In the public domain a woman's significance was based on her power to seduce, her appearance, her image as a passively pretty thing on display. This was the crux to suffrage – the necessity of being taken seriously as equally valid human beings. Feminist debate therefore hinged on how women should represent themselves in the public domain and the importance of constructing and instilling a positive public image for women.

Realizing the potent power of spectacle, feminists in the USA utilized pageants at their first convention at Seneca Falls in 1848 (when the women's rights' movement was officially initiated in the USA) as well as a series of pageants sponsored by the Woman's Party between 1923 (the 75th anniversary of the Seneca Falls Convention) and 1925. The pageant held in 1923 was lavishly produced, with hundreds of women in purple robes or holding purple, gold and white banners (the colours of the Woman's Party), arriving in procession by foot or in barges, singing the 'March of the Woman'. The symbolic climax of the evening saw Lucretia Mott and Elizabeth Cady Stanton recite to the sound of trumpets the same list of principles (the 'Declaration of Sentiments') that had been read out in Seneca Falls.[12]

All of the pageants were lavishly and theatrically undertaken, with a view to transforming cultural values and attitudes towards women. Cynthia Patterton and Bari J. Watkins point to a prominent shift in tactics between the radical feminism of the early years and those of the 1960s. The 1920s pageants 'depict women in the positive image of equality', whilst the 1960 beauty pageants 'presented an image of women against which women activists rebelled'.[13] This difference in tactics, one constructive and the other destructive, underlies the strategies of intervention that women have used to challenge images they have found to be oppressive. Feminists have employed both tactics as vehicles for change. Kathleen Rowe states that if 'public power is predicated largely on visibility', then women must 'use it to negate [their] own invisibility in the public sphere'.[14] Within the ranks of feminism and post-feminism women have used both strategies in order to transform their negative, powerless image, utilizing their 'visibility' in order to legitimize a public power that was not based solely on their sexual identity. By doing this they addressed the possibility for transforming their own discredited visibility into a powerful legitimate source for accessing power.

Both strategies realize how spectacular display dramatically impacts on the mind of the spectator. The suffragettes' guerrilla tactics included Mary Richardson axing Velázquez's *Rokeby Venus* in the National Gallery in 1914 – her reasoning: 'I didn't like the way men visitors to the gallery gaped at it all day.'[15] It was a protest against the persecution of Mrs Pankhurst, 'the most beautiful personality of this age'.[16] By way of destructive guerrilla tactics, the suffragettes and the second-wave feminists were attempting to create a new image through spectacle. On the other hand, by way of the pageant, feminists hoped to transform values and ideology from within the dominant system of representation. Whether subverting through pleasure or through displeasure, both were marked by spectacular display and knowledge of the constructive/destructive power of public image.

By outlining these reactions to woman's public image, I hope to have laid bare the foundations of a bipolar tradition that perpetuates in contemporary feminist debate. The modern perspective on this debate moves into more explicit terrain where the body becomes a tug of war between those feminists who denounce all explicit imagery as pornographic and defamatory, and those feminists who would like to re-appropriate these images to express their own pleasures and sexual desires. Andrea Dworkin, more than any other feminist, represented that faction within the women's movement who rejected all sexually explicit imagery of women. In her view these images degraded, objectified and reduced women down to their basest sexual elements. Pornography was like the caricatured superficial graffiti that is scrawled over walls in public toilets: breasts, nipples and 'cunt'. Women are reduced to sexually subordinate 'vile whores'.[17] What she found most disturbing about these misappropriated images were their potential for exposing women to sexual abuse, harm and oppression. Dworkin, along with Catharine Mackinnon, founded the anti-pornography ordinance, Women Against Pornography (WAP).

In opposition to this stance was the pro-porn FACT group (Feminist Anti-Censorship Taskforce) that was formed in 1984 and spearheaded by activists Anne Snitow, Carole Vance and Ellen Willis, as well as the lesbian feminist group Samois,[18] who published their alternative expressions of sexual pleasure in a collection of essays and narratives based on the practice of sadomasochism (S/M). *Pleasure and Danger: Exploring Female Sexuality* (1984) edited by Vance also sought to challenge the image of woman as passive victim. These essays celebrate women's sexuality. Yes, sexual abuse exists and, yes, some images do degrade, but this should not prevent women from being able to represent their experience as sexual beings:

> If sexual desire is coded as male, women begin to wonder if they are really ever sexual. Do we distrust our passion, thinking it is perhaps not our own, but the construction of patriarchal culture? ... Or are we purely victims, whose efforts must be directed at resisting male depredations in a patriarchal culture?[19]

A polarized viewpoint in relation to sexual depictions of women is repeated again in post-feminist debates. Camille Paglia proclaims in *Sex, Art, and American Culture* in her usual cut-throat style: 'I am radically pro-pornography and pro-prostitution.'[20] For Paglia, sexual exhibitionism displayed by women like the pop star Madonna is an expression of 'the whore's ancient rule over men'.[21] Women are the 'dominant sex' who have bewitched and destroyed men since Delilah and Helen of Troy. Feminism has, she argues, 'cut itself off from history and bankrupted itself when it spun its puerile, paranoid fantasy of male oppressors and female sex-objects victims'.[22] Naomi Wolf in *The Beauty Myth* (1990) on the other hand uses the mediaeval instrument of torture, the Iron Maiden, as a painfully explicit metaphor for the tortures inflicted on women by images of ideal beauty. The Iron Maiden consisted of a wooden casket in the shape of a woman, on top of which is painted the figure of a beautiful fair maiden, inside of which are metal spikes. The victim is encased in this casket and either dies by impaling herself on the spikes or though starvation. This late twentieth-century debate expressly inculcates capitalism and patriarchal power as the oppressors. For Paglia, this is pure 'whingeing'. Women have the upper hand and any talk of victimhood sends shivers up and down her empowered-tycoon-feminist spine.

I have reduced these feminists' thoughts to their bare bones, however. Their arguments are by no means this simplistic, but what I am attempting to express is a dichotomized perception that has been created in relation to these writers that has modelled and framed a divisive chasm within feminism and postfeminism. This chasm between those that see sexual depictions of women as positive and pleasurable, images to be appropriated for positive change, and those that reject these images as oppressive and harmful exploitation is replicated in the 'high' art world of fine art, especially within feminist body art and performance.

How did feminist intervention into such images challenge the objectifying male gaze and reinstate women's desire in the historical picture? And from a similar standpoint, how did these images demonstrate the friction that was enveloping the women's movement? And what about the weighty problem of the negation of female subjecthood?

Histories of female performance

According to Jeanie Forte, all women's performances are derived from the 'relationship of women to the dominant system of representation, situating them within a feminist critique'.[23] Forte is a strong believer in the capacity of women's performance art to disrupt this system of representation by forwarding 'an alternative discourse'.[24] Any practice, however, that uses the female body is working within a cultural system that is not value-free. Attempting to reconfigure or reconstitute the meanings produced by the already tainted female body by using that very same body is obviously problematic. In *The Explicit Body in Performance* (1997) Rebecca Schneider argues that 'any body bearing female markings is automatically shadowed by the history of that body's signification, its delimitation as a signifier of sexuality'.[25]

Women's body performance art of the 1960s and 1970s attempted to create alternative images of the female body, making visible what had been historically excluded or veiled in traditional art and claiming back the right to self-representation. Cixous exhorted women to subvert, revolt, disrupt and 'write the body' with a 'feminine text'.[26] The early push to re-appropriate the female body was grounded in 'consciousness-raising' groups where women were trying to explore what their bodies and their femaleness meant to them. Female performers wanted in some way to symbolically give women back their bodies, bodies they felt had been hijacked and violated by the media and patriarchy. *Our Bodies, Ourselves* written by the Boston Women's Health Book Collective relays many of the burning issues of the early 1970s. In a nutshell, what these women were looking to do was to explore and get to know their 'body as home',[27] a body that they could no longer relate to, felt estranged from, ashamed of, disgusted by. They felt that their body had been misappropriated by the media, men, the church, the family, consumer culture and the movies: 'we are always making comparisons, we're never okay the way we are. We feel ugly ... There is little encouragement to love our bodies as they are.'[28]

Whether the artist was part of a consciousness-raising group or not, women's performances were seen by Moira Roth as rooted in these honest, sometimes painful and collectively shared personal investigations and explorations of their lives. It was seen as the ideal art medium for sharing and investigating these fresh and at times taboo insights before a supportive audience. As a result many performance artists created work that celebrated the sacredness and taboo of the female body. Ana Mendieta produced poetical ritualistic pieces (*Siluetas*, 1973–7). Her performances included both the presence of her naked body strewn with flowers in grave-like spaces or the absence of her body through the use of its imprint or indentation in the earth. Other performance artists concentrated on the female body as an object of violation. Yoko Ono in *Cut Piece* (1964), Maria Abramovic's *Rhythm 10* (1973), Gina Pane's *Azione Sentimentale* (1973) and Adrian Piper's *Food for the Spirit* (1971) dealt with power imbalances and the insidious violence created by stereotypes, myths and judgments, and the desire to escape from them.

Ironically this period in women's performance has been criticized for its essentialism, for reducing women to their biological, domestic and reproductive functions and therefore also reducing women to victimized objects. However, as Anette Kubitza argues in her essay on Judy Chicago's *The Dinner Party* (1974–9), this work with its symbols of female genitalia celebrated (like Schneemann or Wilke's performance pieces) woman's experience, not her essence.[29] Kubitza argues that Chicago's piece was a feminist landmark and should be respected as such.

Carolee Schneemann and Hannah Wilke created work in the 1970s that celebrated women's sexuality and pleasure. One well-known piece by Schneemann, *Interior Scroll* (1975), saw the artist naked on stage extracting a scroll from her vagina that she then read out to the audience. Wilke's work included, *I Object: Memoirs of a Sugargiver* (1977–8) where she is photographed full-length and naked. Her work challenged feminists who denied and decried the imaging of her 'pretty', heterosexual, pleasure-giving body as politically incorrect and treacherously anti-feminist. It is frankly easy to criticize some of this work retrospectively but what these performances did was mark the beginning of an important stage in feminist art, the beginning of a process, an educational stepping stone towards wider public awareness of women's art, history and experience.

By the mid-1980s some artists had rejected the use of the naked female body altogether. It was not possible to use that image any more; it was not a clean canvas but was loaded with culturally determined meanings and values. To try to represent 'woman' as sacred, as passively feminine, was naive and regressive. Anatomy was not destiny. These anti-essentialist tendencies materialized in works by Mary Kelly and Barbara Kruger, who tried to avoid the actual use of the naked female form. Kelly instead opted to exhibit objects relating to her motherhood – stained nappies and journals recording her son's first few months. Denise Riley in *'Am I That Name?' Feminism and the Category of 'Women' in History* (1988)[30] states that the word 'woman' itself was an essentialist trap whereby women lose their agency. Kelly follows this line of thinking with her representation of herself as the subject of her own discourse by using the objects and journals that described her quotidian experiences as a mother.

Some performance artists tackled this dilemma differently. They would re-present themselves through the very same images cultivated by patriarchal culture, inserting back what Linda William calls 'a provocative feminist agency'.[31] Artists were challenging the disempowered image of woman's passive 'to-be-looked-at-ness',[32] seeking to reverse, challenge and make blatant this power relation. In body art, to use Elinor Fuchs pertinent description, the 'sacred body had been replaced by the obscene body'.[33] Karen Finley performed the violence of the relationship between performer and spectator in the scatological and pornographic *Yams Up My Ass* (1986) and *I Like to Smell the Gas Passed From Your Ass* (1986). The performances seem to recreate a sense of the poetically abject world of Julia Kristeva's *Powers of Horror* (1982) or the spectacle of the grotesque Rabelaisian body where boundaries containing the purity of the self (in the same way as the nude tradition contained the pure image of womanhood) collapse, releasing a flood of pus, blood, mucus, urine and faeces.

Annie Sprinkle on the other hand transformed herself from bored suburban housewife Ellen Steinberg into sex educator, prostitute, porn queen, pleasure activist and performance artist Annie Sprinkle. The only way in which her film *Deep Inside Annie Sprinkle* (1982) differs from traditional hardcore porn is Sprinkle's smiling and direct address to the camera. In her *Post Porn Modernist Show* (1992) she talks her live audience through her transformation from Steinberg to Sprinkle, discussing in detail her forays into prostitution and the porn industry (and her involvement with 200 porn films). Part of her stage show includes Sprinkle inserting a speculum up her vagina for the audience members to look at her cervix, and with no one forthcoming the 'educational' simulation of oral sex on a dildo. This was actually an interesting take on the 'peep show' format – the cervix not being considered a desirable 'part' of women's sexual bodies (unlike the vulva or the breasts).

Here we are sitting on uneasy territory, however. By performing such an explicit spectacle, both Sprinkle and Finley opened up their art to extreme misinterpretation and abuse. With Finley, the college students – the 'blokes out on the piss' – that congregated at her performances assumed that this gave them free rein to hurl abuse at her, and with Sprinkle, explicit sexual education sat precariously near to sexual voyeurism and pure titillation. By using an already appropriated patriarchal genre and representational system, critics felt that these artists would never be able to move beyond the negative connotations but would just continue to reconfirm traditional standpoints.

Artists in the 1990s moved away from the 'obscene' body and the actual 'live' performance of the purely physical, visceral self or body in order to depict how the contemporary era created bodies or selves that were now thoroughly 'mediatized' (imaged via the media) and technological. Amelia Jones in *Body Art/Performing the Subject* (1998) refers to this position as 'posthuman'.[34] Artists utilized technology to move way from any fixed notion of the 'self' and the 'body', representing identity as more complex and less easy to pin down to one place, one nation, one gender, one culture and so on. In terms of feminist performance practice, in the late twentieth and early twenty-first century this translated into work that dealt with a body that was both made neurotic and empowered by and through the use of mediatized images. This includes the plastic facial reconstructions (later broadcast by webcam) of Orlan. Orlan's body becomes material that she sculpts, testing out ideal images from the media and art on her own flesh. The act of marrying and jarring the mediatized ideal and her actual body seemed to create a sense of both neurosis and empowerment. This dichotomy is also mirrored in Jenny Saville's painted nudes. *Branded* (1992) and *Plan* (1993) are at once depictions of self-loathing as well as luscious and pleasurable painterly depictions of corporeally fleshy women.

The dislocation between the 'ideal' and the 'real' is created in Vanessa Beecroft's media-perfect naked or semi-naked white, slim, young and pretty 'Aryan' living sculptures who force us to flicker uncomfortably between looking at these bodies as images or art and as flesh-and-blood women. The desire to image the parallel but seemingly opposite concepts of image and flesh, lust and love, art and life has been emerging boldly as a discerning feature of other female artists. Natacha Merritt's *Digital Diaries* (2000) show the promiscuous 'whoring' of her body: the shallow, quick Internet connections of consumer 'have it all' culture and virtual love. This contemporary work reveals a desire for sexiness and an erotic zest for life's experiences but it also could be seen to recreate a regressive depiction of female sexuality. Merritt shot to fame when her work was discovered on the Internet by Eric Kroll, a veteran of obsessive erotic photography, which leaves one questioning how these images, with their maximum exposure of the genitals, challenge, subvert or even offer any alternative to traditional erotic representation.

Jemima Stehli's work opens up the same dilemma for the female viewer. Stehli's work sets out to explore via self-portraiture the issues that arise from the representation of the nude female body. She makes reference to the nude in art history as well as many familiar works by male artists and photographers including Helmut Newton. *Strip* (2000) is a photographic series that shows Stehli stripping in front of a male (who represents the male gaze of critics, dealers, writers and curators) who is enjoying what he sees. By resolutely including herself as the female subject and 'sex' object she is insisting on her authorial presence, and we know that Stehli has set up this choice of shot. Yet her decision to image herself from behind to focus on the male gaze as he looks on in appreciation perhaps forces one to question its subversive qualities. Like Merritt, Stehli is youthful, slim and pretty. How therefore do these images challenge, subvert or even question stereotypical representation? Or is the work showing an unresolved complexity in that Stehli is both the subject who is enjoying her own objecthood and the artist who is acknowledging that in her art, and as a woman, she is also intimately trying to please men.

The history of women's body art has pivoted awkwardly between two extreme points of view. Staunch deconstructionist Jill Dolan is scathing of this kind of art, which she describes as naive.[35] Using nudity in performance could further entrench women's position as objects and therefore reinforce existing engrained ways of thinking and seeing. Is therefore the work by Jo Spence of her larger, older, ill, desiring body in fact more subversive than that by Merritt or Stehli because it moves away from stereotypically acceptable, desirable representation? Lisa Tickner conversely suggests that the solution is 'to grasp and reconstruct it, through the exposure and contradiction of the meaning it conveys'.[36]

Hannah Wilke's *I Object* clearly seeks to intervene in this manner. In two photographs, Wilke's body stretches out, luxuriating in its nakedness, with the words 'I OBJECT' printed at the top of the image. The word play is obvious: the female body as a site of paradox. She both takes pleasure from 'giving' her (stereotypically 'pretty') body as a sexual object whilst 'objecting' to the capitalist and patriarchal circuit of cultural exchange that seeks to promote her as nothing but an object. Rosalind Krauss describes proactive interventions, such as for example this piece by Wilke, as 'guerrilla actions'.[37]

However, both ends of the argument seem insufficient. Is *any* representation always positive or always negative? Or could it be that some representation is subversive and others actually conformist whilst imagining themselves to be subversive? Is this perhaps the case with Stehli's *Strip* or Merritt's *Digital Diaries*?

Turn-of-the-millennium body artists have started to create work that permits a more complex reading of representation, pleasure, self-image and the gaze. Undeniably the position is grey and ambiguous, and it seems impossible therefore to adhere convincingly to either of the stances (voyeuristic/exploitative/disempowering on the one hand and empowering/desiring/sensual on the other). Young female art students are now at the point of wanting to explore and express this very emotive and complicated issue in their own work. These young women want to be desirable and sexy but realize also that it is naive not to be aware of the sometimes negative and harmful effects that can come from that very same sexualized image. A question that perhaps needs to be explored is why are women so concerned with *being* sexy and are less concerned with sexy men – with who they *find* sexy? Where is the desire in the work by Merritt or Stehli? Why do (straight) women not ever make work about men they desire? Is there such a thing as a female heterosexual gaze? Sam Taylor-Wood's video of David Beckham, *David* (2004), and Carolee Schneemann's video *Fuses* (1964–7), which I will discuss later in this chapter, are perhaps pieces of artwork that do address this point.

The tradition of women's body art practice gives women in the here and now a rich pool of knowledge from which they can cultivate a self-reflective awareness of both stances.

This ambivalent position shows itself clearly in the two female performance artists Carolee Schneemann and Hannah Wilke, to whom I will be referring. What is particularly interesting about these artists, as representatives of early feminist body art, is their exclusion and marginalization in the histories of contemporary art. According to Amelia Jones, this exclusion came from a fear of 'femininity, physical seduction, and the dangerously chaotic pleasures of the flesh'.[38] The difficulty and point-blank denial of Schneemann and Wilke's work was not only that they represented danger, chaos and seduction but that they represented an image of femaleness that had always been class-bound. Seduction and public display of sexuality had always signalled a woman of ill-repute, sluttishness, disrespect and abuse.

By questioning why the 'sexy feminist' was an oxymoron these artists evidently moved into a territory that provocatively connected the female body with class, money and sexuality. Investigating these particular body artists will give us a deeper understanding of the complex historical cultural backdrop of feminist politics that was taking place in the early years of the second wave of the women's movement. What will be gleaned by looking at the work of Schneeman and Wilke is the slippery, tense nature and purpose of displaying a sexual, conventionally beautiful body.

THE FEMALE BODY IN PERFORMANCE

Carolee Schneemann

In 1964 Schneemann posed as Manet's Olympia in Robert Morris's action *Site*. This particular action complicated the traditional notion of active male artist and passive female model as this model, posing for the well-known artist Morris, was in this case herself an established female artist. What this brought into play was a paradox: as a performance artist Schneemann was challenging rigid, gendered categorization, which was consolidated in the nineteenth century, of artist, artiste and artisan. The label *artist* included painters, sculptors and later on composers and writers. *Artisan* meant a skilled manual worker and *artiste*, an entertainer. These rigid divisions meant that the middle and ruling classes were staking a claim to the qualities of the intellect and the imagination and jealously protecting a male, white, bourgeois identity that was feeling threatened by changes in gender, sexual, class and cultural relations. By blurring boundaries between subject and object, male and female, the artist and artiste Schneemann was also bringing into play the faint line dividing the display of the female body and prostitution, the female body and its rate of exchange.

The nude tradition delineated rigid gendered roles and boundaries between the artist and the model (artiste). As part of *le grand art* tradition of the late nineteenth-century Paris Academy, the nude was understood to be a male preoccupation. Women were said to have a greater eye for detail and were therefore more suited to domestic subject matter such as scenes with children and still life. The small number of nudes that were painted by women in the Salon des Femmes (the first was held in 1882) were idealized depictions and acceptable within the rigid conventions of the day.[39] Male critics criticized the artists for their lack of originality and bemoaned the fact that there was no original feminine aesthetic and perspective, only poor imitations of masculine art. However, women artists who did fill this remit were excoriated as scandalous.

Camille Claudel's sensuous renderings of female erotic desire were seen as indecent. *The Waltz* (1892–5) was in fact refused for a commission by an inspector from the Ministry of Fine Arts, Armand Dayot, on the grounds of this 'surprising sensuality of expression'.[40] Her lover Rodin's obsessive drawings and sculptures of female genitalia, whilst much more explicit and close to the edge of decency, were seen as acceptable, however. This unwillingness to work within masculine regulation clearly marks out both Claudel and Schneemann. Other female artists in relationships with male artists, the 'Significant Others',[41] frequently chose domesticity and inferiority. Historically it was difficult to reconcile their art with their 'femininity'. Sonia Delaunay spent her life, it seems, willingly in her husband's shadow, speaking of her own accomplishments as secondary. Lee Krasner's paintings were seen as poor imitations of Pollock's *oeuvres*. What was highly combustible about Claudel and Schneemann was their refusal to be victims, their independence as artists and their assertive representation of female sexual desire and pleasure.

In *Site*, Schneemann, as an artist, represented Manet's model, Victorine Meurent (interpreted by Eunice Lipton as a lesbian), who dressed (or rather undressed) as the prostitute Olympia. Manet did not idealize the nude model but showed her in all her shocking reality as a common prostitute: sexualized, economically independent and self-possessed: 'This sexual flesh is frankly available and unromanticized [; she] meets our gaze without apology. She is practical, efficient, a bawdy woman of the world who knows her market value.'[42] The point that is significant is that by posing as Olympia, Schneemann positioned herself as part of a complex historical female lineage of model/artist/prostitute where all sexualized display was equated with the 'selling' of one's body – and therefore immediately equated with stigmatized sexual deviancy and even criminality.

It has been suggested by Charles Bernheimer that the model Olympia may have been a dancer or an actress. So too Schneemann in the 1960s was more comfortably labelled 'dancer' than 'artist'. To some degree, therefore, the label 'dancer' was being used to silence and contain the sexual and individual freedoms expressed in the work, and to undermine the artist. Sally Potter points out that, for women, being an entertainer (whether a stripper, actress, singer, music hall artiste or dancer) was akin to prostitution for the 'display of the female body in performance was considered a form of sale'.[43] Schneemann refuted and challenged this correlation. Her body was to be used experientially as a medium for changing these engrained values. As she states: 'I didn't stand naked in front of three hundred people because I wanted to be fucked.'[44]

In the nineteenth century the public often saw the role of the artist's model as well as that of the artiste as being synonymous with prostitution. The model and the artiste's body therefore became open territory for fantasies of sexual availability. By straddling the artist–artiste axis female performance artists therefore undeservedly aligned themselves with the artiste–prostitute position and, perhaps because of the display of their bodies, the historical impossibility of being accepted as artists. Schneemann took on this legacy: the fear and anxiety provoked by the economically and sexually independent woman and the notion of the artiste as feminized, sexualized and therefore of lesser significance. *Site* excavates and reignites the memory of *Olympia*. It becomes a witness to the life of the defiant gaze that scandalized. However, in the climate of the early 1960s, Schneemann was looking out onto a very different social and cultural context. The impression was that the work was not enough to push bourgeois 'respectability' over the edge, to make a mark. It did not fully reignite the shocking experience of *that* gaze, *that* transgressive female body, *that* unruly sexuality.

In Camille Paglia's essay 'The beautiful decadence of Robert Mapplethorpe'[45] she draws parallels between the shock caused by Mapplethorpe's *Man in Polyester Suit* (1980) with its image of a large black penis poking out from an otherwise respectable suit, and the cultural shock created at the unveiling of *Olympia* in 1863. Mapplethorpe's photograph goaded respectable sensibilities and therefore crossed the line that is drawn by a society to define and protect its morality and identity. *Site* too closely mimicked the traditional model of the still mute nude to cause offence, to shake up the viewer's habitual mode of looking and of thinking. It was nothing new. *Olympia*, by contrast, left the male viewer feeling raw and exposed. They felt passion, but they also felt fear and anger. Looking at Olympia/Meurent, they felt naked. This model was not solely the passive object of the gaze but also assertively a sexual, independent, creative subject.

Marie Lathers speaks about the image of the prostitute in nine-teenth-century French society as the transgressor of 'public and private boundaries'[46] and a threat to middle-class domesticity. Baron Haussmann's newly redesigned Paris of the 1860s had lost much of the working-class district that housed many of the brothels, pushing the *fille publique* (common prostitute) into a more visible presence in the brasseries and cafés of the wide new boulevards. Bernheimer states that the bourgeoisie masked their fears of the *fille publique* through the 'deluxe modern commodity' of the courtesan (nouveau riche prostitute).[47] Her rich and feminine exterior could be used to mask the threat that the sexual female body signified; a defence against their own shameful and perverse weaknesses and vulner-ability. This enterprising woman of the day was feared – she was too powerful and too central economically, sexually and emotionally, for there was also a fear of this woman marrying and therefore polluting their own class. What Olympia did was to deflect these fears back at the male bourgeois viewer, destroying his power and poking fun at the female nude genre.

It was intriguing and appropriate therefore for Schneemann to have been part of the action *Site*. Her desire to express what she called 'a self-contained, self-defined, pleasured, female-identified erotic integration'[48] was at the heart of her work. *Site* demonstrates Sch-neemann's resistances against a masculinist art world but neverthe-less highlights the narrow exclusivity of that 'female-identified' body: white, middle-class and heterosexual. Lorraine O'Grady discusses the two women's movements' inability to embrace their non-white Oth-er's sexuality. This is evident in the glaring omission of the black maid from *Site*. The struggle of black and lesbian women was twofold: like Schneemann they struggled to assert their creative selves as women but as well as this they were struggling to express their own sexuality within a women's movement that was defining desire and pleasure from a hetero-centric, white, middle-class position.

Schneemann later voiced her concerns regarding the project. Col-laborations with men, she stated, only resulted in 'experiences of true dissolution'. In *Site* Robert Morris was the instigator, and Schneemann felt her identity lost and dominated, 'historicized and immobilized'.[49] Where the collaboration was successful, however, was in excavating the memory of *Olympia* and forging a link between the historical gaze and Schneemann and Morris' contemporary context. Comparable to female artists working in the late nineteenth century, Schneemann in 1963 was struggling to assert her independent aesthetic as an artist whilst still being defined and regulated by masculine standards with its restrictive sociocultural conflation of female bodily display with the categories of model or artiste.

What becomes interesting is the comparison between the passive reception of the still mute body in *Site* and the quite hysterical reaction to the erotic, active performing body in *Fuses* (1964–7). By moving out of the artist–model stasis this work was able to reignite the shock that was *Olympia*'s legacy. In the context of the 1960s, *Site* could no longer effect a similar response. What it did, however, was act as a springboard from which to launch work such as the controversial and unacceptable *Fuses*. With no directing male artist, Schneemann had authorial control, as explicit body and artist, object and agent. As a result, *Fuses* was provocative enough to reignite the original sensation caused by *Olympia*.

Fuses, made a year after *Site*, showed the love-making between Schneemann and then husband Jim Tenney. *Fuses* shows fragmented glimpses of both naked bodies including images of Schneemann performing oral sex on Tenney, Tenney's erect penis (an image that is still extremely taboo today) and both bodies as they go through the various rhythms and sensations of sex. Schneemann commented that when she started making *Fuses* there was still the belief amongst many of her 'smart' male friends that women want to be raped and that it was even 'good for them'.[50] This film, however, represents Schneemann's own heterosexual gaze and desire and the erotic pleasure shared between partners. The film is intentionally obscured by scratches, painterly marks, over- and underexposure and abrupt editing, which prevents the viewer from lingering too long on any bodily parts. Schneemann wanted to create an erotic filmic image by turning the body into 'tactile sensations of flickers'.[51]

Schneemann wanted to give the audience 'permission to see'.[52] The film was 'too much',[53] however, for both avant-garde audiences and feminists. She was described as 'a dangerous pornographer' and a 'deranged frigid nymphomaniac'[54] – an intriguing oxymoron (one can only assume that the gentleman describing her thus felt that for a woman to enjoy or depict sex, she had to be mentally disturbed or emotionally cold). A young critic, closer to Schneemann's age, felt that it was an assault on his sexuality and a critic from a more liberal paper shook her hand and commented: 'I'm afraid that we deserved that film.'[55] Schneemann appreciated the reaction, as anything crossing the boundaries imposed by censorship tended to provoke reflection and debate and unearth taboos.

Expressing an active desire, by representing the sexual organs or the sexual act itself, was still taboo at that time. Gayle Rubin states: 'From the late 1940s until the early 1960s, erotic communities whose activities did not fit the post war American dream drew intense persecution.'[56] She argues that sex laws were there to enforce taboos against sexual behaviour that involved homosexuality, money, minors or 'obscenity', which meant direct representation of the sexual act. Pornographic material, prostitutes and 'erotic deviants' were all incriminated by these anti-obscenity laws. So in the late 1950s and early 1960s, when Schneemann was actively working within Fluxus (an association of avant-garde artists, designers and composers that was active in the 1960s), both the homosexuality of members of Fluxus and the 'obscene' and 'pornographic' images produced by Schneemann were incriminated by these sex laws, and they were therefore vulnerable to persecution. The persecution of Schneemann came from her open expression of her sexuality – her erotic pleasure.

This depiction of her female pleasure was extremely radical and caused offence not only to society at large but also to feminists involved in the beginnings of the second wave of the women's movement. Some critics found Schneemann's pure expression of pleasure arrogant or even embarrassing. Joanna Frueh has commented that this reaction was the result of an art world which gave greater emphasis to the abject and the grotesque, and therefore would find anything that was not cut by irony or past pain 'difficult' or 'embarrassing'. She stated, 'an aesthetic of unadulterated pleasure in an aphroditean body is "too much" because it is more than many of us can imagine to be possible for ourselves.'[57]

As Schneemann's work was sexually assertive and bold it was being defined in terms of maleness, 'a stray male principle',[58] that she felt detracted from what she was actually producing by her 'creative female will'. *Fuses* did not fall smoothly into either the male aestheticized tradition of the nude, of 'art', or conventional perceptions of 'femaleness'. Like *Olympia* one hundred years before, *Fuses* clearly disturbed. It kicked up sexual taboos, it transgressed boundaries, it outraged bourgeois sensibilities and pushed against the limits of what constituted acceptability. By doing this, Schneemann's work courageously acted as a testing ground for pre-feminist thinking about class, the gaze, female sexuality and erotic imagery. By using the nude tradition, by being the nude model, Schneemann as performance artist questioned why the fusion of the feminine, the sexual and the 'low' had been historically silenced, negated and submerged.

We will now turn our attention to Hannah Wilke to illuminate post-second-wave feminist debates over the issue of 'prettiness', which reveal a schism not necessarily as a result of white, male bourgeois oppression but as a result of a feminism that was seen to be too severe and unsexy in its condemnation of sexual imaging, prettiness and sensual depictions of pleasure – one which is still an issue today.

Hannah Wilke

At the end of June 2005 an article by Kevin Gibson was posted on a fashion and lifestyle website called 'Rant: the benefits of feminism'. He begins: 'For starters, I try not to think about feminists. Truth be told, it isn't that hard to do in this day and age.'[59] He then goes on to depict 1970s feminists as humourless, hairy, asexual women who eschewed pleasure and ranted about the Equal Rights Amendment.

Today's young modern woman or 'chick', he argues, is someone who wants to be called a 'slut' in the bedroom and who equals men in her desire for casual, wild sex and 'friends with benefits' (FWBs). Courting rituals, he says, are 'as dead as disco'. Because of feminism women can now think for themselves. What that means for Gibson is that they now choose to beautify themselves, wear low-cut suggestive tops, have a Brazilian wax and play the field. Women want to be objectified. In the past, this type of woman would have been labelled an outcast or worse. Today, 'strippers, porn stars and hookers' are the ones with the power, not the victims. This, he concludes, is feminism's legacy.

I do not reference this article as a piece that took itself seriously. Its purpose was to entertain young 20-something men in a quite light-hearted if not facetious way. It does, however, work to register and legitimize a specific kind of contemporary sexual and social female behaviour. Within his argument, stereotypical caricatures of old-school feminists are strongly reinforced, permitting them to become targets for ridicule, scorn and indifference. Men can bask in the feminists' failure. For Gibson, the women's movement fortunately has left its mark only in the fact that women are now liberated enough to be able to enjoy the power that comes as a result of their sexual prowess whilst also expecting equal access to pay and rights.

This article is therefore an extremely pertinent way to kick-start the polemical reaction to artist and 'sex' object Hannah Wilke. Wilke was battling against the strand in the women's movement that she called 'Fascist Feminists'. The feminism denounced and brushed off by Gibson was too severe and unsexy for Wilke, disallowing diversity in the way women chose to enjoy their bodies and their sexuality.

For Gibson, we might presume that seeing a woman without pubic hair means enjoying women's bodies – but is this way of conforming to a porn or nude tradition of images of women often done for male rather than female enjoyment? In 1974 Andrea Dworkin, in *Woman Hating*, perhaps embodied this faction of feminist thought. Her dogmatic and dry approach to solving discrimination and violence against women was to strip culture completely of patriarchal stereotypes of female sexuality. In the same year Lynda Benglis created and

71

paid for an advertisement: a pin-up of herself, naked, greased up and holding a dildo to her genitals. Maria Buzsek states that the force of the reaction against this revealed how much feminists were unprepared for such a medium; it was too close to existing oppressive representational modes. By re-appropriating popular and mass-produced depictions of the female form Wilke and Benglis rallied against patriarchal myths, and indeed against extreme feminist notions that being a sex object robbed women of their agency.

A group of editors from the journal *Artforum* were so outraged by Benglis that they issued a letter condemning the piece for 'its extreme vulgarity ... [It] reads as a shabby mockery of the aims of [the women's] movement ...'[60] Striking comparisons can also be made with comments made about Wilke in the same journal. James Collins states that there was:

> a strange paradox between her own physical beauty and her very serious art. She longs to fulfil her sexuality in an almost Marilyn-Monroe-like way; but her attempt to deal with this dilemma within the women's movement has an air of touching pathos about it.[61]

What, therefore, were the aims of the women's movement? And did these aims have to exclude humour, playfulness and eroticism?

In the early 1970s women contemporaneous to Wilke were coming together on a private level in consciousness-raising groups and at a public level with radical feminist action or 'guerrilla theatre' – such as at the 1968 Miss America Pageant in Atlantic City and the WITCH (Women's International Terrorist Conspiracy from Hell) demonstrations. Women were looking at issues of power, of representation and of authority. There was a perception that women's bodies had been misappropriated and used against them to suppress and oppress. Public action including feminist performance was rooted in and triggered by these 'gut level' experiences and this sense of sharing before a supportive audience. However, there was a small faction of women who were beginning to voice 'politically incorrect' dissidence. In a sense, there was a listening and supportive audience *as long as* the feelings of anger and pain were the 'correct' ones of 'Everywoman'.

In *S.O.S. Starification Series* (1974–5) Wilke was professionally photographed in flamboyantly stereotypical pin-up poses. The poses that she adopted were those that she used during a series of performances in which she flirted, topless, with an audience. During these performances she handed out chewing gum and then after retrieving it moulded it into what she called 'chewing gum cunts' that she stuck to her body as both wounds or fashion accessories. Wilke played with the motif of femininity and played on her role as seductress. She parodied as well as revelled in the assertion of herself as a sexual object. Women's bodies and their sexuality were depicted popularly as either dirty, pornographic and offensive or passively perfect. Both ways were reductive and restrictive. Female sexuality had been hijacked and was now steeped in negativity. Wilke's objective was, as she put it, to create 'a positive image to wipe out the prejudices, aggression and fear associated with pussy, cunt, box'.[62]

The problem was that she was considered a little too good to be true. Was she using her 'prettiness' to titillate or critique? By playing with the male language of the nude, Wilke was seen to confuse her roles as beautiful woman and artist, flirt and feminist. This exposed her to criticism. At this point in feminist history an equivocal position was not up for discussion; it was not feasible to bridge both polarized roles and it was therefore impossible for many critics to comprehend Wilke's contradictory stance. For the viewer 20 years on, this work remains contemporary because of this challenging and problematic position. By embracing the tropes of 'femininity' Wilke willfully antagonized that element of the women's movement that she thought restrained a woman's erotic desire for pleasure. However, by seeming to collude with the representational system Wilke was seen to be doing more harm than good.

In the earliest second-wave feminist anthology, *Woman in Sexist Society* published in 1971, Alta in a short narrative called 'Pretty' exclaims: 'the first thing i do … is to look around at all of you to see who is prettier than i.'[63] The literature of the period makes clear that female gratification and attainment were perceived to be measured by how closely they compared to media images of what Firestone, in 1970, called 'The beauty ideal'.[64] Stannard in the same anthology states, 'The little boy is asked what *he's going to become* when he grows up; the little girl is told she *is* – pretty.'[65] Truth be told, Wilke was annoying – a fly in the ointment, because she was beautiful and that hurt. If women were to be judging their success solely on their looks, then Wilke, the ideal beauty of the time, was painfully accentuating their insecurities, their weaknesses, their failure. She fulfilled all the stereotypical requirements for the prototype 'beauty' and to rub salt in the wounds was proud of and relishing the pleasure gained from this objecthood.

Did Wilke therefore, whatever her stance, have a political responsibility to not collude with this representational system that was disempowering many women? By exaggerating her 'femininity' as the beautiful woman, the flirt, the 'cunt' queen, Wilke in *S.O.S.* tried to underscore how 'being pretty' was equally oppressive and reductive. Her 'pretty' label neutralized her significance as an artist and as a feminist. She was pretty; therefore she was stupid. To this extent labelling, external judgments and presumptuous gazes are wounding and scarring and become how we express ourselves, forming our subjectivity. As she states, 'Even in my sleep I was posing.'[66] By conflating her 'self' with her body through her excessive display of 'femininity', Wilke's work expressed that antagonistic disjuncture current in the literature and activism of the period between body as representation, as femininity, as 'appearing', and body as 'self', as 'being'.

In 1972 John Berger in *Ways of Seeing* described the way in which a woman splits her 'self' in two, the surveyor and the surveyed, as she tailors herself to be what she thinks she ought to be. Jo Spence speaks angrily about this betraying and conflicting self. Spence's shame came from many years of trying to 'pass' as middle class. For bell hooks the 'hurt' was caused by 'desire and complicity', having to 'forget racism' and to a large extent sexism, in order to enjoy the pleasures of the cinematic experience.[67] To this extent the traditional conventions of the pin-up genre and its forebear the nude, betray women's sexuality and agency by setting a homogenized standard of perfection. Women compete with each other to be this stereotype in order to procure their own pleasure, success, power or advancement as objects of desire, despite the consequences of this action. Their public presence becomes a threefold tussle between their self, their self-to-the-other and the gaze. This becomes their art. And as Berger states, 'Her own sense of being in herself is supplanted by a sense of being appreciated as herself by another.'[68]

Wilke's work attempts to reinsert her own pleasure, her own sense of agency into our way of seeing the female body whilst enunciating this as an inevitable struggle. By conflating 'appearing' with 'being' she playfully accentuates and painfully encapsulates her 'self' as dissonant, as contradictory. By inserting the 'self', women's sexual agency and subject position back into the nude Wilke attempts to restore the power imbalance in the interface between the self and the gaze. Re-appropriating the cultural imaging of the female body can control the way women are perceived and therefore help to liberate and revitalize how women perceive themselves. Maria Buszek writes about the early 1990s post-feminist interventions into male dominated spaces by *The Riot Grrrls* with their prolific recycling of the pin-up genre in their 'zines (their magazines or fanzines). From Geekgirl to Minx, sexiness, wit and intelligence infused the display of these bodies to inspire and Buszek states they 'contribute a feminist voice to ordinarily male-dominated spaces in which they felt silenced'.[69]

Joanne Munford in 'Wake up and smell the lipgloss' poignantly argues, however, that these feminists were still young, 'pretty', healthy, white and middle class, thus they risked repeating the second wave feminists' mistakes.[70] By continuing to 'rubber-stamp' the existing stereotypes, the group, like Wilke herself, risked distancing, alienating and ultimately disempowering a large percentage of women who could not or did not want to conform. They also, presumably, would have been shocked themselves once they got older and could not or would not do this anymore. By attempting to recode existing motifs they not only risked perpetuating and reinforcing a crushing exclusivity but also failed to intervene at the source of this exploitation where they would have had the most effective political, economic and social clout.

Wilke's work acknowledges this checkmate. In *Portrait of the Artist with her Mother, Selma Butter* (1978–81) Wilke succinctly expresses this contradictory multiplicitous self through the smile. She pleasurably affirms herself as a sensual subject whilst acknowledging her complicity in a representational system that denies her mother's and indeed many other women's existence. This smile is poised at the epicentre of pleasure and displeasure. It is 'knowing' rather than liberating, and formed within contradiction. Parallels can be drawn with Jo Spence's *Beyond the Family Album 1939 to 1979: Twenty Nine Years*. With reference to this image, Spence recalls: 'Twenty nine years: a last fling at being "beautiful". By now I had learnt to tip my head back slightly (saves retouching), and to smile in a way which hid my dreadful teeth.'[71] Like Wilke, Spence's smile acknowledges the ambiguity of pleasure. She is simultaneously both enjoying and acknowledging the ephemerality and artificiality of being 'pretty'. Ultimately, this kind of personal empowerment comes at a price.

We return to the article quoted at the beginning of this section, in which Gibson spoke superciliously about the benefits of feminism. If the modern, young feminist is assertively matching men in her dominant ravenous sexual conquests whilst holding down equal rights and pay, does this sense of agency now mean that we have a post-colonized body? Or if we can interpret the young female body as the most nubile and effective commodity of exchange within the capitalist system, does the social encouragement of her sexual excess open her up to further abuse and exploitation?

Gibson assumes that ravenous sexual conquests are something women actually want or should want. Is this in itself not a gendered view of sexual pleasure and rights? What if many prefer monogamy? Additionally, strippers, porn stars and hookers are all *paid* to be sexy. Surely, shouldn't sexual liberation mean being sexy for free? Or does

Gibson's triptych of 'strippers, porn stars and hookers' actually work seriously to infiltrate the heart of this exploitation by taking control economically, socially and therefore politically?

What Wilke's legacy demonstrates is that it is our power as readers and visual artists that determines how we use these images. There are no simple answers. The tenuous balance between power and desire is never going to be resolved. The objecthood of the body gives us the potential to be both empowered and co-opted back into the system. A question that both Schneemann's and Wilke's work raises is whether 'equality' would really involve women negating their beautiful bodies or whether it might rather involve both sexes enjoyment of their own and each other's beautiful bodies. Why are men who revel in their own beauty assumed to be gay or considered 'girly'? And why when a female artist or filmmaker portrays beautiful men, for instance Sam Taylor-Wood or Claire Denis who directed *Beau Travail*, is the work immediately labelled homoerotic, as if a female desiring gaze (for a man) cannot exist?

This chapter has demonstrated the historical incompatibility between women's attractiveness, 'prettiness', and their subject power as socially active decision-making agents. We now return to our exploration of burlesque. The last three chapters will be dedicated to unravelling how burlesque glamorously, disrespectfully and 'unnaturally' married these historical opposites. First, Chapter 3 will look at this incompatibility within the world of business. The connection between gender and business is a very new and thriving research area and has opened up a new perspective on how women and 'femininity' operated and operate in the world of work. The combination of 'femininity' and 'business' has always implied prostitution: women selling their body. This is what burlesque performers challenged in their 'leg business'. They brashly and brazenly forwarded a different meaning of the association of money and sex, which tried to eradicate or at least highlight the pitfall of stigma. Chapter 3 will therefore explore this explicitly female and feminine intervention into the world of business.

Gypsy Rose Lee (Culver Pictures).

3.

The 'Leg Business'

MONEY

The man's world of business

The emergence of burlesque performers expressed a new burgeoning model of womanhood that encroached on the male domain of business, challenging the truism of business being a man's world. Burlesque and female opportunism flourished at the cusp of boom and bust because the stuff of male entrepreneurship and risk-taking during the boom had been weakened. Between 1870 and 1930 there was a huge increase in women entering the business world and the labour market in the USA. The clerical sector typified this expansion, with female labour increasing from 2.5 per cent in 1870 to 53 per cent in 1930. This signalled an important shift in the status of women. Kwolek-Folland states: 'For the first time in American history women could choose a paid career or occupation rather than wifehood and motherhood as their life work. Some could even attempt to combine the two.'[1] The new stages and growth in capitalism began to open up opportunities for women, changing the structures of the family and workforce. Women began to have a more visible presence in the public domain.

Women who had become cut off from making a living and had taken on the roles of housewife, mother and wife were now being challenged into more resourceful and enterprising 'gendered endeavours'.[2] A vivid illustration of these endeavours with its sense of risk and self-reliance is illustrated in Gypsy Rose Lee's memoirs. Her mother's inventive but not always successful money-making schemes included an egg business, 'jelly that didn't jell, turkeys that didn't thrive, guinea pigs that didn't multiply'[3] and taking in paying guests at her farmhouse, whom she crammed into all the rooms in her house including the sun porch. She also convinced them to do the chores by explaining that part of the 'fun' of living on a farm was to experience it firsthand. 'It was all good, wholesome outdoor activity, Mother said, and slenderizing besides.' That way she managed to get her barn re-roofed, her chicken coop painted and her driveway widened free of charge.[4]

This example is useful for demonstrating a shrewd female entrepreneurial spirit and a different, more resourceful kind of female role model. During periods of depression, daughters and wives have explored alternative avenues for earning money in order to keep the household afloat. Mothers and wives in the depths of depression would have frequently sold their possessions, produced moonshine, grown their own food, made their own clothes and relied on a network of other female friends to help ends meet. Women have not only had a key role bringing money into the household but have also had a substantial say over how that money was spent. In fact, Margaret Walsh comments that in the late nineteenth century 85 per cent of household expenditure was determined by women.[5] Forced to concede or at least challenge his role as the sole provider, the father/husband was also forced to concede some of his control over the household, sparking off re-negotiating debates over gender and sex roles.

In the 1860s and the 1870s male white bourgeois culture was restructuring and reasserting itself in reaction to the changes in production, class, immigration and the social demands from women. It was a period of extreme insecurity. The 'naturalness' of the bourgeois order was being consistently challenged. In the UK, feminists were using the essentialist notion forwarded by eugenists and the cult of sensibility,[6] of women's weaker, passive yet morally superior nature and man's aggressive, lustful nature, to force change in relation to the power imbalance and make men legally and socially accountable for their actions. They took on the role of moral torchbearers for purity, a higher, more civilized order and spiritual enrichment. Similarly, across the Atlantic feminists were using this role of moral torchbearers to champion many causes including abolition, suffrage, prohibition, anti-prostitution and anti-burlesque campaigns.

However, if fragility, purity and frigidity were being harnessed as a strategy – a tool for certain late nineteenth-century middle-class women to assert themselves publicly[7] – then it only acted as a hindrance and a psychological bulwark for other women who were of a different class, sexuality or ethnicity, or women from a similar background who did not want to uphold these puritanical values. Female performers of burlesque expressed this alternative model via a backlash again restrictive and exclusive conceptions of womanhood. Their performance was 'low', overtly sexualized, loud and feminized. They were revelling in their 'unladylikeness'. These performers demonstrated a kind of feminine behaviour that was pushy, assertive, sexual and free. They were reflecting a new kind of working-class woman, such as the Bowery Gal, who was becoming more visible on the streets and in the workplace. She wanted to make a point ostentatiously of her new status as a more financially independent worker as well being a sexual, young single lady who wanted to be on view. As Christine Stansell iterates, this public presence did not give these girls any real formal power in terms of trade unions or party politics but it was a presence that held considerable 'imaginative and symbolic power'.[8]

By virtue of their small contribution to the household, young women were also exacting some power over their 'free time'. Although some girls would have been expected to hand over all of their wages at the end of the week, the son, as a matter of course, would have been allowed to keep a portion of his to do with as he wished. Some young women were therefore having their own adventures and enjoying the social and personal powers that financial independence brought. By 'making a living' women were getting a taste of their potential as able, competent subjects and as a consequence were beginning to achieve a greater sense of power and agency. Women who earned a living – the burlesque strippers, the working-class and some middle-class women (who were the first to lose their jobs in the 1930s depression) – were blamed for the onset of depression, for taking men's jobs or for an overall degeneracy in society, whilst simultaneously being labelled money grabbers and the bane of man's economic existence by male burlesque comics.

With the system weakened, women were both quietly and loudly challenging the legitimacy of 'Business as a Man's World', what Margaret Walsh would describe as a 'gendered flow of decisions, events and consequences'[9] and the power and dependency implicit in this. In contrast, middle-class feminists were using their female status as fragile and de-sexualized beings paradoxically, to acquire more power and experience in the public domain as fund-raisers, orators, politicians, negotiators and businesswomen. They were using a particular femininity, what Joan Rivière would call a 'masquerade of womanliness' in order to acquire more power and be more accepted in the man's world of business, politics and public speaking. Rivière's example (some say it is autobiographical) is of a woman who wanted to be accepted as a 'user of signs' (a speaker, lecturer and writer) and an equal rival to man. However, to do this she had to reject her body as a sexual 'sign object' whilst still wanting to assert her femininity to ensure her standing as a heterosexual woman.[10]

This paradox of superiority through weakness has, Melanie Philips argues, always been at the heart of feminism.[11] Power acquired through this conjecture of victimhood was permitted because it was laced with a non-threatening uselessness and helplessness that demanded paternal protection. This correlates also with Angel Kwolek-

Folland's description of the early twentieth-century sales and management workplace, where acceptable 'feminine' qualities for young unmarried women such as 'sauciness', 'impudence' and 'inconsistency'[12] were being inverted to suggest that these were business strengths rather that womanly weaknesses.[13] 'Impudence' became an acceptable version of male aggression, therefore, Kwolek-Folland argues, accommodating 'aggression into the canon of feminine business behaviour'.[14]

Post-feminists in the 1990s (Roiphe, 1993; Paglia, 1992; Wolf, 1991) drew parallels with Victorian women's espousal of 'victim-womanhood' and the 'victim-feminism' that they saw emerging in the campus date rape and sexual harassment furore. These popular feminists saw this as damaging: representations of these intelligent, future professional, female students were being created that were based primarily on their sexual and physical weakness and vulnerability, and not their success in the academic arena. Post-feminists like Camille Paglia and Katie Roiphe believed that by always emphasizing victimization and subordination women were never going to be able to arrive at a point whereby they could freely accept their own sense of equality in the public arena and responsibilities as independent, desiring women.

These post-feminists were criticized, however, for their limited, closeted gender and sexual politics. They risked making the same mistakes as the nineteenth-century middle-class activists whose 'universal' conception of womanhood and feminism elided or negated any worthy and necessary critique of class, race, capitalism or unbridled individualism. As white, middle-class, 'Ivy League/Oxbridge' educated and privileged women, their assertive 'call to arms' for more power and more pleasure left a severe lack of room for other models and created a negative impact on other women. As black cultural critic and author bell hooks has argued, this feminism belied any attempt at being inclusive.

Second-wave feminists' desire for equality and inclusion for all women appears to have ended up inadvertently privileging one particular set of values, one particular perspective on 'empowerment' and 'equality' and an individualist approach that promotes one particular kind of 'individual'. In the desire to bring all women together as independent, self-assured and fulfilled women, feminists seemed to have fed and inflated the very system they set out to challenge. They have also perhaps in the process helped to promote and create an even larger chasm between privileged and underprivileged women. Barbara Ehrenreich and Arlie Russell Hochschild spell out a similar hypothesis in *Global Woman*:

> Only it does not bring them together in the way that second-wave feminists in affluent countries once liked to imagine – sisters and allies struggling to achieve common goals. Instead, they come together as mistress and maid, employer and employee, across a great divide of privilege and opportunity.[15]

The system promotes and rewards particular values. Women who choose to work every hour under the sun, follow a career and leave their children with an underpaid nanny are loudly applauded as exemplary, for they serenade the establishment's value system. When middle-class women do this, it is iconic and empowering, even though frequently the 'care' is provided by Eastern European underpaid women, so the unpaid/underpaid childcare just shifts onto another 'Other'. Madeleine Bunting in an article in the *Guardian* in June 2004 drew an interesting parallel between the rise of neo-liberal capitalism and the rise of a feminism that 'articulated itself in terms of professional success, helping to promote a concept of the self only available through high-status paid work'.[16] There is, however, an undercurrent of venom in the establishment's promotion of the strong, independent, professional woman.

Women who encroach on male power and succeed in the 'male' professional domain still have to perform 'womanhood' correctly: they must know their place and they must look good. If they do not perform this role impeccably then this very deviation is held up to underscore their ultimate failure as 'women'. News coverage about Cherie

Blair consistently focused on how she looked, not what she achieved, as if this is ultimately how she, as a woman, is going to be judged. The infamous morning-after-the-election shot of a ruffled Cherie Blair as she opened the front door to collect the milk in May 1997 perhaps supports this argument. Kirsty Scott, in an article entitled 'This isn't what we really, really want', in *The Herald* in 1997 comments on 'the distressing sight of one of the country's most able lawyers reduced to the role of tailor's dummy as she trailed around the UK after her husband with instructions to look mute and adoring'.[17]

As an extremely able woman in her own right, Cherie Blair was expected, like a 'diplomatic wife', to consistently look good and be servile. Cynthia Enloe in *Making Feminist Sense of International Relations* recounts the story of Lady Fretwell, wife of Britain's former ambassador to France, who kept a picture on her bulletin board of the stylish and slim, Mme Giscard d'Estaing greeting the 'lumpy, unkempt' wives of Brezhnev and Gromyko 'as a reminder of what can happen if you let yourself go'.[18] How one looks becomes politically significant. This was exemplified in the 2006 'cash-for-coiffeurs' scandal that erupted after Cherie Blair handed the Labour Party her £7,700 hairdressing bill.[19] She was meant to fulfil her role as the wife of the Prime Minister unobtrusively yet on command ... to make no waves ... and expect nothing in return. It was pivotal that she successfully fulfilled her role as a 'woman' and as a wife because if she did this well she could act as an asset to her husband; however, if she did this badly, she could be an absolute liability.

The key point that I would like to make here is that women seem to get caught in a balancing act when they enter the public arena of entertainment, corporate or political business. They have to negotiate traditional gender parameters and conform to expectations ... seamlessly.

In the 1860s and 1870s Lydia Thompson's troupe pushed against the 'correct' gendered boundaries for 'womanhood'. They parodied and sexualized both masculine and feminine genders, combining their male costume that delineated their womanly curves and sex appeal with their 'masculine' characteristics such as bawdy language, assertiveness and humour. They did not reject their sexuality but in fact used and exploited this very play on gender and sexuality to further their success as businesswomen. In the 1930s Gypsy Rose Lee also fully exploited her sexualized stage personae, an example being when she tantalizingly auctioned off one of her costumes sequin by sequin. This self-conscious manipulation of an unmanageable but ultimately career-lucrative combination of sexuality and femininity was also used by women to gender-orientate the labour market in the 1930s. As Kwolek-Folland states, 'Women's clothing reminded managers of the explosive potential of sexuality and of management's ultimate inability to control the social construction of a worker's gendered self.'[20]

The British Blondes set a physical standard for burlesque performers. These were no wilting violets. They were described as 'beefy', in a similar way to Eva Tanguay who performed in vaudeville in the early 1900s and was described by Jessica Glasscock as looking as if she 'could hold her own in a barroom brawl'.[21] From the Blondes onwards the weight requirement for burlesque performers was 250lb (approximately 114kg) – a stark contrast to the conventional 'ideal' figure of the slender waif of the day who tried to take up as little room as possible.

Interestingly, Rubens' nudes include female figures that are butch and most frequently seen in action, in contrast to what we think of as 'Rubenesque', which is now simply taken to mean 'overweight'. The Blondes' 'transvestite' voluptuous combination of 'masculine' and 'feminine' was popular in the business world of the 1980s, too, with the idea of power-dressing that included padded shoulders, body-hugging suits, red lipstick, a see-through white blouse and intimidating attitude. Chris Straayer argues that the transgressive potential of the 'she-butch', best symbolized by 1980s icon Annie Lennox, came through the appropriation of 'male action'. These figures not only achieved 'a postmodern dismantling of gender and sex difference but also a greater sexuality'.[22]

The burlesque performers drew upon as well as inspired what was happening in the workplace. This 'greater sexuality' was how they differed from the professional 'new women' of the 1920s/1930s and 1860/1870s, who believed that that they needed to renounce their 'feminine' sexual power in order to be taken more seriously intellectually, politically and in business. The 1920s *garçonne* look, however, did also have a certain type of sexiness and prettiness, too, as well as certain transvestite elements (especially with the bob and smoking, both of which were provocative at the time). This look nevertheless modelled itself on reining in, containing or even excluding voluptuous curves, flesh and excessive 'feminine' sexual display. This may have distanced many women who wanted the independence of working but without having to compromise their sexuality and 'womanliness'.

By combining gender and business, burlesque or the 'leg business' communicated wider vistas of possibilities for female agency. Burlesque theatres were one of the few 'legitimate' businesses where there was an unquenchable demand for women. There was no need for skills or qualifications. These women were profiting to some degree by the unregulated market demand for cheap entertainment and sexy 'girls'. However, it was the 'soubrettes', the older, more experienced strippers, with the sharp business mind, the witty, biting politicized repartee and intelligence who could reap the biggest financial rewards. As I will now explore, these 'stars' were seen as ruthless and unfeminine in their drive for self-publicity and control over their public image, and immoral in their masculine assertion of their sexual awareness.

Ruthless tycoons

In 1990, Camille Paglia, in her stark, pull-no-punches manner, pronounced Madonna as 'the future of feminism'.[23] As 'an international star of staggering dimensions' and 'a shrewd business tycoon' it is Madonna who is, she states, 'the true feminist' and a pure exemplary model for young girls and women.[24] As with many of Paglia's essays, her argument is bite-sized, headline-grabbing hyperbole ('greatest', 'best', 'most perfect', 'brilliant', 'most enduring') that somehow deprives the argument of needed subtlety. This sensationalism puts Paglia in much disfavour with many feminist scholars. Her thinking, however, holds an incisive, entertaining, no-nonsense clarity that gives her audience an argument to kick against. In this particular argument Paglia reproaches old-guard feminists for their self-damaging and wilful blindness to one woman's phenomenal success.

Feminist denunciation of Madonna boiled down to a view of her undeservedly successful position as a talentless and tacky opportunistic exploiter of femininity and sexuality. Madonna 'degraded' womanhood: 'she was vulgar, sacrilegious, stupid, shallow, opportunistic'.[25] Here was a woman who had smashed through the glass ceiling that prevented women from reaching the top in terms of pay, reputation and success. Here was also a woman who riled feminists because her success was not secured (in some feminists' opinion) by legitimate and worthy means. 'Femininity' and 'business' were therefore not seen to be compatible bedfellows. To be taken 'seriously' you had to be seen to be rising to the top through your talent and intelligence, not your sex appeal or prettiness. This is what gave your success real substance. Being phenomenally successful by virtue of your pushy prettiness was shallow, flimsy and easy: a backward step.

The same critical assumptions and aspersions maligned and marked Lydia Thompson and the British Blondes. Their rise to stardom was mired by accusations of vulgar opportunism, and implications of ill-gotten gains. At the period in which the Blondes were huge, burlesque performers could earn up to $1,000 a week (Sobel reports that the Blondes earned $6,000 for their final three shows at Niblo's Garden in New York).[26] This is a staggering amount if you bear in mind this is what headlining strippers were earning in 1969 when union wages started at $175 a week, an amount that was still much more than many unskilled women could get.[27]

Earning such a substantial amount and ostentatiously parading these gains in the form of jewels and furs would as a matter of course have been regarded as tasteless and disreputable. These women were aggressively marketing their sex appeal and exploiting an unquenchable thirst and demand for exciting, sexy entertainment. In the aftermath of war and on the cusp of depression, with many marriages and families fraught with tension and fractured masculinity, they were assured success and outstanding financial gains: men wanted to *feel* like men and women wanted to *be* like these women.

The 'leg business' astutely cashed in on this need for escape, sensation, entertainment and titillation. Lydia Thompson's act filled this gap in the market and exploited it to the full. Thompson's rigorous self-promotion and clever exploitation of new modern technology and media reconfigured the word 'business'. As Mary Yeager points out, the word 'business' may well be one of the more stubbornly gendered words and activities of our time.[28] When combined with 'femininity', 'business' could only have one meaning – that of prostitution – and it was this interpretation that the Blondes were trying to shake off.

Their success came because of their driving ambition and intelligent colonization of media that was in its infancy (particularly photography and newspapers) and therefore without ground rules. This was seen as the reason for both Joan Crawford's astonishing amount of leverage in Hollywood in the 1920s and 1930s and Lucille Ball's success as a producer and writer in television in the 1950s.[29]

Lydia Thompson had sharp business acumen and realized the power of publicity in the furtherance of her status and career. Before her arrival in America from England, Thompson had her press agent send out releases to be published in American journals, exaggerating her importance and stature:

> At Helsingfors her pathway was strewn with flowers and the streets illuminated with torches carried by ardent admirers ... At Lember, a Captain Ludoc Baumbarten of the Russian dragoons took some flowers and a glove belonging to Miss Thompson, placed them on his breast; then shot himself through the heart, leaving on his table a note stating that his love for her brought on the fatal act.[30]

As a result, her long-awaited tour beginning in 1869 at the Wood's Theatre in New York had people queuing up at the box office. The Blondes became an overnight phenomenon, attracting huge audiences in every city in which they appeared. Dita Von Teese also used this astute sense of business and theatrical publicity by arriving at Harrods to sign her book in a horse-drawn carriage.

Dita Von Teese's official website reveals her huge success as a businesswoman. She sells her own brand of lingerie, photographs, videos and her book via her website, with help by way of the free advertising in newspaper articles, fashion magazines, celebrity bash paparazzi shots and references to her relationship with Marilyn Manson which help to add to her popularity and appeal. Her website oozes with sexuality, created for optimum business impact; it lures you in and then demands hard cash to see more. Her glamorous niche of sexiness has created an unquenchable market demand. Her image is everywhere. She is cleverly filling a lack, a gap she sees in the market for the dressy glamour of old, and is making the consummate icon out of these missing ingredients.

Gypsy Rose Lee also knew the power of the media to further her career and employed her own press agent, apparently the first stripper to do so. She played the media to her own advantage, with articles being written about her almost daily. *Variety* remarked: 'Miss Lee has received more free space in two months than the rest of the burlesque business, including everybody in it, usually gets in two years.'[31] Gypsy Rose Lee knew that she had to titillate as well as stand out from the crowd to make her act seem special. She constructed and primed herself as an 'intellectual stripper', putting her own slant on quotes from philosophers and literature. Morton Minsky and Milt Machlin write about one example in their book *Minsky's Burlesque*. After quarrelling with her lover in public, Gypsy was asked by the press whether she hated men:

> Why the little rascals. I adore them – some of them. Let me freshen up a little on my philosophy. Wasn't it St Augustine who said, 'Man is born in filth and predisposed to evil?' Well, I don't subscribe to that.

I incline more to Clement of Alexandria, who wrote that 'man should not be ashamed to love that which God was not ashamed to create'.[32]

It could be argued that the burlesque performer treads a fine line between using an overtly bold and aggressively entrepreneurial manner to 'sell' 'femininity' and falling back on old dominant stereotypes that equate 'selling femininity' with prostitution, or at least a looseness of morality. Rather than undermining and reinterpreting old gender assumptions and stereotypes of women in 'business', the influential figure of the burlesque performer could have ultimately hindered other women who were pushing for success in the public 'masculine' world of business. Lydia Thompson and another British Blonde, Pauline Markham, fought vehemently against this presumption that if women were earning a living by displaying their sexualized femininity they must therefore be whoring their bodies. They fought to protect their morality. They were businesswomen, they were performance artists; they were therefore not prostitutes but independent women who were challenging these traditional gender assumptions.

The performance of their constructed, staged, female sexuality was about 'selling' an attitude, an idea and entertainment that was pleasurable to watch; however, the display of their female bodies did not equate with the 'sale' of these same bodies. Tracy C. Davis writes about this in relation to actresses in Victorian England: 'Like prostitutes, actresses were public women; their livelihood depended on their attractiveness and recognizability.'[33] Davis argues that the expectations and assumptions made about actresses, dancers and artistes were in part determined by 'the geography of the sensual activity in the neighbourhood', which reinforced how women were read as female bodies in the public arena. Up until 1857, the market for pornographic imagery was unregulated and theatres would have been situated next to shops that sold a whole array of explicit and erotic material. Actresses were therefore being 'defined by what pornography and its marketplace relayed'.[34] In mid–late nineteenth-century America, the assumptions made about actresses were also being made about other working women who were venturing out into the workplace. Sexual display in a male environment was understood as a woman's rate of exchange.

Even without overt sex appeal, however, the assumption that businesswomen sleep with their bosses in order to move up the ladder remains rife. When women were moving more conspicuously into the business world in the 1980s this same equation was still presumed. Corporate business was a sexist environment and there was always the assumption that women had earned their success by virtue of their sex. This was the case with US Bendix Corporate Vice President Mary Cunningham, who in the 1980s was snidely accused of sleeping her way to the top – how could she be *that* talented or *that* deserving? The well-publicized romance between Cunningham and the then head of Bendix was blamed for ruining the company's attempts at a hostile takeover of Martin Marietta, which in turn destroyed Bendix. The director of Martin Marietta said at the time: 'We'll burn this company to the ground before we let that [woman] have it'[35] and then consequently turned the tables with their own hostile takeover of Bendix.

As an attractive 29-year-old woman, only a few years out of Harvard, Cunningham's promotion was immediately attributed to sexual manipulation. Susan Lee sarcastically commented in her article 'Goodness had everything to do with it' in the *New York Times* (1984) that Cunningham described herself as coming from a new Yuppie generation where sex was not 'a necessary corporate skill'.[36] Must one assume from this comment, therefore, that up until this new generation of businesswomen 'sex' *was* seen as women's key corporate skill? Lee argues that Cunningham never did say 'what she did do to make it to the top', aside from 'pouring coffee, writing college applications for Mr Agee's daughter, finding cleaning women and hostessing parties'.[37] Finally she comments that perhaps Cunningham is in fact innocent because she comes across as 'awesomely prissy' and 'boring and whiney'.[38] Succeeding in business without sexual manipulation is therefore seen to equate with sexual frigidity and lack of character.

From the late 1980s, exploitation of feminine wiles and assets began to figure more in the language used in popular magazines to describe successful female executives. What was formerly seen as oppressive and restrictive, such as female sexuality and motherhood, was now perceived potentially advantageous to women:

> They don't act like men or think like them. They never dress in androgynous suits ... they don't golf ... This new female elite is definitely not your parents' paradigm. Remember when executive women used to be overwhelmingly single and childless? All of [these women] have children. Five are married and two ... used to be ... These women skilfully exploit [their sexuality].[39]

What these examples of 'career women' illustrate is how women have been squeezed between a marketplace that reduces the visibility and success of 'woman' to her sexuality (sexualized whore or desexualized mother) and her own private and public need for integrity, fulfilment, pleasure and success.

We still sit between the two extremes of mother (desexualized) and whore (sexualized male fantasy). On the one hand we have the mother/career woman who is sensible, responsible and hard-working – exhausted – and on the other hand that 'pneumatic, take-me-now-big-boy fuck-puppet of male fantasy'[40] with no in-between and a divide that is ever increasing. Feminist aspirations of equality, of women wanting to 'have it all', translate at the turn of the millennium into middle-class women who are 'all-slog-all-speed'. America has coined both Super Woman Syndrome and the Hurried Woman Syndrome to describe this phenomenon of all-work-no-play contemporary womanhood. We are also, however, simultaneously surrounded by sexualized images of women on advertisements, cable stations, internet sites and so-called lads' mags.

As described by Angela Phillips in her article 'The rise and fall of silent girly-girls in G-strings' (2006), young women are buffered between the need to be 'good' – controlling their body and their life by way of education, postponing motherhood to establish a career and deferring gratification (being mindful of the media's constant messages of the perils of binge drinking) – and a marketplace that promotes the idea of the 'bad' girl who needs to dress sexily and provocatively in order to feel wanted.[41] Dita Von Teese seems, like Madonna before her, to integrate both the 'good' girl (successful, astute businesswoman, motherhood on hold and moderate alcohol intake – but never losing control) with the 'bad' girl (sexy display). Could her popularity therefore be attributed to her absolute success at embodying the pinnacle of this contemporary equivocal ideal?

At the beginning of this section Camille Paglia was quoted as forwarding Madonna as the future of feminism. Her strength and ability as a business tycoon, like the burlesque queens Von Teese, Lydia Thompson and Gypsy Rose Lee, was indeed something laudable and inspirational. Yet what must be asked is whether this individualist model of behaviour is challenging the status quo. Are our contemporary sexualized, rich and professional burlesque 'queens' still permitting and encouraging the old analogy between femininity, sex and money? How liberating can your sexuality be when you need to make money from it? If your income depends on a certain type of 'sexy image', what happens if you step outside it or, indeed, get old? Would this therefore mean that you lose your livelihood? This 'image' disallows for experimentation or life's changes. Is the burlesque performer therefore irresponsibly blocking women's potential for being or doing anything bar earning by virtue of her sex? It seems that if this type of business is not backed up by some kind of informed debate, it could expose some women to abuse and just encourage more relentless images of pure greed and pure 'cunt'.

The second half of this chapter will intertwine and explore the relationship between the burlesque phenomenon and the sex business.

SEX

The unholy trinity (strippers, hookers and porn stars)

The sex industry is now worth an estimated $20 billion a year.[42] Globalized and denationalized as a result of the Internet, pornography and prostitution are now less regulated and much more easily accessible, particularly with international tourism and business travel also making commercial sex a booming trade in poorer countries. The dramatic growth in the sex industry came with the advent of industrial capitalism, with businessmen travelling away from home and in need of 'comfort'. This underbelly of society now tempts customers via cyberspace. Its nefarious actions are monitored but cannot be completely controlled. 'We can pay to see live sex, watch a woman pee, or book time with an e-prostitute.'[43] As a direct reaction to this major expansion in the sex industry in the late 1990s Major Rudolph Giuliani banned legalized forms of commercial sex in zoned areas of New York. This was an attempt to 'clean up' areas that he felt had been adversely affected by sex-related businesses such as X-rated adult video/magazine shops, strip clubs and adult cinemas. Pro fam ily values were at stake.

It was in the midst of this furore over legitimate and illegitimate, respectable and disreputable, clean and dirty 'business' that the new wave of burlesque performers erupted into the middle-class imagination most prominently during the turn-of-the-millennium years. Fantastically lush, sensual, colourful, naughty and cheeky websites tempt the viewer like a peeping tom into their burlesque world of tease. With names that mimic their contemporaries in the world of Internet porn and e-prostitution (Dita Von Teese, Dirty Martini, Catherine D'Lish, Southern Jeze-Belles) these performers give their viewers a glimpse, a taste of their extravagant excess and glamour, that leaves them clambering for their credit cards to buy a DVD, a photograph, go to a gig or join a dance class. These women use cutting-edge technology. They are contemporary businesswomen who make their websites the cornerstone of their money-spinning businesses.

What the explosion of the new burlesque phenomenon does is to force the mainstream to reconsider its interpretation of disreputable, pornographic or sleazy entertainment. These strippers and fetish models seeped into respectable circles to cohort with the rich, the famous and the elegant stars of the high world of fashion and 'A'-list celebrity. I am not arguing that the recent burlesque revival in New York was in direct protest to Giuliani's clean-up campaign but rather that it was an indirect, hybridized result. What Giuliani inadvertently created was an environment that permitted and encouraged burlesque to cross over from the underground into the mainstream.

Like the contemporary alignment of sexualized 'low' flesh with social decay, the nineteenth century also blamed the 'leg business' for diseasing and polluting the nation's morality. Burlesque stars of the 1930s, such as Gypsy Rose Lee and Mae West, were blamed by some for the cause of the depression and subsequently were arrested on many occasions. The Production Code (Hays Code) of 1930 banned any mention of 'loose' women from cinema as well as nudity and suggestive dance. Similarly the eruption of burlesque into the nineteenth-century middle-class arena came directly after the banning of the honky tonk (with the Anti-Concert Saloon Bill of April 1862). This was seen as a direct reaction against the 'waiter girls' who by the use of alcohol and their sexual powers were seen to be tempting respectable men out of their senses and out of purse. Junius Henri Browne describes an encounter with a 'waiter girl' in *The Great Metropolis* (1869):

> She tells you that so good-looking and nice a gentleman ought not to be alone, or go without a drink ... then you have another drink, then another, then another ... The scene of repulsion is replaced by one of attraction, almost of fascination ... The tones of your attendant Circe change. They appear soft, and low, and sweet; and her once harsh face grows lovely in the glamour before your eyes. The tawdry

hall becomes a place of enchantment ... You call for more liquor. You sing; you dance; you are happy. You whisper tenderly to the nymph at your side ... There is a floating, swimming motion before your eyes and then complete oblivion.[44]

When this gentleman regains consciousness he realizes he has no money, he has been cheapened by this 'foolish experience' that has cost him morally and financially. His account sounds more like a date rape in its narration of voluntary lure and involuntary exploitation. This gentleman wants to buy into the short-term thrill of living life on the edge of his safe, middle-class, respectable cocoon. He wants to be seduced but feels disgust and revulsion at being at the mercy of this pariah of respectable society and her sexual charms. It is this desire to willingly and extravagantly pay out for this transgressive, dangerous, edgy experience that makes the sex industry such big business. Judith Lynne Hanna writes about the experience of one erotic dancer called Nancy who feels both psychologically and economically empowered, when 'crazy bastards pay money to goggle at your body ... It is an interesting dynamic to have almost total control over a man and his wallet by manipulating him with our sexual energy.'[45]

Why is it that topless bar patrons spend so much money 'just to look at naked women'? Or to rephrase this question, why is it that men tip so generously when they are not actually going to get any physical sex? 'What exactly are patrons buying – or buying into?'[46] Historically, women's 'respectability' may have stripped them of their sexiness. You could therefore see why a man might have wanted a more overtly sexual woman. However, in the post-feminist era would you not think that women would be more sexually open and therefore men would not need to 'escape'? The answer to this is perhaps that women have not become so – or is it that what women want sexually is not what men would wish them to want? Burlesque expresses this tension between the sexes, bridging that huge chasm between 'respectability' and sexual 'escape'.

With the USA apparently a nation of absolute extremes, with fervent conservative politics and strict religious beliefs on the one side and a thriving sex industry on the other, is it no wonder that the new phenomenon of burlesque erupted first into the American cultural arena before filtering out globally? Burlesque with its innocent, humorous raunchiness seemed to accommodate that middle ground between the two groups. Turn-of-the-millennium American society, like Victorian society, is a society of double standards. On the one hand, adult establishments of a sexual nature are banned because of the imagery that is seen to be promoting violence towards women and children. On the other hand the USA, and other countries in its stead, use the female sexualized image to sell everything. Religious and conservative values of the family passed off as feminism are unable to be reconciled with pure venal animal lust and sexual gratification.

A hard core of feminists continue this sentiment into contemporary history. Such feminists, described by opponents as the anti-sex campaigners, include the likes of Catherine MacKinnon, Karen Davis and Andrea Dworkin, who have written relentlessly against the objectification of women in any form and its harmful effects on women and children. MacKinnon has been strongly opposed by Parveen Adams and Mark Cousins. In one chapter in *The Emptiness of the Image* (1996), entitled 'The truth on assault', they critique the definition of abuse in MacKinnon's 'world'.[47] For MacKinnon, words and images should be considered as sexual acts for they are directed at woman even though she is not there. Pornographic images and/or texts have a message to relay, which is 'get her'. As MacKinnon states, 'This message is addressed directly to the penis, delivered through an erection and taken out on women in the real world.'[48]

For Adams and Cousins, though, there is a vast difference between representation and the event, between fantasy and crime, between the wish and the act. This debate has again come to the fore in the UK, with new laws being put in place that will make it a criminal offence to download explicitly violent pornography. This was a victory for the mother of 31-year-old teacher Jane Longhurst, who was murdered by Graham Coutts hours after he had viewed legal Internet pornography sites that contained scenes of necrophilia and hanging (snuff movies).[49]

When Mayor Giuliani attempted to eradicate legal commercial sex in specific zones in New York he was forced to prove that these businesses were having an adverse affect on local communities, to get around the Supreme Court decision in 1991 that allowed nude dancing a modicum of protection under the First Amendment. By proving that erotic dance was a form of legitimate artistic expression the dancers were able to procure some access to legal rights and protection. In the 1930s, Ziegfeld was allowed to continue displaying nude women because it was seen to be artistic; this kind of entertainment was therefore considered more wholesome. Minsky's burlesque theatres, on the other hand, contained similar acts, with perhaps even less nudity and less titillation, but this brand of burlesque started its life in the rougher parts of the city and was known for being a working-class sleazy entertainment, not 'art'.

The famous Minsky brothers created their brand of burlesque when other burlesque houses were losing their audiences to the cinema and to the more risqué Ziegfeld theatre. From 1913 Samuel Scribner and I.H. Herk ran a censored and 'clean' circuit of burlesque houses called the Columbia Wheel. The Minsky brothers managed to avoid censorship and remain cheap. They therefore flourished. Columbia finally was forced to stop censoring in 1925 due to poor profits and allowed bare-breasted tableaux and the removal of tights – but the damage was done. They had lost their audience to the movies and to burlesque houses like Minsky's.

By 1937 the Supreme Court ruled that burlesque should be banned from New York City, as it was 'the cause of many of our sex crimes',[50] and to simply use the name 'Minsky' was prohibited. However, even if you had legitimacy, if you rose to stardom at Ziegfeld, if you had been given 'artist status' and you had been exonerated of your 'whore' stigma, surely the basic facts remained the same? Whether under the guise of art or not, whether the work is seen as intelligent and cultured or not, women were still getting paid 'to get their kit off'.

Rebecca Schneider suggests that the buying and selling of women's bodies by way of sexual representation and entertainment just creates a situation whereby women become the sexual property of men.[51] Arguing from this perspective, surely whatever the context, selling sex is selling sex and if some women are abused or oppressed socially and politically in society in general as a result of this activity, is it not then pure irresponsibility to continue in this line of work? Many young girls turned to burlesque during the depression because it was work and they needed the cash and at that point in history pretty 'girls' were in demand. Equally, I was told by an American professor that many of his female undergraduate students did pole/erotic dancing or stripping to pay their way through university. Is this worrying? Why do some of us now find this acceptable? Is this kind of labour liberating? Is it all fine now because women are empowered enough not to be bothered or exploited by any of it anyway?

The figure of the burlesque performer clearly demonstrates the balancing act women play between empowerment and exploitation by revealing or selling their nakedness. In order to continue with this debate I shall move back in history, to an argument set out in 1879 by August Bebel (German social democrat and one of the founders of the Social Democratic Party of Germany) in his book *Women Under Socialism*, rephrased by Dorothy Rowe in her book *Representing Berlin* (2003). Under industrial metropolitan capitalism women were caught up in a 'double burden'. First, they were 'socially and economically dependent on men in a male-dominated society but together with proletarian men especially, they were also in thrall to the mechanisms and superstructures of bourgeois capitalism'.[52] Has this subordination and oppression always been the case? Is it still the case?

The shift in scholarly research begins to reinterpret this historical double bind by introducing the contemporary reader to the powerful if controversial luxury, the capitalist commodity figure of the courtesan.[53] Influential and staggeringly charismatic, the courtesan acts as an ideal means of trying to understand, from both a historical and contemporary stance, the power dynamic and the possibilities for female agency when the female body is on hire.

To conclude, I now wish to explore this ambivalent figure of the *demi-monde* from a contemporary standpoint. What does the present fascination with the new burlesque female performer and her take on the courtesan role say about contemporary young women's sexual, social and economic status and value system?

The courtesan

In a 2005 edition of the 'lads' mag' *FHM*, the question was posed: 'How much are you paying for sex?' A form was included to let the reader work out how much he had spent on taking women out. This included travel to and from the woman's or women's home(s), cinema tickets, drinks such as Bacardi Breezers and ad hoc gifts like sexy underwear. He then had to divide the total by the number of 'shags' he had had, to calculate his 'pay per lay'. Under £5 was regarded as 'too cheap – she's about the same price as a Cambodian whore'; up to £20 was 'about the going rate of a Cypriot tart ... Each shag now needs to be a better purchase than a new CD.'[54] For more that £31, apparently, a man should expect feminine sexual skills on a par with a high-class, nipple-twirling Cuban show girl!

Of course, this form was to be received and filled out in a tongue-in-cheek fashion – in fact, the whole of the magazine's content is passed off as 'harmless fun'.[55] A *Guardian* journalist was left feeling as if she should apologise for her 'archaic feminist mindset' when she quizzed *FHM* editors about whether images such as that of 'Abi Titmuss on all fours, offering her thonged bottom doggy-style' were degrading to women ... The reply was: 'You are imposing outmoded sexual politics on a world that doesn't fit [them] any more.'[56]

The message that comes across from the 'pay per lay' questionnaire is that, like anything you buy, the more you pay out, the more you should expect for your money. The skin and bones of what sexual relationships boil down to, for lads' mags, is the rate of exchange ... wining and dining becomes a calculated business deal. You pay up and she'll put out. Women have to be bought, and just as you would expect within the commercial marketplace, the higher your expenditure the better-class whore you will get in return. Why are women still allowing themselves to be bought? Now that women are earning more and attaining social status through their careers, should relationships and seduction not be more equal with regard to 'gifts'? Women want to feel like a million dollars. Women expect to be wined and dined. This is how men mark themselves out as gentlemen...*still*! How many drinks have you had for nothing? I doubt there are too many (straight) women who have never accepted a free drink.

It is still assumed that when men date women it is men who pay for the date. It is also women who get in free to many clubs – they are paying by their presence. They attract the male clientele like bait and those men who 'pick them up' will pay for all their extras. Young men realize quickly the bonus of having a flashy car, their own flat, a fat wallet, and women know or should know that the acceptance of gifts, free drinks, car rides and sexy dressing can signal sexual interest and therefore sexual willingness – the unsaid rule of the sexual encounter. It seems to be naive, greedy or even dangerous not to consider it. Can we assume, therefore, that until women give up these privileges, these freebies, they cannot expect to be thought of as anything less than whores?

A strand of contemporary women's fashion found in the celebrity world and on the high street cements this assumption, with women playing on and subsuming the aesthetic of the whore or erotic worker. The hair extensions, breast enlargements, Brazilian waxes, thongs and long, white-tipped nails come straight from the lap dancing and American porn industries. This appropriation of the fashions of the *demi-monde* was also evident in the mid-nineteenth century and the turn of the twentieth century, when the working-class female subculture of the Bowery Gals and Tough Girls appropriated the styles of prostitutes. The prostitute symbolized a combination of confident sexual allure, self-governance and financial independence with a particularly attractive detachment and singularity. She was hard and sassy, and could look after herself. As young women who were beginning to establish themselves as independent wage earners in the public domain, clothes, attitude and social visibility became the means by which these women could cast aside, even if symbolically, female dependency.

This seepage of the *demi-monde* into everyday living and loving consequently, and perhaps dangerously, blurred the line between courtship and commercial sex. Women's more visible presence 'out on the town' became equated with an expectation that they were easy game. Christine Stansell states:

> In so far as sex retained its associations to exchange and money, women's presence in a *commercial* culture of leisure, based on the purchase of pleasures, could in itself imply sexual willingness ... Commercial culture promoted the assumption that women owed sexual favors in return for men's generosity.[57]

What was interesting at this point in history, with women moving away from traditional gendered roles within the family and into the public domain as bold interlopers, was that each heterosexual encounter held the possibility of veiled and murky interpretations from both parties. In the past relationships were formed within close-knit communities and allowed time to grow over several meetings before the sexual element was negotiated. Away from this safety net, sex could be expected after one night at a dance or even forced upon a girl whilst out alone.

Gang rape was virtually never recorded before 1830; yet from this date on it occasionally would appear in court records. Obviously this did not mean it did not exist...but that women, if gang-raped, were now realizing their power to report it as a crime. Men could not now see it as their right. Of course, non-gang rape has been reported as early as during the Renaissance. In 1612 Agostino Tassi was accused and convicted for the rape of the painter Artemisia Gentileschi, and in the 1630s the painters Nicolas Poussin and Peter Paul Rubens were portraying the *Rape of the Sabines* as brutal rather than 'heroic' or 'patriotic'. Rape in the late nineteenth century became an issue between a man who seriously felt that he had earned his right to sex because of his 'gifts' and a girl who, whether 'knowingly' or 'unwittingly', found herself in a dangerously misunderstood and inherently powerless situation.

The new territory being mapped out by women left sexual interchange charged with ambivalence. Young working-class women were seen to be sexually willing simply by socializing in a commercial culture that associated female visibility with prostitution. The buying of gifts, although still indicative of woman-as-whore, nevertheless gave these young women, who perhaps would have otherwise been forced into sex, some leverage. New sexual codes were being put in place, supported by a network of female peer groups to negotiate levels of decorum and respect and when it was appropriate for women to acquiesce to sexual demands. Angela McRobbie and Jennie Garber comment that girls were strikingly absent from literature on gangs, the only mention often being how pretty or how unattractive they were. Girls and young women were only there, as perceived by outsiders, to please the boys or young men, as eye-candy or simply as the gang 'bike'. In this uncertain terrain of gender relations women eventually came to delineate the boundaries as negotiating subjects rather than as objects that have been negotiated.

Interesting parallels can be drawn with the contemporary situation. There is an absolute plethora of sexual images of women being used to sell just about everything from coffee to sofas, with images of pornography and lap dancing permeating the mainstream. Women again need to take stock of their own position and lines need to be renegotiated. This splurge of pornography demeans meaningful connections between heterosexual couples by deluging our screens, our billboards and our magazines with empty images of 'fuckable' women which promote guiltless sex devoid of tenderness yet intent on profit. And it is being promoted as hip and cool to boot. The frontier between love and 'insensitized' lust is not just being crossed, it is being brutally colonized. Despite the fact that this blurring of the lines benefits male corners of the business world – because, as the cliché goes, 'sex sells' – women also seem to *want* to be sexy. Many hundreds send in pictures of themselves clad in knickers and bra to these lads' mags for free, wanting to show off their sexual appeal, their youth.

Many young women want sexual adventures. However, does this desire to be seen as sexy emerge from a desperate need for approval in a world where if you are female and not 'fuckable' you amount to nothing? The sex industry is heavily reliant for profit on women revealing all. Consumer capitalism is heavily reliant for profit on the promise of pleasure that a product will bring by using the tantalizing combination of women and sex ... is it fortunate (which it is, according to the lads' mags) that many women appear to be gagging to strip their clothes off and engage in casual sex at the drop of a hat? Does this mean therefore that we will all now live happily ever after?

It is an interesting and extremely problematic dilemma, because if we claim that all women who send sexy photos to these magazines are victims of the system, are we not also implying that women lack free will, thus stripping them of their responsibility for their own actions? Within the tension between archaic, humourless, uncool feminism and the free-for-all sexual gluttony of the lads' mags, the porn industry and the excess of sexual images in our quotidian existence, where do young women actually stand? Does the explosion of burlesque say anything more revealing about young women's contemporary postfeminist or post(-)feminist condition?

The burlesque performer crystalizes that reckless thin line of double standards and murky mixed messages. Her appropriation of gender and sexual stereotypes both challenges and adds to that empty, endless procession of 'sexy' images. Rather than mimicking the common whore, the porn star or the lap dancer, burlesque stars like Dita Von Teese, Gypsy Rose Lee or Lydia Thompson, glamorous and rubbing shoulders with the glitterati, more closely approximate with the seduction, allure and power of the historical courtesan. The 'low' has been made more easily digestible for the middle classes. The sluttishness has been upgraded. The tastelessness and vulgarity have been given a touch of glamour, and she reflects the spirit of the time: 'moneyed, sophisticated and ebulliently nouveau'. [58]

The courtesan made 'femininity' *her* business. (Further proof that this artistic business of 'femininity' touches a contemporary nerve is the present fascination with the geisha. Contemporary burlesque performers *Velvet Hammer Burlesque* and Miss Erotic World runner-up Kalani Kokonuts have also incorporated this figure into their acts.) Witty, intelligent, voraciously sexy and powerful, this aristocrat of harlots[59] was admired and feared by both men and women. The courtesan (from the male term 'courtier', meaning 'to the court') was a prominent figure in classical Greece, Renaissance Italy, eighteenth-century Japan and late nineteenth-century France. She was known for her artful and irresistible combination of sexual, political, social and poetical skills. She propelled her way to power, money and fame by her associations, whether by marriage or by way of her select lovers.

In classical Greek life (*c.* 479–323BC) the Athenian courtesans (*hetaera*, meaning 'companion' or 'friend') were rich and famous escorts to respectable and powerful poets and statesman like Pericles, Alcibiades and Socrates. Within Athenian culture, the courtesan lived in the fragile economy of the gift. She represented a pleasure that was neither pure sex nor procreation and was seen to exercise complete control over who she slept with. Unlike the common prostitute, or *pornai*, who had to have sex with *ho boulomenos*, 'whoever wishes', the *hetaera* would give herself to whoever 'persuaded' her.[60] In terms of visibility and perhaps also in terms of 'the gift', the Athenian courtesan was closer to a wife than a common *pornai*.

Margaret F. Rosenthal discusses what was seen as a problematic blurring between 'respectable' women, prostitutes and courtesans in sixteenth-century Venice. Rosenthal argues that the courtesan (*cor-*

tigiana onesta) 'projected a highly sophisticated public image which she used to move beyond the domestic space of the family into the public spheres of Venetian life'.[61] Courtesans were also wealthy and so could afford to dress themselves in clothes that made it extremely difficult to differentiate them from married women or the upper classes.

The Parisian courtesans, referred to by the French as *les grandes horizontales*, were living in France as 'mistresses' or employees of the elite and were seen as the ultimate commodity. The most highly regarded of courtesans, Cora Pearl, La Paiva and Catherine Walters (known as 'Skittles'), moved swiftly up the social ladder by virtue of their erotic artistry, charisma and clear shrewd business sense. Cora Pearl describes her movement along 'a golden chain of lovers'[62] until she reached the bed of Prince Jerome Bonaparte. These women knew how to sustain a luxurious lifestyle, the most exquisite fashion and jewels, expensive establishments and extravagant parties. The quintessential prerequisite for a courtesan was leading the life of a lady and making it her 'art' – even though she came from a low-status background and was seen as vulgar by the rich and privileged of the time. One of the most famous courtesans, residing in France but of English origin, Cora Pearl, became one of the richest women of mid–late nineteenth-century France.

Burlesque 'stars' on the other hand, do not actually whore themselves but sexualize and lampoon the social, sexual and economic conditions of their rate of exchange. Like the courtesan and the call girl, they exploit to the full their market value in order to cohort with the higher echelons. However, unlike the courtesan or call girl, burlesque artistes luxuriate in the pleasure gained by displaying their body-as-object whilst also clearly challenging the viewer by using retro styles with varying levels of irony. In Katharina Bosse's book *New Burlesque* (2003) we see sexualized tropes of 'femininity' that have been deliciously subverted to suit a quite modern aesthetic and attitude. Honey Corday dresses as a 'stripper' showgirl in black pants, tights and bra and slippers and stands astride a pussy cat. Ruby Darling is photographed in her Moulin Rouge music hall costume and provocatively looks at the camera whilst hoisting up her dress to reveal a large tattoo that snakes its way up her inside leg.

Dita Von Teese's style, on the other hand, seems to lack that sense of irony. She instead has built up her business excessively embracing and artfully perfecting this retro-femininity. She has fully appropriated and embraced the persona and lifestyle of the courtesan: 'a model of impeccable beauty, captivating style and mysterious feminine power. She was a careerist, a society girl, an emulated celebrity … [and she was] not dependent on any man.'[63]

How does this art of femininity subvert or upset the conventional mainstay of 'the fuck-me puppet' of male fantasies? Is there any real disturbance of the status quo or is someone like Dita Von Teese merely consolidating what young women are already constantly told to aspire to – a painfully thin waist, pale complexion and large breasts?

The next chapter will delve further into the questions of glamour and unveiling. I will try to ascertain, through the figure of the burlesque star, the subject power that potentially comes from enhancing and exploiting one's constructed 'femininity'.

West End bill poster advertising *Immodesty Blaize and Walter's Burlesque*, 2005.

4.

Powers of Seduction

PAINTED LADIES

Artifice

When the British Blondes hit the headlines in 1868 their selling point was not just the tantalizing and shocking sight of their legs but also their artificial 'look'. Actress and women's rights activist Olive Logan, in her scalding critique, described them as 'coarse, indecent, painted, padded and dyed'.[1] When the British Blondes first performed in America their thick white paint, cheek rouge and eye make-up reflected and expressed the contemporary trends. The periods of time during which burlesque peaked also, intriguingly, paralleled the short bursts of time during which, in women's fashion, the natural gave way to the artificial.

Simone de Beauvoir describes the period of the 1920s to the 1940s as a time when French women were 'addicted to physical culture',[2] and the late nineteenth century is described by Kathy Peiss as period when: 'The strain between appearance and identity – that women are not what they seem ... deepened substantially.'[3] Women in both eras were reacting against a limited conception of beauty, that of pale skin, blushing cheeks and a slight, fragile build, as well as reacting against a women's movement that seemed to be equating equality with sexlessness. This could also be the reason (post-suffragette) for the reaction outlined by de Beauvoir, when women were fanatically reconstructing and refashioning their look by way of obsessive exercise, diets and laxatives. In the late nineteenth-century Civil War era in the USA, young women rebelliously and defiantly wore make-up and bleached their hair in direct opposition to the 'natural' look of the antebellum years.

At a time of greater visibility for women, the art of spectacle, of how best to represent oneself, became a pressing concern. Constructing the best 'look' became a liberating and pleasurable experience. Women could now use cosmetics and artifice as a 'dramatic performance of the self'.[4] The competitive display of their bodies as spectacle playfully married with a visual commodity culture that was more than ever before fuelled by spectatorship and consumption. What this also meant was that women could now choose to transform their bodies into that superior, 'pure', much sought-after beauty.

'Beauty' had always been women's escape route, their ticket to success. Men had their career opportunities and women could catch the eye of a rich, successful prospective husband. Being pretty was a woman's envied talent that transgressed class divisions because her objecthood could provide her with status in society and a better standard of living. The opportunity therefore to imitate artificially this 'ideal' womanhood, and therefore increase one's visibility and future prospects, was consequently liberating.

This liberating artifice was thus read as deception by men seeking purity of heart in spirit and morality by way of women's 'transparent' beauty. This lack of transparency was the cause of much anxiety. In late nineteenth-century America, men were given advice books outlining how to differentiate the natural real beauty from the counterfeit, the 'Venuses and the viragoes'.[5] The real fear was that cosmetics could hide racial, sexual, moral and class differences and allow these illegitimate women to mingle and blend seamlessly and freely into bourgeois respectability. They would be able to stake an illegitmate claim to power, wealth and connections by seducing, marrying and procreating above their allotted station. Now that both 'ladies', the 'pure' and the 'impure', were painted, how could one differentiate between the pure of heart and the impure of spirit? This uncertainty thus assumed that purity would 'show' in the face and features if unadorned.

Cosmetics have been used as far back as the days of the Roman Empire. What differentiates the periods under discussion in this book from other periods is that there was a heightened importance placed on images, image-making and performance. The blurring of difference could act as a leveller for women who would otherwise be excluded from any source of real power. On the other hand, there was a danger in this homogenizing effect in that the image that women sought to create emphasized and accentuated the superiority of one universal 'look'.

Contemporary female trends in the USA and Britain have recently moved towards the 'plastic' and the 'unnatural', with the fashion for cosmetic surgery that kick-started in earnest in the 1990s. During 2005, cosmetic surgery procedures in Britain increased by one third. As in the late nineteenth century and the 1920s–40s, women can now adapt and accentuate their body to enhance their career or social appeal.

Contemporary culture also abounds with debates about the inferiority of the 'artificial' as opposed to the virtues of 'natural' beauty – 'Yes, her breasts may be beautiful but *mine* are 100 per cent natural'.... This debate had also reared its head in relation to the Blondes. The media frenzy obsessed over whether their blonde hair was 'real'. Recently the debates have, in certain corners of popular culture, taken an about-turn. Artificial breasts are now applauded by many for their perfection – they are seen to enhance a woman's natural beauty.

In fact, for some, cosmetic surgery now adds to a woman's sexiness and her standing as a sex object, since she has been willing to go under the knife and spend so much money to prove that very fact. Dita Von Teese is a paradigmatic example of this fêted artificiality. Originally named Heather Sweet, Dita is admired for her white, flawless complexion, her black hair, her perfect formidable breasts, her beauty spot and her very thin waist. However, this body – 'And what a body! (Vital stats: 34, 24, 33)'[6] – is a diligent construction. Her hair is naturally blonde but she dyed it blue-black for her first *Playboy* photo shoot, her beauty spot is painted on, her breasts are 'fake' and her waist is corseted (although she already has a naturally small build).

However, now this artificiality is seen frequently as enhanced sexiness by glossy magazines such as *Elle*, *Vogue* or *Cosmo*; although the key is to not look artificial, but to get it visually spot on. That is the *enviable* quality – to get it 'just right', without showing the strings, the cuts, the stitches: 'But you wouldn't know it; they're not huge round modern melons. "They hang just right," she says matter of factly.'[7] Von Teese seems to use the artificial to accentuate, to take ownership of and give character to the sensual. She performs 'erotic theatre'[8] perfectly. *Elle*'s November 2005 UK edition excitedly describes Dita as a 'modern day Snow White', 'a ballerina with breasts'[9] and 'an exquisite porcelain doll'.[10] It really still seems as if little girls want to grow up to be light-boned, graceful, 'feminine' ballerinas and princesses but with impressively large, perfectly sized breasts. This 'look' conflates a pre-adolescent skinniness – in order not to lose the 'lost-little-girl-please-help-me-act' – with womanly sexual weapons to enhance a wickedly seductive allure.

Contemporary consumerism heavily immerses little girls in 'ballerina' and 'princess' culture. Disney offers up *Cinderella,* a nauseating, regressive depiction of femaleness, and television offers up Barbie, who continues to be advertised between children's programmes. Barbie going skiing, Barbie riding her horse and Barbie driving her sports car adorn the screen, with five- to seven-year-old girls strutting up and down the catwalk with their red lips and long blonde hair, demonstrating Barbie fashion. What does this say about our contemporary culture? What claims do these images make? Advertising on television and in magazines helps to nurture a seemingly 'correct' and 'normal' gendered model that both girls and boys seek to emulate. Are young girls still being confronted with the early nineteenth-century ideal of the 'Cinderella Myth', whilst women's success in life depends solely on her ability to imitate this particularly restrictive beauty and gender ideal?

The Cinderella tale is described by Sarah Banet-Weiser as one of the many claims made on the origins of the modern-day beauty pageant. She states, however, that tracing the history of the pageant, although interesting, becomes almost irrelevant, because women's physical appearance has in many cases always been competitively judged. The Greek myth about the Judgment of Paris could perhaps be the first 'beauty contest' in Western culture (and prolifically painted throughout art history). In this myth, Paris is asked to judge who is 'the fairest' out of three goddesses: Minerva with her wisdom and knowledge, Juno with her majesty and power, or Venus as the goddess of beauty. The winner would be able to claim the golden apple. Venus draws Paris aside and promises him a bride 'as fair as herself'[11] if he should select her. Whether as a result of her beauty or her bribe, Venus wins the coveted golden prize.

The truth of the matter is that our culture and childhood are littered with references to who is the fairest of them all – the fairest being the one who gets to marry the Prince or win the coveted prize. Miss America proudly displays how 'appropriately gendered'[12] young women should typically look and act: 'fixed in age, a changeless body and the embodiment of heterosexual desire'.[13] The trick is to make this construction of 'femininity' look painless, natural, easy and effortless (a trick that is not discussed openly, so as not to destroy the ruse). As Banet-Weiser states, 'Disciplinary practices such as dieting and other beauty practices are assumed by most women as femininity; the practice *is* the production.'[14] It *is* hard work and the invisibility of all this torturous hard work can even be a point of pride.

Sustaining the illusion is what many if not most women aspire to achieve: not staying over at the boyfriend's house for fear of him seeing you without make-up the morning after, silently starving whilst protesting that you eat what you like and never put on a pound – or stuffing your face in the safe, unsurveilled comfort of your room but never letting *that* image, or *that* dressing gown, see the light of day. This is the source of the humour in the book *Bridget Jones' Diary*, published in 1996 and filmed in 2001: the frank, losing battle between being 'natural' and looking 'naturally feminine'. The healthy message of the film starring Renée Zellweger was that when they sit back and act 'naturally', many women could be perceived as being unfeminine and inappropriately gendered. This was jeopardized, however, by Zellweger's emaciated appearance shortly after the making of the film. The urgent and persistent plea that came to us by way of her publicity machine was that she was not a natural size 12 – she had to work hard to pile on so much weight! The illusion could not be ruptured.

Simone de Beauvoir speaks about the obsession with physical culture in the 1920s–40s period as akin to 'a horror of life itself'.[15] Some women sustain their neurotic desire to ward off signs of decay, maintaining a clean, dust-free house and a streamlined, wrinkle-free, fat-free body – even to the negation of life's joys and indeed of the erotic:

> This negative obstinacy makes them enemies of their own existence and hostile to others: good meals spoil the figure, wine injures the complexion, too much smiling brings wrinkles, the sun damages the skin, sleep makes one dull, work wears one out, love puts rings under the eyes, kisses redden the cheeks, caresses deform the breasts, embraces wither the flesh, maternity disfigures face and body.[16]

It is interesting and perhaps disturbing that de Beauvoir's words, written almost 60 years ago, are still so relevant today. As a result of trying to prolong youth, the opposite effect instead is realized – a life that is inert, sanitized and risk-free. The woman's life and self-image relies too heavily on her slim, youthful beauty. Her home symbolizes this fanatical quest to stop the flow of life, to maintain her ageless-ness. In the timeless zone, life is deadened, conserved and actionless, like a tin of preserved fruit. These beautifying measures are about *looking* sexy without *being* sexy or sexual. We see this in the current cosmetic fashion for Botox, where a deadly poison is inserted into each wrinkle to relax the muscles and smooth over lines on the face, deadening facial and individual expression and personality: a desper-ate battle to keep death and impurity, and indeed personality, out.

The fanatical quest to 'stop the rot' is not shaped purely by fe-male competitive neurosis or by the simplistic assertion that we are 'victims' co-opted into a commodity culture that feeds on our inse-curities in order to bolster profits. Many women continue to feel the pressures to conform, to be that ideal woman. Botox is the one of the fastest growing sectors of non-surgical cosmetic procedures. In the UK in 2006, 415,000 procedures of Botox and chemical peels were carried out, a 240 per cent increase on the 2001 figures. Also, 90 per cent of these procedures were carried out on women.[17] In America, nearly 3 million Botox injections were given in 2004, with these fig-ures rising to 4.1 million in 2006.[18]

However, there is for many also pleasure in colluding with this same system. We can construct, control and define our identity, our own image. We can use dieting, make-up and even Botox to po-tently assert our sexual selves, not necessarily just to comfort our neuroses but also as a liberating self-conscious tool, enhancing our sensuality.

There is a blurred line between empowerment and neurosis, plea-sure and collusion, coercion and wilful choice. Part of our empower-ment should also come from knowing how precariously we balance on this fine line. Some of the imagery by the contemporary painter Jenny Saville contests this ambivalence with neurotic and empower-ing paintings of undulating sensual flesh that simultaneously show the lines through which a surgeon's knife will shortly make its 'beau-tifying' incision. She describes them as 'half alive, half dead',[19] anxious and neurotic. Saville condemns women's magazines for these mixed messages, on one page promoting breast cancer awareness and empowerment and on the next page having an article showing skin products that make you look younger (encouraging neurosis).

Whilst sitting awaiting my fate in the hairdressers' Toni & Guy's, in an attempt to test the liberatory potential of artifice, I was handed the January 2006 edition of *Harpers & Queen*. In 'Confessions of a Botox junkie', Sharon Walker posed the question whether paying for a new face had now become as acceptable as getting highlights. She spoke about the 'age maintenance' of losing her Botox virginity and argued that 'looking old is starting to seem optional, a bit careless, like forgetting to brush your teeth'.[20] Is it this desire to be forever beautiful that attracts women to the new contemporary burlesque performer? How are Von Teese's bone-crunching, breathlessly tight corseted waist, artificial breasts, arched brows and scarlet lips empowering? How is burlesque subverting the acceptable mainstream values and the 'universal' ideal? Or does it not really matter now, as long as she/we look divine?!

Perhaps that contemporary twist is created through Von Teese's fusion of Snow White with the Wicked Stepmother, giving her image a touch of SM subversion and danger. She queers up Snow White by injecting a bit of the Wicked Stepmother to upset the equilibrium. Burlesque performers delight in standing out, in behaving in excess of the 'norm', in cajoling expectations. There is a hint of the unbecoming, a glamour brimming over with understated subversion, with many new burlesque performers coming out of the fetish, transvestite and punk subcultures. Dita Von Teese's own background is in the fetish scene. However, the controlled, self-conscious, constructed glamour of the new wave of burlesque performers expresses an extremely seductive *joie de vivre*.

Before exploring and questioning this glamour further I would like to end this section with a story that was injected as an informal aside at a recent conference, in a strand called 'Camp as cultural strategy'. Dr Roger Cook, a senior lecturer in fine art at the University of

Reading, asked his student why, as a gay man, he did not embrace the glitz and glamour of camp culture. The young man replied that he did not want to stand out in that way, and added that he felt that this was, in any case, now passé. To this Cook replied that he thought (paraphrasing): 'it was such a shame because he was missing out on such fun!'[21]

Glamour

When my mother was a teenager growing up in a small town called Toogoolawah in outback Queensland, a town predominantly made up of one sandy track and a small number of Queenslanders (living in houses on stilts with verandas), she used to frequent the local cinema, or 'flea pit', as she refers to it. Like many teenagers with access to the cinema at that time (the 1950s), cinema and magazines were the only sources of escape from quite a harsh life. Sitting on their deck chairs watching glamorous stars such as Lana Turner, Barbara Stanwyck, Veronica Lake, Rita Hayworth, Joan Crawford, Betty Grable and Joan Fontaine would have been a mesmerizing experience. My mother would collect their images, cut them out of magazines and paste them into her scrapbook. The potent allure and glamour of these women gave the young girls in the audience fantasy, dreams and hopes for exciting adventures, when at that point in their life the 'city' (Brisbane) and its excitement was an expensive, once-a-year, four-hour journey by rail motor. These were pleasurable and powerful images that opened up a tantalizing space in their heads of new modes of living, of behaving and of being.

Lydia Thompson, as 'the first mass-consumable sex symbol in American culture'[22] held similar appeal to the cinematic femme fatale in offering up a tantalizing glimpse of another 'femininity' that was strong, assertive, sexy, pleasurable and – most importantly – independent. But what did this glamour mean? Glamour as defined in *Collins Dictionary*[23] literally means: 'charm and allure'; 'fascinating or voluptuous beauty, often dependent on artifice'. Yet this modern usage is seen as a Hollywood corruption of the original Scottish word 'glamorous', meaning magical or supernatural, and 'glamerie', meaning witchcraft. 'Glamer' was therefore to bewitch or put a spell, or a 'glammer', on someone. This original meaning perhaps gives us more of a sense of how these 'screen goddesses' were seen to have a more threatening control and power over their audience.

What was it about these women that gave them such an allure? And, cutting straight to the chase, what is the difference, if any, between the glamour offered up by the female burlesque performer and the glamour offered up by the cinematic 'sirens' of the 1950s?

In order to explore this difference in allure, I am going to digress momentarily by referring to Woody Allen's self-confessed favourite film (of those made by him), *The Purple Rose of Cairo* (1985).

In this film Mia Farrow as Cecilia, a film buff, goes to the cinema to escape both the bleakness of the Great Depression and her dreary, loveless marriage. Mesmerized by this more romantic celluloid world, Cecilia literally draws the screen character (Tom) out of the black and white film to join her in the coloured reality of 1930s America. In the film the actor who plays Tom's character, himself called Gil, comes to find Tom, and makes Cecilia choose between them. Woody Allen states, 'she chooses the real actor and he dumps her; that was the time it became a real movie. Before that it wasn't.'[24]

This précis of the film's narrative perfectly encapsulates all of the elements that will be pivotal to my discussion of glamour and burlesque. First, what you have here is female fantasy, illusion, spectacle and consumption. Second, there is the active blurring of the private 'feminine' world of intimacy with the public sphere of action. Third, you have the man duping and ditching the broad! And finally, there is the seductive, empowering, interactive pleasure of looking and being seen, off-set and accentuated by the disgruntlement, dissatisfaction and transformations brought about by depression and suppression.

All of the boom periods for burlesque have been set against a backdrop of severe dissatisfaction with the status quo. The above sequence was set during the Great Depression. One can only imagine the impact created by a burlesque performer who was not only sexy and independent, like the femme fatale, but also gave vent to these women's communal sense of disillusionment and yearning. Both the late nineteenth century and the years of the Great Depression were eras when the relations between the sexes were fraught. For women who had been hidden away indoors, scrimping and saving, with their arms up to their elbows in washing, dirty nappies and cooking fat, life had lost its sparkle! The glamour, the diamonds, the furs, the sexual allure and the witty repartee in classic burlesque demonstrated a self-reliance and a steely sexual character who did not kowtow to male authority; she both embraced and exceeded social conventions.

At a time when money was tight these women were decadently wasteful; when women were feeling the claustrophobia of four walls, these women were exploding outrageously into the public arena; when women were seriously beginning to question the narrow re-strictions of 'femininity', these women were flamboyantly yet elusively expressing a sexual vibrancy that could not be conventionally categorized. They appeared to be in control of their own destinies and got what they desired.

The fashion of the 1950s, modelled on the New Look created by Dior in the 1940s with its bejewelled full skirts made from luxurious silks and satins, also did this but was not so sexualized. Many new burlesque performers reference this pre-feminist look in their own retro styles. Re-contextualizing a dress that formerly simmered with only just contained sexual energy clearly underscores the contempo-rary performer's more unashamed, freely sexual, erotic expression. But it also ironically highlights that, at this historical point where second wave feminism has already happened, paralysing stereotypes of 'prettiness' and narrows conceptions of female eroticism still per-sist with their restrictions and limitations.

Burlesque performers like Lydia Thompson also symbolized the fears and anxieties prevalent from the mid-nineteenth century of the voracious carnivorous female consumer who was draining man sexu-ally and economically. The French term 'consommation', described by Rita Felski, Professor of English at the University of Virginia, as both 'economic consumption and erotic consummation',[25] was used by Emile Zola to describe this all-consuming woman represented through his character *Nana* who symbolized the dangerous, 'feminized' pleasures of the modern city. We see these fears expressed by the male comics in the comedy 'bits' of 1930s New York burlesque, where women are seen as gold-diggers. Whether they love men, or dupe men, women are seen to be only after men for their money.

In 1930s burlesque, the routines involving male comics often focused on women's greed: 'That's my wife, she's always after dough';[26] 'Yeah, gimme, gimme, gimme'.[27] In these routines, women are all manipulative gold-diggers and are only after you for your money – 'That was no lady, that was my wife!'[28] Women are depicted as cold, heartless and wasteful, with an insatiable ability to spend money on luxuries. As now, shopping was linked to women's lack of control. The glitz and glamour of the shop window had become the new 'surrogate lover', with the husband seeing himself metaphorically cuckolded, financially wrung dry and sexually manipulated.

Women in the comic 'bits' comment on the strenuous rigours of marriage and motherhood on the body: 'I don't know whether you are married or not, but if you're not don't do it. I used to have a beautiful shape once ... Now I look like half past six.'[29] Men are depicted as untrustworthy, unreliable and unfaithful. In one sketch a women's lover, when found in the cupboard by her husband, answered: 'Would you believe me if I said I was waiting for a taxi?' The sketches also comment on men's sexual impotence:

> Are you Mr. Myers? I've heard all about your lovemaking.
> Oh, it's nothing.
> That's what I heard![30]

All in all women were now feeling more able to voice their unhappiness and were finding a more glamorous life outside of the home, at work and in the department stores. In both the late nineteenth century and the 1920s and 30s, shopping became the legitimate means of channelling women's unacknowledged needs and desires into a harmless if trivial pursuit. However, this activity – the gendered activity of shopping was part and parcel of women's domestic duties – backfired with seriously unforeseen and permanent social consequences. This self-indulgence triggered off a sense of fatigue and even antipathy towards the traditional relationship between the sexes and the hierarchical order. Desires and needs became channelled by some middle-class women into luxury objects and frivolous spending, which acted perhaps as a substitute for marital coitus.

A contemporary example could be women's erotic self-indulgence in bath-time candle-lit pampering. In his book *A Theory of Shopping*, Daniel Miller, Professor of Anthropology at University College, London, discusses self-indulgence in relation to 'the treat'. In this discussion, Miller discusses how buying a 'treat' acts as a re-affirmation of the self. If depressed, an academic may treat him or herself to a book, a food shopper may choose chocolate, a teenage girl, cosmetics or accessories.

According to Miller, this behaviour is more typical among housewives in their weekly shop, where 'the self is particularly unacknowledged'.[31] A key point that Miller makes is that even though this treat is a reward for what is perceived to be unappreciated hard work, it, 'is also clearly regarded as a hedonistic act of materialistic self-indulgence'.[32] Women, therefore, were short-circuiting and questioning the usual sexual and economic connections and dependence where their 'self' felt unfulfilled and ignored. Yet simultaneously, this assertive push for recognition and pleasure was being undermined and attacked as frivolous and self-obsessed.

In twentieth-century popular culture the diamond, the symbol of romance and weddings, became the metaphorical symbol of this combination of female aspiration and disgruntlement, of achievement and indulgence. In such songs as Marilyn Monroe's rendition of 'Diamonds Are a Girl's Best Friend', later sung by Nicole Kidman in *Moulin Rouge*, and Shirley Bassey's 'Diamonds Are Forever', diamonds become that reliable, ever sparkling object of desire – 'But square-cut or pear shape. These rocks don't lose their shape.'[33] These are interesting lyrics because they are saying that even when *I* am no longer a commodity and have lost my 'shape', I will still have the money to keep from when I *was* a commodity. The diamond was re-launched to reflect a new found, blossoming, hard-toothed economic independence ('A kiss may be grand but it won't pay the rental on your humble flat or help you at the automat'[34]) and erotic self-reliance ('They are all I need to please me, they can stimulate and tease me'[35]).

As for our contemporary femme fatale Dita Von Teese, here is a woman who has come from being a stripper – 'being a fancy-pants stripper got me here!' – to wearing 'millions of dollars of diamonds!'[36] and gaining the admiration of young women who aspire to be that successful and that glamorous. She gives women an erotic boost, allowing them to daydream beyond the dowdy daily routine, beyond the clinical rota of working existence.

Burlesque addresses this lack, this need for female-inspired erotic imagery. The erotic pin-ups of Dita Von Teese are not pornographic; there are no men, no genitals, no male orchestrator enforcing the pose and raking in the cash, just images that offer up a sensuous, pleasurable, self-defined glamour. She delights in her self-conscious detached yet intimate 'femininity', in her heterosexual appeal and potent sexual agency.

Laura Herbert, burlesque enthusiast and webmistress for the Exotic World Burlesque Museum, comments that burlesque is now very much a female form of entertainment. New burlesque audiences are made up of 50 to 75 per cent women, depending on the venue. Herbert comments that 'Modern burlesque is all about a woman's fantasy.'[37] It is about revelling in a variety of body shapes and having fun. Burlesque performer 'Kitten on the Keys' satirizes body image pressures where one moment she is a precocious girl and the next, 'a neurotic thirty-something dumpling who laments weight gain and sexual frustrations' with the lyrics, 'Why did I eat so much bacon?... Oh no no no no no no / It's not a pretty princess day.'[38] Another illustration of this social satire is The Fat Bottom Revue's humorous subversion of 'Wonder Women' with the whole cast dancing confidently to the sound track dressed as Wonder Women yet with very different figures to the 'ideal look'.

The 'bawdy beautiful' imagery forwarded by new burlesque performers is therefore a welcome relief from limiting glamorous 'ideals'. Amongst the performers there is a plucky desire to re-image sexiness, to reformulate 'prettiness' and to insert a sexual subject and female erotic pleasure into stereotypical sexual imagery and identities. It must be said, though, that within this positive imagery there are still only a few black burlesque acts (Cocoa Mae, UK, and Harlem Shake, USA). The mainstream's wholesale mis-appropriation and promotion of acceptably pretty female display (Von Teese) somehow undermines the radical wider message of new burlesque. By taking this erotic imagery out of its context (where it represents a small yet significant part of a much wider and richer expression and array of glamour) and holding it up as *the* tone, the media again are able to overexpose one crippling standard of erotic attractiveness and pleasure.

The next section will look more closely at the agency that comes from this expression of pleasure. The point that needs to be explored is the contradictory edge on which this pleasure precariously balances. Walking down the high street, waiting at the bus stop, women feel alienated and discomforted by images of perfectly posed, perfectly empty models. Women have no choice but to accept this visual onslaught. It has become 'normalized', and to say anything will stigmatize you as regressive, prudish and narrow-minded, or old and envious. Waiting for a bus to go to work, standing next to naked women 'wanting it now', there is a disturbing chronic sense of severance and disengagement. We do not figure in this representation. Where is our sense of self as living and breathing, sensual erotic agents? Who is in control of these messages? Who is benefiting from this hijacked imagery? Does the burlesque performer liberate women from or just contribute to this onslaught?

VEILING AND NAKEDNESS

Democracy

Whilst the USA and its allies were joining forces against the 'Axis of Evil' in January 2002, democracy was being pushed even harder through the symbol of the veiled woman. Veiling came to signify oppression and undemocratic tyranny and acted as justification for the USA's push for empire and domination. George W. Bush's keynote speeches in relation to the Afghan war mentioned 'free expression' and 'human dignity' in tandem with women's freedom. In the media, the liberation of Afghanistan focused on women's sexual and physical freedoms, and to this end news articles spot-lighted women's subversive domestic activism – including a group of women who gathered together to experiment secretly with make-up. This tension crystallized in the symbol of the female *hijab* (worn for religious modesty) or veil, perceived by many in the Western world as a threat to individual freedom of expression. This culminated in a dispute where a French school insisted that a Muslim girl stop wearing her veil in the interest of acculturation and national security, with the girl insisting that it was her religious and cultural right to wear one.

This perceived threat raged on into the British election campaigns of 2004. 'Freedom', 'democracy' and women's rights and their freedom of expression were being used as a Trojan Horse to hide the actual issues of imperialism, power politics and dominancy.

A spoof newspaper, the *Hate Mail, Immigration Special 2005*, was posted through my letterbox. The 'Female' section was entitled 'hatelife'. In one 'article', the 'Total Citizenship Makeover' showed two images. The first image was of a Muslim woman dressed in black *purdah* with only her eyes on show. The caption read 'BEFORE: A poor oppressed foreign woman'. The second image was of a Hooter girl, with vest and orange shorts, blonde hair, an insipid smile, cleavage and buttocks hanging out, with the caption: 'AFTER: A liberated and self-respecting British woman'. Resident fashion guru Charles

'Home Secretary' Clarke advised women: 'Let's ditch that repressed woman look and go for today's new Freedom™ style. I'm thinking tighter, shorter and brighter! After all, truly liberated women should be happy to expose themselves freely. If you've got it – flaunt it. And hey, we all know you can't hide seven tonnes of semtex under a micro mini!'[39]

This humorously cutting article exposes several interesting points. First, the journalist makes a dig at the assumed presumption that levels of democracy can be simply equated with levels of dress or undress, and second, that women's 'look' can transparently reveal the culture's national identity, morality and freedoms. Ultimately women are used to demonstrate the country's permissiveness, how much freedom of expression the individual is permitted under a particular national governing body and constitution. The article quite pertinently sums up this sense of attempting to hijack Freedom™, Democracy™ and Roots™ through the image of the unveiled 'free' woman. This cannot help but erupt into other questions of legitimacy, morality, economics, identity, ownership and geopolitics. The dominant power becomes the one who can 'legitimately' trademark freedom and democracy and the image of woman is used to gauge and symbolize that country's superior, more civilized and open and tolerant stance. This also becomes entangled with issues relating to power, capital, freedom of movement and freedom of expression.

It is revealing that at the point when national issues about democracy, exploitation, morality, and hierarchy are loudly resounding and fiercely debated that burlesque rears its ubiquitous head. Issues related to morality, legitimacy, boundaries, respectability, freedoms, limits and identity are all expressed and lampooned by burlesque and the female burlesque performer who makes a spectacle out of all that should not be seen. The unveiling of her legs, the lower stratum of her body, alluded to all that was 'low': sexual urges, the irrational, impertinence, a lack of control and sexual femininity. This uncouth insubordination was also coupled with the humour of verbal sexualized, 'uncultured' double-entendres and working-class city slang. This direct address, based on Gypsy Rose Lee's heckling of the audience, is something that Dita Von Teese talks about wanting to incorporate more into her act.[40] Yet I question whether this heckling acts as a social critique or whether it is just a good solid gimmick to make Von Teese's act stand out.

What was directly unsettling about the classical burlesque performer was her refusal to submit to hierarchy and authority. Her humour was indiscriminate and, Allen argues, 'became an affirmation of the right of a nobody to question the stature of a somebody'.[41] Unveiling in this instance became a symbolic uncovering of false veils, sexually, socially and politically, erected to exclude, oppress and divide. A test case in Luton in the UK in April 2005, which culminated in victory for 16-year-old Shabina (who was represented by Cherie Booth, QC) highlights this very contentious issue of inclusion and exclusion through the symbol of the veil. Formally addressing the press after the trial, stated:

> It's amazing that in the so-called free world, I have to fight to wear this Islamic dress ... As a young woman growing up in post 9/11 Britain, I have witnessed a great deal of bigotry from the media, politicians and legal officials. This bigotry resulted from my choice to wear a piece of cloth.[42]

belittles the hullabaloo which arose over a simple 'piece of cloth'. The 'piece of cloth', however, has become the defining symbol of her cultural and religious identity as a young Islamic woman living in Britain. Reducing the issue to a piece of cloth clearly sets it up as a boundary between her belief in freedom and the undemocratic beliefs, as perceived by the Western world, of the non-Islamic culture within which she participates. It is a carefully selected statement that is clearly meant to criticise, redefine and hold to account Western definitions of democracy and freedom. The symbol of the veil challenges the authority of patriarchal white capitalist values in the same way as the 'nudity' of the burlesque performer challenged the authority of nineteenth-century bourgeois culture to maintain her sexual, social and intellectual invisibility.

This challenge to the authority of the veil as a democratic symbol exposed contradiction and hypocrisy in the West. Democracy permits certain levels of undress. There is a point where unveiling becomes indecent in the same manner that veiling can become a spectacle that disturbs and therefore provokes suspicion. Women need to strike a careful balance between veiling and nakedness to hit that point of transparency, of control, of comprehension. The 'compulsory unveiling' of Islamic women could easily verge on a sort of forced stripping – since to the veiled Islamic woman the removal of the veil could feel like an exposure or an indecency.

The case was defined as a victory for democracy ... staged by Britain and the prime minister's wife. France's decision to make illegal all cultural symbols in the interest of acculturation (spearheaded by the test case of the banned headscarf) unhappily coincided with tension between Muslims and non-Muslims and riots in Paris. Britain's choice to strike a balancing act between order and disorder demonstrated the struggle in trying to redefine or at least re-image itself as a liberal nation. It seems that female propriety and correctness must be so tightly orchestrated in order to ensure the correct imaging of that nation's 'democratic' values.

From that perspective, with the tidily orchestrated speech and images of her flanked by her brother (an Islamic fundamentalist activist), we are left unsure as to 's domestic 'freedom' and how much personal 'freedom' her cloth actually gave her. The struggle between prohibition and freedom of choice continued into the Netherlands, where Dutch minister Geert Wilders announced in January 2006 the government's decision to ban the *burqa*. The reason he gave was that covering up was mediaeval and a way for terrorists to hide. These women frightened the elderly and made children cry. In interview with the BBC, a woman attired in a *burqa* exclaimed that Western values stood for freedom of choice, freedom of expression and freedom of religion and that she would also fight for these universal values. The news bulletin concluded that this was a country obsessed by identity, with a government which felt that all its residents should act and behave Dutch.

What was strikingly bizarre and perhaps even shocking about this scenario was that it was happening in a country labelled by its European neighbours as liberal because of its open-minded views on drugs and the sex industry. The 'universal' democratic values expounded by the young woman in the news bulletin seem only to extend to *un*veiling (even to the level of prostitution), since covering up became an act of sedition. In this cauldron of mixed messages new burlesque acts as the cloudy, transgressive edge where boundaries blur. Positioning itself at a halfway house between erotica and pornography, between morality and immorality, glamorous veiling and seductive unveiling, teasing and containment, burlesque plays and fuses our fears, anxieties and desires. It subsumes cultural debates in relation to female sexuality and display, and Western hypocrisies and contradictions with regard to what society rejects, accepts or dispels.

The pleasure and parody of the seductive tease is characteristically lampooned in Gypsy's tongue-in-cheek routine 'Lonesome Little Eve':

I'm a lonesome Little Eve
Looking for an Adam
Gee I wish I had him
Cuddlin' me,
'Neath the shade of the tree
And in our garden we would be so happy

Would you ... for a big red apple?
Would you ... for a piece of mine?
Would you ... for a big red apple?
Give me what I'm trying to find.[43]

This parody of the tease, the temptation and the disobedience of the original sin, humorously and bitingly directs us to the Christian mythical roots of shameful nakedness and modest covering up. Woman's punishment is that she is now made to become man's chattel: '...and thy desire *shall be* to thy husband, and he shall rule over thee'.[44] The shame of unveiled flesh is thus related to woman's lack of morality and easily bought-off pleasures. Interesting parallels can be drawn between Christian and Muslim traditions in relation to this shame and female disobedience. Fatima Mernissi identifies the two major concepts in the modern Arab psyche and political consciousness, *qaid* and *hijab*, which cite women's sexuality as the source of a potentially rebellious and seditious disorder. *Qaid* is the sexual power that emanates from women, which holds potentially destructive consequences for the social order. The institution of *hijab* acts as a protective barrier concealing women within a forbidden space.[45]

The Christian world, like the Muslim world, upholds a controlled binary system of decency and indecency, visibility and invisibility. Burlesque utilizes the controlled act of veiling and unveiling to question stigma, to question shame, to question restrictive disempowering roles and sexual, gender and class relations in society. By the use of irony and parody, the performer is knowingly accepting that the 'freedoms' that come from unveiling do not acknowledge the fear of this woman and therefore the potential dangers for that woman.

Julie Atlas Muz often deals specifically with these freedoms and dangers by the use of black, bawdy humour and direct address. In a piece that she performs to Leslie Gore's 'You Don't Own Me', Muz starts off blindfolded and bound tightly in rope and then strips out of it. Michelle Baldwin argues that the piece had poignancy at a time when almost a third of all US women were physically abused by husbands or boyfriends. Muz's mixture of bondage and self-release is, Baldwin comments, 'feminist, sexy, and darkly funny all at the same time'.[46]

Why is Western democracy linked to women's unveiling? Nawal El Saadawi argues that 'veiling and nakedness are two sides of the same coin. Both mean that women are bodies without a mind and should be covered or uncovered in order to suit national or international capitalist interests.'[47] Leila Ahmed states that the veil in Islam signified women's place in the class hierarchy, with harlots and slaves prohibited from wearing the veil. The veil acted as a marker of women's sexual activity and their relationship to men, unlike men who gained their status 'on the basis of their occupation and their relation to production'.[48] Veiling held similar significance for Victorian society; indeed, revealing one's face or even one's ankle was considered a sign of a woman's 'availability'. It is ironical therefore that the veil at exactly this time was being held up by the colonial powers as a symbol of oppression.

Intriguingly, Haideh Moghissi states that Muslims have justified veiling in the name of Islam 'but only after it was promoted by the colonials as a symbol of Muslim societies'.[49] It was, she argues, only at that point in the nineteenth century that the veil grew in popularity and importance. On home turf, the Victorian establishment extolled the virtues of their veiled Ideal Woman, who was the domesticated servile and virtuous Mother and Wife; this was the measure of the model of their superior civilization. Abroad as colonizers they were using the very language of feminism that they were seeking to suppress and disprove at home in order to chastise Other men and Other cultures. As Leila Ahmed exclaims in her chapter 'The discourse of the veil':

> The idea that Other men, men in colonized societies or societies beyond the borders of the civilized West, oppressed women was to be used, in the rhetoric of colonialism, to render morally justifiable its project of undermining or eradicating the cultures of colonized peoples.[50]

By the 1930s, the question of whose interest these anti-veiling initiatives served was beginning to be asked. These conflicting mixed messages were again repeated in the 1930s, in Palestine, and with the Reza Shah's government-led anti-veil offensive in Iran that was resisted by the Patriotic Women's League. On 7 January 1936 Iran became the first Muslim country to ban the veil in a bid to 'modernize' and secularize the country. Azadeh Namakydoust comments that, 'the resistance of women proved to be much stronger than what the government had predicted',[51] with women refusing to leave the house for months or defiantly going out fully covered, knowing that they risked being beaten or having the veil forcefully removed. For many women the veil signified femininity, dignity, honour and, for some, comfort. One slant in feminist discourse pushes towards this positive, empowering perspective on the veil. Moghissi, however, is wary of this new liberal streak in Western feminism that could threaten to be the next brave new ideology and does not consider the women 'who are persecuted, jailed and whipped'.[52]

There seems to be something tantalizing and poignant therefore in new burlesque's self-directed combination of covering and uncovering that dissects and intersects the male-driven notions of femininity that seem to confuse and contradict. Nawak El Saadawi remarks that, 'women in Islamic societies are caught between the globalized image of femininity or female beauty as commodity in the West and the Islamic notions of femininity "protected" by men and hidden behind the veil'.[53] Burlesque sits at the interception between 'feminism' and the public face of female sexuality. The last section of this chapter will look at unveiling and freedom in relation to this feminist trajectory of self-determination.

Freedom

What is truly liberating about exposing oneself? Does this revelation of flesh equate with some kind of personal victory? Does flesh, the ability to dance naked, frolic nude or strip in a public place make you free, give you real freedom? The length of a woman's skirt has slowly risen with each feminist battle won. In the mid-nineteenth century the 'cage-crinoline' skirt was seen as extremely erotic clothing and taken on board first by the courtesans before becoming a craze with the more gentile ladies.

The 'cage-crinoline' was made up of a hoop of light steel that permitted women to do away with the heavy, cumbersome layers of petticoats that had slowly built up over the 1840s, which were stiffened and padded out with whalebone, split sugar cane and horsehair ('*crin*' in French).[54] The steel hoop maintained the fashionable fullness of the skirt without the weight. As well as giving women freedom of movement these dresses had another bonus. What added to their allure and appeal was that when walking the swaying of the skirt gave onlookers a tantalizing glimpse of the lady's ankles. So historically, over approximately 150 years, we have moved from allowing a sensually erotic glimpse of one's ankle to flashing our G-string knickers!

What does this mean exactly for women? Is this pushing against the boundaries of decency counter-productive?

In the mid-nineteenth century the exposure of one's ankles was an erotic gesture but it was also a politicized gesture and was evocatively explosive at a point when women were breaking out of their restrictive four walls and moving into the public domain. It became a non-verbal form of resistance at a time when verbal forms of debate were perhaps reserved for those women of a particular ilk, those from a particular social standing who were articulate enough to be given a platform, even begrudgingly. The Blondes' cheeky exposure of their tight-clad legs expressed and reflected working-class female resistance to both bourgeois male restrictive thinking and prejudices and to white middle-class women's personal and exclusive slant on freedom.

Women activists still fervently believed in covering up, which explained why the mid- to late nineteenth-century symbols of new women's emancipation emanated from male attire: the back necktie and the bloomers. The bloomers or 'rational dress' were introduced by US social reformer Amelia Bloomer in 1849 and consisted of a split skirt similar to Turkish trousers that gathered at the ankles and was worn under a shorter skirt.

These dress reformers also campaigned against the corset, a symbol of a controlled 'femininity': a 'femininity' that restricted and caged women's bodies. Young women wanted to be freed of these instruments of torture, of having to be the 'perfect' woman. For modern burlesque, this instrument of torture becomes part of the forbidden fun and pleasure. In some of Dita Von Teese's more bondage- and fetish-based imagery she has exposed breasts above a tightly corseted waist. Her corsetry is therefore both constraining and restricting. The exaggeration of 'femininity' is what attracted Von Teese to the image of the 'damsel in distress' who is never cruel, never harsh, never aggressive. It is this vulnerability, this gentleness, this disciplined 'femininity' (getting the seam perfectly lined up the back of the leg), this self-attentiveness and this glamour that is a source of self-pride that Von Teese argues is missing from our current daily lives.

In the late nineteenth century, dress reformers wanted to be freed from having to put on the daily public face of 'femininity', something that you had to do to be an attractive or at least presentable woman and future wife. This daily routine reminds me of my own Nanna who was born in London in about 1907 and worked as a milliner in Luton. She would have her routine, every single morning without fail; after a pot of tea, she used to put on her stockings and suspender belt, her corset (which was more like today's body-sculpting elasticated knickers but with tightening straps 'to keep you in place'), put on some powder with puff and 'set' her hair, pulling on her hairnet until it was ready. Even the day she died, she was impeccably made up. If I compare this routine to most people getting ready nowadays, there is a certain lack of attention to detail, a careless speed that seems to miss something, lack something. Men, likewise, dress less carefully now: no more suits and bowlers, waistcoats and gloves.

Are we freer now that we have got rid of the drudgery and labour of love that represented the early forms of 'femininity'?

Mid-nineteenth-century reformers wanted a style of dress that was practical, comfortable, easy and light, something that felt liberating. They wanted to be able to express their new sense of life, which was urban, fast and independent. Similarly, in the 1960s the bra became the core symbol of feminist resistance, a symbol that has dogged them ever since, however. These feminists, like the anti-corset campaigners, used non-verbal resistance against engrained sexism and a male-dominated culture that robbed women of their agency. The term 'bra-burning feminist' is now used as a derogatory term, however, to label as puritanical, sexless and humourless any feminism that is at all critical of woman-as-object.

Hannah Wilke created art that lashed out against these 'fascist feminists' – in her view their negation of femininity denounced and therefore rained on the 'spice' of sexual play and the sexual chase. There was a contradiction. Feminism advocated that women should be allowed freedom of expression whilst disavowing the traditional erotic codes of heterosexual exchange, as Muriel Dimen points out:

> On the one hand, since women have been traditionally seen as sex objects, feminism demands that society no longer focus on their erotic attributes, which, in turn, feminism downplays. In this way it becomes politically correct not to engage in any stereotypically feminine behavior, such as putting on make-up, wearing high heels, shaving legs and arms, or coming on to men.[55]

In the 1990s, lesbian theorists and activists explored gender roles and power play as a means of challenging the gender–sex–sexuality axis that ascribed 'femininity' to heterosexual women (with Judith Butler standing as the 'Queen Bee' of this debate). Gender was a construct, a performance that had mutable meanings, and queer theories helped to revitalize how 'femininity' and femaleness was perceived and exploited.

Clothing, behaviour and the way we approach and construct our gendered bodies can enhance and fashion our sexual agency. Burlesque performer Dita Von Teese uses style and fashion in this way to construct her excessively gendered body. Her use of classically 'sexy' lingerie and traditional erotic accessories such as stockings, stilettos, corsets and a beauty spot are used to play with and play to her image as a desiring and desirable sexual subject. As the mainstream 'look' of the new burlesque scene, we are, however, again faced with the same seemingly pre-given, although more exaggerated, aesthetic.

Why must women be desired for specific reasons? An 'ugly', un-kempt, hairy, masculine woman can still have an orgasm. Actual physiological sexuality is not really connected to looking good, to 'feeling' sexy. When Carolee Schneemann created art during those pre-feminist years, she was expressing her female-centred erotics by way of her naked and unrestrained body. What does it now mean to go back to this overt 'femininity'? Is it a backward step?

Consumer culture pushes women as pure sex objects but society punishes any woman who attempts to pursue this sexual agency. In relation to this dilemma Seph Weene, a feminist and former stripper, comments:

> I thought I was crazy because both the conventional, male-domi-nated outlook and feminist doctrine defined what I did as bad. I was having forbidden fun ... In order to reclaim the feminine power for my own, I gave it a name: *feminissima...*'[56]

In relation to new burlesque, some of this exaggerated reclama-tion of 'feminine power' feeds out from the drag and transvestite subcultures. The World Famous *BOB* was first described as 'wom-an-to-woman' drag. Before moving into burlesque, *BOB* used to perform as a Marilyn Monroe impersonator in a gay bar called The Cock in New York's East End. Kitten on the Keys comments that her 'role models have always been drag queen and trannies because they are burlesque performers in a nutshell'.[57]

It is interesting that Roger Baker in *Drag* (1994) comments how 'drag' culture flourished in both the 1860s and 1920s. Baker argues that these were times of crisis in relation to sexuality and gender. The late nineteenth-century burlesque performers constructed their sexuality via both a masculine style of dress and behaviour and 'fe-male-to-female' drag. Gypsy Rose Lee was inspired by gay cultural icon Dwight Fiske. His 'blue'-style ditties clearly influenced her own witty monologues.[58] Roger Baker draws parallels between these eras and the early 1990s, when he argues 'women were making strong demands and men, in reaction, [were] thrown into doubt and confusion'. The drag queen therefore became, he asserts, 'a symbol of sexual uncertainty and in many ways an agent of release from it'.[59] The exuberant play on 'femininity' by new burlesque performers could equally come from a need for self-invention and pleasure at a time when gender–sex imagery is becoming increasingly suffocating and colourless.

Forbidden fun, a sense of rescuing the female body from institutionalized shame, is what female performance artist Carolee Schneemann explored in her work. Most women did not recognize themselves in the one-dimensional imagery that surrounded their everyday lives, with the nude tradition being emblematic of this masculine-identified desire. Joanna Frueh describes eroticism as a 'sensual dimensionality' and a 'self-conscious aesthetic/erotic attentiveness', a 'self-love' and a 'self pride'.[60] Returning to this sensual sense of self meant unashaming the body, unashaming the heterosexual interchange integral to eroticism, unashaming the sexual act and unashaming the sexual gaze. As Frueh argues, 'The erotic requires a connection in which the gaze of another is essential and not necessarily alienating.'[61]

Striptease or erotic dance, Liepe-Levinson argues, replicates this very everyday ritual of surrender and control that is the sum of heterosexual seduction and chase. '"Desiring", "desiring to be desired by others", and even vicariously or narcissistically "desiring oneself" through the image of another'[62] is staged in the highly controlled environment.

Within the striptease routine, the power oscillates between the audience and the performer. The performer can feel the power that comes from manipulating the audience with her sexual energy as well as knowing that their voyeurism is only made possible through her wilfulness. She can also be made to feel like the most beautiful woman in the world with hundreds of men wanting and desiring her. In the strip joint, power is distributed and you can experience the thrill of 'incorrect' fantasies: being 'taken' as a man and 'taking control' as a woman. Liepe-Levinson points out, however, that the striptease scenario still demonstrates an engrained notion of gender norms. Women are still the sex objects who seduce through their beauty, their 'femininity', and the men – fully dressed – are the onlookers, the audience. The striptease scenario therefore upholds the status quo; it does not challenge it.

Men know that they can only look and enjoy being noticed as a desiring man because they have paid for it. The stripper has been bought. This is the kind of place that permits this kind of thing. This is the *kind* of woman that allows you to openly stare at her sexually. It follows therefore that women who strip, who 'give out', ultimately want it and deserve to be ... 'given one'. Burlesque however differs from this scenario in that the woman embraces and enjoys her sexual power, spinning a web of seductive manipulation with her erotic energy, but also puts question marks around the whole interchange. The word 'pazazz'[63] that Ann Corio used to describe Lydia Thompson is a perfect way of describing the dazzling charisma and fascination traditional burlesque performers held, where the art of the tease took precedence over the revelation of flesh or any 'giving out'. Through the tease, the tantalizing seduction of veiling and nakedness, she both confirms her sexuality, her feminine pleasures and the intimacy of the exchange, as well as maintaining a critical, self-conscious distance.

On Radio 4's *Woman's Hour* in March 2006,[64] Miss Immodesty Blaize performed her 'Reverse Strip', relayed to the listeners by a panel that included Rachel Shteir, author of *Striptease: The Untold History of the Girlie Show*, and Lynda Nead, Professor of Art History at Birkbeck College, London:

> Immodesty begins her act lying down naked under a black silk sheet. With many tantalizing glimpses and flashes of her flesh, she slowly stands up entwined in silk and shimmies forward. With a twang of elastic, she smoothly pulls herself into a pair of diamond-encrusted panties. She stands up, naked back to the audience and slides with a wiggle of her derrière, into a black evening dress. As a finale Immodesty then turns to the audience, winks and blows them a kiss.

There is a gentle humour to this performance. Nead describes it as 'flirtatious', 'beautiful' and as 'companionship'. Shteir and Nead agree that this show did in fact cater to the 'female gaze'. Indeed, as Immodesty previously pointed out in an interview for the *Evening Standard* in 2005, many of her audience are women who enjoy the show and 'walk out visibly two inches taller'.[65]

Women are engaging with and defining what is erotic. Immodesty Blaize's act – the reverse strip, the diamonds, the feathers, the humour, the glamorous womanly curves, the strong Rita Hayworth/Ava Gardner-like personality (in short, the camped-up femininity) – speaks to women in its pleasurable erotic parody of the 'sex object'. As Nick Curtis from the *Evening Standard* asserts, Immodesty's look veers on the 'cartoonish', 'classic Fifties American bombshell, with a bit of wry British wit thrown in'.[66] She exuberantly takes pleasure from this act, flirting infectiously with the audience who are affectionately seduced by the imagery. It is a female erotic form with the female gaze challenging the male gaze as the only available erotic outlet. However, as Lynda Nead commented, women are still defined by their bodies and striptease is still part of that exploitation. Immodesty's performance, her smile, flirtation and the female gaze leave these questions open, raw and exposed.

Burlesque is more that just individualist quenching of female pleasures, it is more than just a tantalizing feast for male delectation, it is more than just humorous parody. The burlesque performer's unshrinking direct gaze questions the basis of the viewer's desire, turning the tables so that viewers must look deeply at their own values. Chapter 5 will take a historical look at the female performer's politicized address. Her 'knowingness' moved beyond the theatrical space by way of her pin-ups, her reported antics and word-of-mouth, allowing this rebellious woman to reach out to a large network of women. Her individual transgression became a creative communal critique of the system in which she lived.

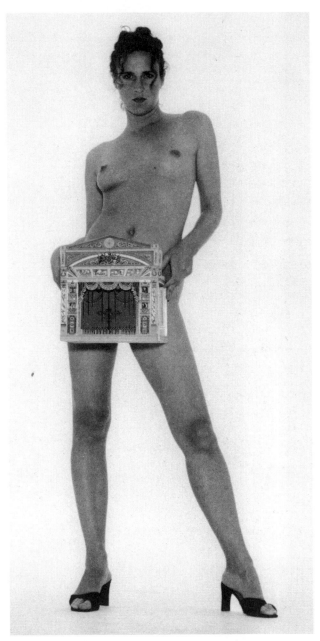

Ursula Martinez in *Show Off*, 2001.

5.

Guerrilla Theatre

THE FREAK

Subversive submission

'So should I embody your ideal?'[1]

In his essay 'Coldness and cruelty', Gilles Deleuze discusses Sacher-Masoch's *Venus in Furs* (1870) and the 'pleasure–pain'[2] of the power relations between the cruel female despot in fur, Wanda, and her self-elected lover-servant Severin. Severin is devoutly in awe of Wanda's beauty, a 'suprasensualism' that is heightened by her cruelty and his desire for her to wear fur. He goads her into becoming his ideal yet when she begins to act in this way he shudders at her coldness and lack of care. She questions whether she will be corrupted by the power he has given her over him. She also questions whether she is becoming his fantasy or breathing life into her own. This narrative is therefore extremely relevant because it resonates so concisely with contemporary feminist debates. As with Pauline Réage's *Story of O* (1954), where 'O' is subjected to her lover's sexual sado-masochistic whims, or the imagery of Dita Von Teese adorned in quintessential erotic accessories, breasts on display and whip in hand, there is an uncertainty in relation to who holds the reins of power. Who does this fantasy of erotic submission belong to?

Von Teese states that feminism for her is 'being as feminine as possible'. 'As my friend Ernest Greene says, "Feminine submission is the last stereotype to be liberated."'[3] Does Von Teese's desire to be an ultra-feminine sex object, with her tightly corseted waist, exposed breasts and high heels, translate into the ultimate objectification of women? Or does her artful embodiment of her erotic image as fetish allow Von Teese to represent her own liberated willing and wilful sexual agency, controlling of her own objecthood?

If we look specifically at the burlesque-inspired trend of the corset, which I have briefly addressed throughout this book, we see that an article of clothing that formerly signalled female repression, and this tyranny of 'femininity' is now being worn as a sign of sexual liberation and self-conscious eroticism. Valerie Steele in *Fetish: Fashion, Sex and Power* (1996) comments how the discourse on lingerie-style fashion is polarized. On the one hand, designer Josie Natorie comments: 'It used to be you could just express yourself in the bedroom, now you can express yourself all day long. Women are saying, "I used to burn my bra. Now I'm going to flaunt it."'[4] On the other hand, fashion journalist Charlotte DuCann complains that the fashion industry:

> Assumes that by flaunting her crotch, a woman is asserting some kind of individual freedom. Well, she isn't; it just makes her look like a prick-teaser. Nor is the fashionable flirting with S&M a sign that woman is strong, for there she is using her sex not as a liberating force but as a controlling power.[5]

What does the purposeful adoption of sexually submissive roles by artists like Dita Von Teese tell us about contemporary female sexuality and erotic attraction? In the early 1990s, Madonna's use of Jean-Paul Gaultier's conically breasted corset expressed a hard dominatrix 'ball-crushing' glamour. Like punk's re-appropriation of bondage, Madonna ironically and self-consciously re-appropriated women's erotic underwear, 'the stuff of male fantasy',[6] and transformed it into an iconic symbol of women's sexual empowerment and pleasure. This upfront re-appropriation of 'femininity' was seen to be an act of self-governance and self-fashioning that struck a nerve with many of her young female fans. The corset, an erotic accessory that had been formerly equated by feminists with antifeminist or prefeminist sexist ideas and attitudes, became a postfeminist symbol of women's sexual freedoms.[7]

New burlesque performers' use of the corset and other objects of desire now perhaps reveals a more ambiguous relationship to overt demonstrations of objecthood. Australia's Lola the Vamp argues that her acts allow the audience to make up their own mind as to whether burlesque objectifies women or indeed the performers:

> I prefer to tease out the ideas of objects and objectification – I use masks ... I become a doll. Some of my shows dive headlong into objectification to see where it leads, what it means to play intimately with objects, toys, items that are inanimate but can inherit a world of meaning – fetish toys like corsets.[8]

Burlesque performers explore their very objectness. It is, as aptly described by Lola the Vamp, a 'performance of the fetish',[9] with all its permutations, complications and erotic pleasures. Lola includes a wide assortment of 'objects' in her acts, including feather bowers, corsets, a giant red satin flower, a flower-encrusted swing, a unicorn, a swan called Vivien, as well as Lola dressed up as a caged bird and as a doll.

Lola's performance of the fetish is grounded in nostalgia (including late 1800s Paris, *La Belle Epoque* era of La Moulin Rouge, vintage 1920s lingerie and the bacchanalian antics of Josephine Baker). Other burlesque artistes reference the powerful personalities of the 1940s or 1950s such as Rita Hayworth and Ava Gardner (Miss Immodesty Blaize) or the glamorous 'stars' of the 1930s such as Sally Rand and Lili St Cyr (Dita Von Teese). These artistes invest the past with erotic possibilities for the future. They reconstruct images and narratives of what are believed to be more elegant, gentle, glamorous and sensuous eras, but by inserting their contemporary bodies and sexuality into this vintage utopia they point to a desire that is only based on non-attainability and absence. The creation of a 'future-past'[10] is a yearning for erotic potentiality and possibilities. It is a spectacle of desire and lack.

Lola the Vamp's carefully orchestrated performances include the tantalizing *Serpentine Dance*, inspired by late-1800s artiste Loie Fuller. In this act Lola dances with long veils on an extended pole. She has also reproduced this act as a sepia, grainy film. Another of her performances, *Moondrunk*, is a homage to Josephine Baker in which Lola sojourns on a suspended candy-striped hoop and performs a striptease whilst holding a Venetian mask to her face. She then removes this at the finale. The complex, rich layering of veiling in Lola's performance – cultural, historical (heavily referenced nostalgic sets), aesthetic (sepia, grainy distant shots), material (veils, make-up, masks, costume), physical (her body is always moving, whether swinging or dancing) – pointedly debars and obscures a voyeuristic devouring of the body as sex object. On the other hand there is a real pleasure, a real desire to 'show' the 'girl',[11] to transcribe the body and its sexuality by way of textures, colours, aesthetic appeal and traditional erotic temptation.

This is a paradoxical pleasure. When new burlesque performers 'spread their legs' to ride inanimate objects such as a unicorn (Lola the Vamp), a carousel horse (Dita Von Teese) and an 8ft rocking horse (Miss Immodesty Blaize), there is a sense of fun, a gentle humour, even an innocence about this gesture. The performers use artifice to exaggerate and artfully construct themselves as erotic object, as fetish. For contemporary philosopher Giorgio Agamben (Lola quotes his name as an influence), the word 'fetish' comes from the Latin meaning 'beautiful, pretty' – 'that which, in a human body, seems made by design, fashioned with skill, made-for, and which thereby attracts desire and love'.[12] For Lola the Vamp, over-elaboration and masks (to hide and then reveal identity) are used to emphasize how being a subject and an object are both 'distinguishable and the same'.[13] Her performance demonstrates how she is both immersed in and defined by artifice, by her erotic mask (described as 'abandonment' and 'thrownness' by Agamben).[14] She is sensually submerging herself in her objecthood yet she is simultaneously immersing herself in traditional male fantasy forms that reduce and fix her to this very objecthood.

Lola the Vamp's aesthetic and philosophical 'performance of the fetish' probes, embraces and opens up questions of identity – of subjectivity and objecthood – by way of veiling, exposure, masks, costume, props and nostalgia. On the other hand, Dita Von Teese uses exposure and concealment to exploit her use and exchange value as commodity fetish (in the Marxist interpretation of the word). Her use of the tease is framed within an astute awareness of her market value in the economic, scopic (visual) and libidinal economy. James Davidson's discussion of courtesans (*hetaeras*) in classical Athenian culture is extremely poignant in relation to this careful manipulation of sexual allure and the pleasure and power play involved in the (often) heterosexual erotic exchange.

Within classical Athenian society, Davidson (Lecturer in Ancient History at the University of Warwick) argues that looking was 'linked automatically to possessing'.[15] Visibility correlated with sexual availability. Wives were therefore invisible and prostitutes wholly visible. Davison argues that women could 'place themselves at various points along this continuum of exposure, turning visibility to invisibility'.[16] A prostitute's openness and complete exposure to the male gaze therefore equated with the simplicity in being able to 'have' her – her 'cheapness'. Athenian courtesans knew how to manipulate this scopic economy: 'Complete invisibility and complete exposure arrest movement along the continuum, and thereby neutralize desire.'[17] By keeping her clothes on, or giving rare glimpses of totally exposed flesh, the *hetaera* remained within that scopic economy and therefore was able to arouse a longing for what was hidden. However, as

Davidson argues, 'the *hetaeras* unlike the decent wife covers herself up not out of chastity but to mislead and delude and to maintain her market value'.[18]

Dita Von Teese, like the courtesan, is similarly emotionally detached in her carefully self-constructed, lovingly imbued style. She is a businesswoman who knows her own market value and is scrupulous in the marketing of this 'mysterious' femininity. This is why I still find Von Teese's imagery problematic. Without being coupled with an ironical, critical or reflective questioning of sexual power, erotic display risks falling immediately back into unchallenging, stereotypical 'off the shelf' readings of female sexuality – vulnerable, silent and fake.

When Gypsy Rose Lee exclaimed, 'Sweet? Submissive? Me?' She was clearly coupling irony and humour with her stripping, her sexual display. Like both Lola the Vamp and Immodesty Blaize she combined an informed distance with a sense of submissive pleasure. Her act is both self-effacing and self-governing. What appears to be missing from Von Teese's imagery that is clearly evident in other burlesque acts is this self-mocking critique. Iconic model Bettie Page perhaps best encapsulates this self-effacing questioning 'knowingness'. Bettie Page, smiling brightly and cheekily from the many photos taken of her, epitomizes for me a powerful and playful use of humour and an ambivalent smile that marks both collusion and resistance. The recent revival of this fetish pin-up queen as demonstrated by the film *The Notorious Bettie Page* (2006) directed by Mary Harron and starring Gretchen Mol, the re-distribution of the films by cult film-maker Irving Klaw, and the newfound interest in Page by new burlesque fans and performers perhaps point to a changing perspective amongst many young women as regards female nudity, display and erotic imagery. Both Page and the burlesque phenomenon sum up for young women the desire to both counter and take pleasure from the male gaze.

Bettie Page in both *Striporama* and *Varietease* embodies a cheeky glamour and an innocent saucy naughtiness that seems to fuse *Hammer Horror* theatrical kitsch with *Carry On* double entendres. Erotic submission or domination is always acted out in a delicious tongue-in-cheek manner. Whether stripping, spanking or being tied up, Bettie Page carries it off in an exhilaratingly 'normal' manner that somehow deflates the whole situation. She is both an active participant, enjoying acting out the erotic scenario with other female actors, as well as blatantly communicating to her viewer the absurdity of the whole scenario. In one story two young women tie another young woman up and carefully lift her into the boot of a car before kidnapping her and driving her to a remote wood. There they tie her to a tree to gently give her another spanking. All of the women are clad in stockings, high heels and black underwear. The acting sends up the whole genre, mocking the viewer and the performance, with any seriousness being diffused by the female voiceover that exclaims: 'One can only guess what the hapless victim did to provoke this inter-sister dominance.'

This 'acting' is not, however, delivered in the same vein or with the same intent as the panting boredom in Paris Hilton's now infamous sex tapes where we see Hilton taking a phone call during sex. Ariel Levy discusses how these tapes catapulted Hilton to celebrity status, with her films clearly epitomizing the current climate of being 'fuckable and salable',[19] but not sexual. The worry though for me comes not necessarily from Hilton's sexual submission but from the fact that she does not seem the least be bothered by the encounter. She is utterly uninterested and certainly not in the throes of pleasure. As Levy exclaims, 'Passion is not the point.'[20] This is what sexy girls do. It is what makes them 'hot'. 'Hotness' is not about pleasure, connection or allure but about 'being worthwhile'.[21] It is about the appearance of sexiness rather than sex itself; it is about appearing like you are constantly soliciting attention and approval for your physicality. This is a sexual freedom that is divorced from any real erotic or emotional connection with oneself or another.

In the imagery and bondage or S/M films of Bettie Page she is clearly coming across as having a good time. Yet it is also blatantly parodic. New burlesque performers who demonstrate this sense of self-parody include the anarchic acrobatic Wau Wau Sisters (with a BLEEP sign over each breast) or Sidney, Australia's Imogen Kelly, attired in aristocratic crinoline, high pink wig, white face paint and beauty spot, and cheekily winking whilst stripping off layer upon layer of pants. This is a subversive submission – pleasure–pain – that humanizes rather than idealizes. These women are letting their hair down yet they are also subverting and making fun of this 'hotness' by way of excessive femininity or female-to-female drag, tattoos, bondage, SM, humour, cartoonish make-up and even acrobatics. There is, however, a danger with this bawdy beauty in that it risks distancing a mainstream audience who are lulled by habitual 'normalized' sexual stereotypes. It risks inflating the gap between acceptable and unacceptable glamour, style, sexiness and body shapes. As Michelle Baldwin argues, 'sometimes the gaze is just not so kind',[22] with many men and women who (whether this is because of the figures or the tattoos) do not like the 'look' of the new burlesque movement.

As 'self made "freaks"',[23] are burlesque performers achieving what they would like to achieve or by creating a subculture out of 'unconventional glamour' do they risk creating a larger gulf between men and women in this increasingly sexist society? And if so, does burlesque imagery like that of the perfectly sexy Dita or the youthful Pussycat Dolls thrusting their just-covered genital area toward the camera not exacerbate this sexism?

The freak show

In 2006 in the UK *Big Brother* was seen by the media to have taken a turn for the worse, with journalists drawing parallels between the viewers' insatiable thirst for *Celebrity Big Brother* and the Victorian middle-class touring of the Bedlam mental asylum. The curiosity of the Freak and the re-branding of the term as cool seems to be making a comeback, with former stripper and ailing Page 3 model Jodie Marsh wearing a t-shirt emblazoned with the line, 'Do you wish your girlfriend was a freak like me?' tautly stretched over her large '100 per cent natural' breasts. The *Sunday Times* argued that the popularity of *Celebrity Big Brother*, with its largest audience to date tuning in to watch MP George Galloway miaow and lap like a cat, cross-dresser Pete Burns strut around with his surgically enhanced lips and genitals hanging out, and mid-fifties actress Rula Lenska strip, now represented the modern-day freak show.

We pay lip service to diversity but actually many of as cannot live with difference, especially our own difference from the image of ideal beauty. Our desire to watch these 'freaks' is perpetuated by our curiosity about those who dare to or cannot help but be different from what is seen to constitute perfection, whether that be through cosmetic surgery, unconventional behaviour or the 'grotesque' of an old yet sexual woman. The push to conform may be compounded by our feelings that this perfection will bring us greater individual freedom, greater confidence, greater wellbeing. We are pushed, restricted and utterly embedded in competitive conformity. It can be widely observed in today's society that most of us are in the race, whether we like it or not. Many women yearn to live up to the fantasy of the conventional norm even though our difference from this norm is what gives us our individuality. Youth and beauty are the defining aspiring qualities of contemporary living. Nobody wants to be seen as washed up. Everybody wants to be adored. Nobody wants to be ignored.

The fascination with the need to conform to this seemingly perfect ideal is also coupled with the fascination for its opposite – that which does not or cannot conform. It feeds off a voyeuristic desire for difference but also makes us feel better off, prettier or luckier. The Victorian era exploited this fascination for physical spectacle with the freak show, immortalized cinematically in Tod Browning's film *Freaks* (1932). A nation that was reeling from war, moving in or out of depression, deep in debt and finding solace in alcohol was also finding escape through the sensation of the spectacle. And it is not by accident that in the specific eras when the phenomenon of burlesque became an overnight sensation there was a surge and therefore glut of the visual image (Internet, cinema, photography, penny dailies) at affordable prices for both the middle class and working class. (As an aside, the 1950s striptease sirens also coincided with the rising interest in television.)

Historically burlesque dancers, the 'girl shows', were touted in sideshows alongside other human curiosity acts such as Mary Anne Bevan, 'The World's Ugliest Woman', Joseph Merrick as 'The Elephant Man', Anita, the 'Living Doll', 'Titana, the Fat Girl' or midget 'General Tom Thumb', Charles Stratton. These acts became household names and were patronized by royalty – Queen Victoria met Charles Stratton on three separate occasions.

The 'leg business' was seen in a similar light. Olive Logan vituperatively writes about the 'clog-dancing creature, with yellow hair and indecent costume'[24] who shared the bill with other more conventional curiosity attractions such as 'the giant and the dwarf, the learned pig and the educated monkey'.[25] For her debut appearance at Wood's Theatre, Lydia Thompson shared the bill with Sophia Gantz the 'Baby Woman', a giantess, and a dwarf called General Grant. These living attractions were exhibited in a lecture hall, there to be viewed by the audience as they walked through to the theatre. The *carte-de-visite* or postcards of these 'freaks' was just as popular as those depicting the female burlesque stars.

Similarly, 1930s burlesque was filled with stars with extraordinary physiques like the Amazonian build of 6ft 4in striptease star Lois DeFee, who was billed by Walter Winchell as 'Eiffel Eyeful'. Lois DeFee was seen to exploit to the full the 'curiosity' value and therefore the publicity value of her height. She was said to have married a midget solely for the front-page publicity of the wedding. It only lasted a couple of days but, as burlesque star Ann Corio put it, 'how long does it take to make a photograph?'[26] The 'absurd' and 'grotesque' mismatching of the marriage was exploited as comic material in burlesque shows for many years:

> How did that midget make love to Lois DeFee?
> Someone put him up to it.[27]

Burlesque performers played on the audience's need for sensation to highlight their own reputation and stardom, as much as the audience cried out and incited the stars to push further and further against the boundaries of respectability.

Hinda Wassau was purportedly the first artiste on the Western stage to publicly expose her bare breasts, in 1928, as a chorus girl for a burlesque troupe. Wassau claimed it was accidental, the 'shimmy', or belly dance that was made popular by 'Little Egypt' in 1873, caused her clothes to come loose so she then had to remove them completely! Ann Corio found the story dubious; Wassau's explanation was too good to be true. Whatever the story of the event, the crowds went wild at the unveiling – they had never seen anything like this before.

Similarly the Blondes exploited and catered to the middle-class need for raunchiness and a bit of raw with the tantalizing exposure of their tight-clad thighs. These girls were pushing their acts further and further, competing to find that added extra. The 'behind-the-tent' shows, or 'dirty' burlesque (small touring companies that offered one-night stands, with shabby sets and costumes), offered plenty of 'smut' to compete with the travelling country fairs and carnivals, with their 'time-honoured backroom sex displays'.[28] This extra was usually a prize fight or a *hootchee cootchee* (the original label given to Little Egypt's belly dance).

A fascination for 'the freak' re-emerged at the turn of the millennium. Across the Atlantic in the mid-1990s, New York's Great Fredini joined forces with Bambi the Mermaid to explore what Fredini called 'weird nude performance'. From this, Burlesque at the Beach – 'old style burlesque, sideshow freaks, strange women'[29] – was created as an extension of the Coney Island Circus Sideshow, a sideshow that already featured such acts as The Twisted Shockmeister (a glass-eater, escape artist and human blockhead who eats live crickets and lit cigarettes) and Ula – The Painproof Rubber Girl (a contortionist and trapeze artist who lays on beds of nails).[30] Many burlesque performers are extremely skilful entertainers who are classically trained in ballet and tap, performance, comedy, belly dancing, acting, high trapeze, fire-eating and other circus acts. It is not therefore purely about titillating striptease, but more about the spectacle of putting on a visually evocative, entertaining show. Like burlesque, with its old affiliations to the travelling carnival and fair, new burlesque also extravagantly fuses 'girl-shows' with outrageous sideshow acts to produce the same combination of spectacle and humour, sensuality and absurdity.

In the UK in 1998, the Lost Vagueness Ballroom became the most popular field at Glastonbury Festival. In fact it became so popular that it had to be closed in 2003 due to overcrowding and therefore health and safety concerns. The field is now divided into specialized areas that include 'The Big Brother Caravan' and 'The Freak Show', where transvestite lessons are given by Wyn La Freak clad in ten-inch heels. There is also a cabaret lounge where there are radical trapeze artists who swing from chandeliers, 'beautiful freaks', and a honky tonk piano. In 2005 a new area was created called 'Midnight's Carnival', the first ever field to be curated solely by women. This field included Carnesky's Ghost Train, which was filled with 'ghoulish beauties' who enact 'surreal vignettes', the CanBootyCan showgirls with their anarchic take on the cancan, the Pretty Freaky all-female freak show, and the Burlesque Boutique that sells exquisite costumes and burlesque couture.[31]

What is the reason for this current fashion for freak shows, fairgrounds, carnival, circus and other forms of curiosity? Many of Von Teese's own images reference the fairground with a delicious, vibrant use of colour and magical, tantalizing fantasy. Do we maybe again find ourselves, like the 1860s or 1920s, in a sanitized culture where all quirky, sensual, multi-variant qualities have become rare? With a mainstream culture that is made up of manufactured bands, uniform city centres and coffee shop monopolies that feel grey and lifeless, have we lost a rich spectrum of tastes and visual difference?

Perhaps many of us long for more tastes, smell and sights. Andrew Sinclair argues in *Prohibition* (1962) that in the 1930s the speakeasy became the place for the middle classes who were 'bored with boredom'.[32] With the social stigma against alcohol lifted it had become fashionable to drink, and men had to fight their way past young girls and women to get a drink. In a similar scenario to the present-day, the middle-classes were bored with the ethic of all work and no play, with convention and conformity, and pressures and the stress of having to keep up.

Perhaps we yearn for some colour, some variety. We yearn to have our senses re-wakened and re-invigorated. In relation to the original Scottish meaning of the word 'glamorous', as in witchcraft, being spellbound, relating to magic, a spell ... we want to have a 'glam' put on us. Ruth Tutti-Frutti's comment about 'Midnight's Carnival' (as one of the collaborative organizers) is relevant to this notion of magic. She describes this area at Glastonbury as:

> full of weird and wonderful freaks and beautiful artful women. We want the whole experience to be dream-like that starts the minute you walk through the gate ... an experience that when you wake up in the morning you're not sure if it really happened.[33]

Does this dream-like quality mean that burlesque remains, like carnival, the circus or the fairground, a temporary light escape?

Perhaps a way of understanding this desire for dream-like escapism is to track back to what could perhaps be seen as the origins of burlesque – the mid-sixteenth-century Italian *commedia dell'arte*. In fact the word 'burlesque' comes from the Italian word *burla* (meaning a joke or farce), which was first used at this point in history to refer to a particular literary genre that satirized 'high' poetic language and epic narrative. *Commedia dell'arte*, the world of entertainment, contrasted with the *commedia erudite*, encompassed by the high arts, tragedy. It was the illegitimate, 'unofficial' or 'antiofficial' theatre. *'Arte'* was the art of pure entertainment, where farcical antics by the *zanni* would be interspersed with dancing or acrobatics.[34] This is how popular theatrical forms like carnival, fairs and the circus converge; they all belong to that same world of entertainment, of spectacle, of 'low' sensuous pleasures.

At its origins *commedia dell'arte* acted as a direct escape from the 'steadiness' of the dominant 'respectable' Puritan and mercantile bourgeois value system. Its demonstration of tomfoolery, self-mocking outbursts of oscillating emotion and masquerade were seen as 'defiantly frivolous or sullenly crude'.[35] Martin Green and John Swan argue in *The Triumph of Pierrot* that this *arte* was not overtly political but was a 'nonserious dissent'[36] against society's 'truths' and respectability. In certain periods this 'low' form of dissent has burst out of its ghetto to invade the other 'high' world. (As I have discussed in detail, burlesque became one of these eruptions.) At these times, *commedia dell'arte* attitudes and artifice have visibly, yet perhaps half-consciously, penetrated social life, with its challenges to gendered and sexual roles, violent language, artifice, costume, hedonism and parody. One example Green and Swan give is of the 1920s, when metropolitan fashion leaned towards commedia styles with their sexual and gender dissent, androgynous attire, rouged cheekbones and whitened faces, like Pierrot.[37]

Whether as sensuous, drunken, dream-like detachment or visual deviance, this spectacle of dissent operates at the level of the senses as opposed to 'high' reason and truth. It is transgressive pleasure as revolt. New burlesque absorbs and synthesizes these historical half-conscious cultural retorts, including the Rockabillies (1950s), Punk (1970s), Psychobillies and Goths (1980s), Gothic Lolitas (1990s), tattooing and S/M. It also 'pillages' from other alternative decadent visual forms such as art nouveau, the bacchanalian excess of showgirls, or the absinthe (Green Fairy) fuelled creativity of artists. In this sensual world, when we go through the mirror, down the rabbit hole, we catch glimpses of flesh, exquisite costume, fairground attractions, pink candyfloss, and cheeky, anarchic fun ... the Technicolor world of Dorothy's sparkling red shoes. As Immodesty Blaize exclaims, 'our show is a place of absolute escapism, a velvety, decadent cocoon from reality ... a chance to dress up and show off again'.[38]

In her book *Burlesque and the Art of the Teese* (2006), Dita Von Teese refers to the magical draw of lavish spectacle. According to Von

Teese, the 'courtesan' and queen of late eighteenth-century musical hall, Mistinguett, knew, like Liberace, how to create a lavish spectacle and inspire dreams. With her decadence, her 'feminine power', her lavish costume and effervescent personality, Mistinguett re-invented her self – 'I certainly could not rely on my looks. I never have'[39] – into an extremely glamorous, charming and seductive spectacle. Von Teese quotes Mistinguett: 'We sell [the audience] a trip to nowhere, canvas landscapes, moonbeams made out of gelatin.' Von Teese uses this quote to point to what she 'sells' in her own burlesque act … "magic"'.[40]

Von Teese's discussion of Mistinguett focuses on the performer's ability to put on a spectacular show and look sensational, yet Mistinguett was also extremely political. The extravagant show gave her the opportunity to be heard. Spectacular performances by Gypsy Rose Lee and the British Blondes that combined sexiness and bold, brash public speaking also operated in this same political spirit. The question I would like to raise is, does new burlesque's glamorous, lavish, optically edible spectacle have a voice?

KNOWINGNESS

Gossip

Gossip has always been given a bad press. Bitchy and frivolous. What the girls do when they get together over a bottle of wine or over a coffee. What women do over the garden fence. It is depicted as a particularly, stubbornly female pursuit. Men get together to play poker, play games, play football. Women gossip.

Burlesque performers gossiped. They were also relentlessly, prolifically gossiped about. At their peak, as the expression goes, they were the talk of the town, grabbing headline news and monopolizing conversations. Lucy Lippard in *Get the Message* describes gossip as an 'inherently feminist', intimate type of spoken propaganda that subversively disseminates a different kind of message. Lippard argues that gossip is about *'relating* – a feminized style of communication'.[41] It knits us together in our quotidian dealings. This may involve a small greeting in the street, warm chatter with family and friends, or the airing of cross words. As Lippard states:

> The spoken word is connected with the things most people focus on almost exclusively: the stuff of daily life and the kind of personal relationships everyone longs for in an alienated society. It takes place *between* people, with eye contact, human confusion and pictures (memory). It takes place in dialogues with friends, family, acquaintances, day after day. So one's intake of spoken propaganda is, in fact, the sum of daily communication.[42]

The burlesque performer's power to influence came from her ability to directly address her audience with a different kind of message. Her 'propaganda' intercepted and commented on society's cultural and social value systems, making fun of 'high' art, fashion, marriage and divorce – even suffrage and suffragettes. The female performer's questioning of the rules of play penetrated straight to the heart of the middle-class cultural arena. From this 'privileged' position, her politicized running commentary, social asides and irreverent and relentless backchat spread infectiously and uncontrollably, by way of publicity and word of mouth, beyond the confines of the theatre.

Kathleen Rowe identifies a lineage of unruly women who have 'gossiped and cackled in the margins of history for millenia',[43] including Noah's wife (who would only get in that ark when she was good and ready[44]) and Sarah of the Old Testament (who laughed at God's statement that she would have a baby so late in life). The horse-whipping episode (*see* Chapter 1) and consequent diatribe that Lydia Thompson effectively delivered against the editor who had cast aspersions on her sexual morality would have certainly filtered out to other women via gossip columns and in over-the-garden-gate exchanges.

The nineteenth-century burlesque performer's iconic status would indeed have added further weight and credence to her behaviour and words. Her humorous rebelliousness and self-reflexivity, encapsulated in the image of Lydia Thompson – whip in hand, monocle to eye, looking unswervingly at the viewer and smiling – encouraged laughter as a pleasurable shared experience amongst women who up to that point would have been suspicious and even contemptuous of each other. The humour also made the words and deeds pleasurable to digest and fun to recount. With the Blondes' burgeoning popularity it was no longer so taboo to be in allegiance with this type of woman, whose voice would formerly have been silenced as lewd and uncultured.

The softening of stigma meant that this sexual working-class brash woman was now being listened to and setting trends that middle-class women were following. Rachel Shteir comments that the Blondes 'were not radical' because they 'appealed to the male appetite on a visual level. As one reviewer put it, they were "optically edible."'[45] I would agree with this point. Appealing to the male appetite is not radical – but this was their draw.

The Blondes came to New York from London, where there was already a tradition of biting working-class parody in British music hall. In the late nineteenth-century performers like Bessie Bellwood and Jenny Hill, the 'Vital Spark'[46] and 'First Queen of the Music Hall', sung their risky ditties like 'Then You Wink the Other Eye' and 'A Little of What You Fancy Does You Good' and reeled off their comic patter. In the 1860s Theresa was seen to be the Parisian café concerts (*café conc*) equivalent of this working-class icon who performed before mixed audiences made up of 'ladies' and shop girls, top hats and prostitutes. Theresa was seen as vulgar, bawdy, irreverent and 'unashamedly materialistic'.[47] Her songs reflected what was seen as a brash new *petit bourgeoisie*. Andrea Stuart claims that working-class showgirls like Theresa were perceived to be:

> heroines of misrule, an anarchic force which disrupted class allegiances. Truly popular and populist, the showgirl was a be-jewelled Trojan horse, destined to sap the strength of the upper classes by de-

bauching them with pleasure – whilst simultaneously promoting the views of the newly powerful *petit bourgeoisie* ... struggling for their place in the Parisian sun.[48]

Lydia Thompson and the Blondes were following on from this brash, ostentatious and political trajectory. They were sexy, bold and vital, but most importantly, in relation to the stern Victorian society that they were entering, they were also publicized as utterly moral in their sexual purity (these women were astute in business and self-promotion). This combination is what made them so radical. It was because of this convincing fusion of sexiness and 'purity' that the Blondes were (initially) able to speak and be heard, and it was at this early point of entry into this arena that burlesque was at its most infectious. These women were performing a different kind of stubborn and resistant 'femininity' in words and deeds that acted in opposition to the traditional servility and silent passivity expected from the female sex.

These stories of 'resistant performance' were echoed in the public performances of resistance enacted by the 'guerillist' actions of the women's rights' movement in the mid-nineteenth century (their pageants) and later in the guerrilla theatre staged by the first wave (suffragettes) and second wave feminists (*see* Chapter 2). Up until the mid to late nineteenth century, public speaking had been a white educated man's privilege. With the onset of women's rights activism, middle-class white educated women were beginning to take their protest to the public stage, spokeswomen for a different kind of femininity. Also, as Elizabeth Reitz Mullenix illustrates in her essay 'Private women/public acts' (2002), many women were also encouraging private acts of dissent through public displays of rebellion and self-assertion.

Mullenix recounts Amelia Bloomer's tale of a wife in 1852 New York who, fed up with her respected judge husband's drunken behaviour, marched into the bar he frequented in Wayne county, made a 'general smash' of the tavern and gave the proprietor a 'few blows over the head'.[49] In her temperance paper *The Lily* (1852) Bloomer reports:

Such women are an honor to their sex and entitled to public praise. We hope when she got the drunken judge home she did not forget to give him a few lashes too. He deserved them as much as the rum-seller.[50]

According to Mullenix, Bloomer was suggesting that this kind of public performance could possibly set a very good example for women to follow suit in the domestic space. By opening up a dialogue between the private and public sphere women could be given the strength to stand up for themselves and men could see that abuses of their power would no longer be tolerated. The cross-fertilization between the private and public domain at the time of the first wave of feminist activism meant that women were authorizing a healthy disrespect for certain rules and regulations, certain power structures, hierarchies and roles that were seen to be benefiting a select few.

Burlesque 'stars' challenged sanctified male power and superiority over women by deflating their self-importance and bruising their egos. Gypsy Rose Lee was reported to have said: 'Once in a while I hear that old chestnut popping out that us strippers – ugh – loathe the loathsome creatures. Males – ugh – the beasts! Say am I loathing eighty per cent of my audience? ... Why men are even sweet.'[51] With this statement, she was affectionately undermining male authority, puncturing macho egos and establishing her own sense of self-assured control. At the same time, though, this quote could almost be a parody (ahead of its time) of the idea of feminists as 'man-haters'.

The burlesque performer's subverted rhetoric was not only an upfront challenge to dominant patriarchal 'words' but also acted as a challenge to the authoritative middle-class 'feminist' voice. When Thompson stepped up onto the podium in *Ixion* to give a speech about the 'New Woman' she was both parodying their fashion (Grecian Bend, with huge blonde wig) and their modern behaviour – 'She straddles well a velocipede'[52] – as well as asserting her own right to be part of that struggle for freedom.

The recounting of these 'no bullshit' sound bites, jokes, quips and witty one-liners would have moved swiftly by word of mouth in one piece of gossip to the next via chitchat over the garden fence, the gossip columns in the papers, the accounts from someone who knew someone else who had been there, of friends who had heard this, or next-door neighbours who thought that. The memorable parts would have stuck in the mind of the listener who would have added their own slant, their own opinions and their own way of telling it.

Throughout this book, too, I have made clear my own take on these performers. I have therefore added to the gossip. The stories recounted in this book are perceptions of these performers as have been retold on countless occasions. Particular nuggets will stick or be dismissed on variant retellings. And gossip amongst the middle classes about the burlesque acts would have made a mark on the gossiper in just the same way as it would have moulded and altered the behaviour and attitudes of the burlesque performers. By moving beyond the theatre and into women's homes, these burlesque performers gave other women (who perhaps would not otherwise have got the chance) a stake in the creation of their own propaganda.

A participatory space was being negotiated that worked against the mainstream 'male' flow of knowledge. This was a counter-universe of shared information and mutual support that expanded, spread, reshaped and snowballed. These women therefore had a very real stake in shifting public opinion and awareness. This operated in a similar way to the US 'consciousness-raising' groups and feminist performance art of the 1970s or even the British WI (Women's Institute) – although the activities of the WI are now popularly perceived in a derogatory way and rubbished as an insignificant pastime.

However, group activities such as this gave women the space to listen to how others lived their lives, the good and the bad, the success and the failures. It gave opportunities for warm banter, the space to have a good laugh, an undisrupted chat and make friends. It also allowed them space to reflect on their own lives, what they should or perhaps should not be putting up with and what they could yet achieve. It gave them the space to be heard and was an outlet for voicing opinions and beliefs that had been rattling around four walls and submerged under the relentless demands of babies, toddlers, infants and teenagers.

In a similar way the burlesque performer with her goading address, her smile, wink and sassy comments revealed a different, fresh intervening voice. Why shouldn't a 'fancy- pants stripper'[53] like me make it big? Why should I have to put up with being described like that? Why do I need to be ashamed? In saying these things, she was equally implying, why should you be putting up with the way things are? The Blondes were authorizing a particular uncontained mode of existence. In contrast to the middle-class orators of the women's movement, however, the burlesque performers were working-class and therefore their words had to be either curbed or undermined.

In the contemporary era, uncontrollable female voices are still silenced or undermined by making the women out to be mad, ugly or just plain 'over the hill'. Their opinions are therefore not worth their salt. At a talk that was part of a publicity tour for her book *The Whole Woman*, Germaine Greer spoke with acidic humour about a young male driver who called her 'an old bag', as if her age now took away any of her rights to civility or respect. I also remember the late Mo Mowlam, known for being an unconventional politician, who was taunted relentlessly for being overweight (although not so when she revealed the presence of a brain tumour). Her honesty was seen as too forthright, too honest; she was a bit of a renegade, and her tactics, like throwing her wig onto the table to diffuse tension during the Good Friday Agreement discussions, were seen to be a liability. It was Mowlam, however, who ended up being the only one who could broker a deal.

Robert C. Allen argues, however, that the key to the burlesque performer's transgressive potential is their fusion of sexual appeal *and* unmanageable impertinence. And it is this potent combination that made the classical burlesque performers culturally 'too hot to handle'.[54] Allen argues that as soon as these two elements are divided these women became more controllable and therefore lost their subversive edge.

Jennifer Reed claims that the writer/actress/character Roseanne Barr was able to offer up to women new and subversive ways of seeing. This, she argues, was because Roseanne, as author, was authorizing outrageous behaviour, the 'power to subvert existing power relations',[55] for dissatisfied 'ordinary' women living within heterosexual nuclear family life. It wasn't a safety valve, like carnival, but a very real challenge to the system that up to that point wrote these women's scripts, intercepting and controlling what these kind of women actually said.

However, the burlesque performer differs from Roseanne, who is more representative of the belching, farting laddishness of postfeminism, since the burlesque performer seduces and charms the viewer; she is able to get under the audience's skin and catch them off-guard. Allen's argument is that in order to be transgressive the performer *has* to be an object of desire (I would say for women as well as men), otherwise they are perceived merely as comically grotesque. Roseanne therefore, not being a conventionally alluring glamour puss, loses her edge. Men have to fear the performer's sexual power to be compelled to listen.

This is why subversive public speech and stripping, or rather teasing, fuse so powerfully. Whilst tempting to undress, the burlesque performer uses her script-less, free-running commentary to challenge the viewer's control over her and the complicated power dynamic at play. By doing this she controls what we get to see, what becomes visible and what stays veiled – what we get to know and learn. The veiling of the body and sex becomes a metaphor for the veiling of information. At the same time, though, she is questioning knowingly her 'freak', 'low', exhibition trophy status.

Is this burlesque performer, however, not just confirming what we already know? That as women you have to be beautiful, youthful, have sex appeal and be glamorous before anyone will stop to listen? That a woman can say the most beautiful, honest words but if she is ugly, then her words count for nothing? How does this glamorous, sassy woman challenge the system? As the ultimate object of desire she represents both what women want to be and feel like with her female-identified sexuality *and* that ideal pinnacle of male fantasy. Teetering on this knife's edge, how does the performer challenge a selfish, self-obsessed, individualist culture? Is she not just catering to the whims of a media-ideal? Is this not pure irresponsibility – creating tension, pain and envy? How does she break down the suspicious distance between women and start to build a meaningful, politicized, 'knowing' connection? And finally, does she have to be actively informed by political debate to achieve this?

Networking

[Late capitalist society] has contributed to a bitter twist to the centuries of female oppression. Consumerism, suburban residence patterns, declining family size, increased male occupational mobility, increased female education, declining parental control over children … rising divorce rates, and a host of other changes have been interwoven in a dense network of isolation and anxiety.[56]

The 'dense network of isolation and anxiety' written about by Elizabeth Fox-Genovese still rings true resoundingly 15 years later. In fact, Alessandra Buonfino and Geoff Mulgan have argued in their article in the Guardian entitled 'Goodbye to all that' (2006) that Britain now suffers from a 'quiet crisis of unhappiness'.[57] We are at present better off economically (though how much of this is floating on credit?) but suffer from serious and profound feelings of alienation, loneliness, separation and ultimately distrust. Fox-Genovese goes on to question whether feminism will come to be seen to have 'done the dirty work of capitalism'. By uncritically espousing the ideals of individualism feminism may well have helped to erode 'the older communities and bourgeois institutions that blocked the way to a sinister new despotism'.[58] Re-establishing this 'soft, often invisible' network of social support is vital, Buonfino and Mulgan argue, if we want to improve the quality of all our lives. It is, they state, 'channelled energy that makes social progress possible' and therefore is 'one of the great challenges of this century'.[59]

We always assume that Western ideals of unfettered individu-alism are unquestionably the right way for us to achieve progress. Carolyn Sorisio argues that sex, race and class oppression cannot be challenged seriously 'until we also interrogate unchecked capitalism and American individualism [and] recognize the inter-connected-ness of structures of domination'.[60] This can be achieved, she argues, by exploring other 'strategies of resistance'[61] from historical prece-dents in order to build more inclusive solidarity. In the 1990s, iconic post-feminists (Wolf, Paglia, Roiphe) were criticized for batting on the side of rich, white, middle/upper-class visibility. When Naomi Wolf incited women into action with 'Be greedy. Pursue pleasure', 'female is beautiful',[62] this was not an inclusive incitement, nor did it address serious problems of power. They were seen to be glorifying their success and power as Americans. But this was somehow fine, because they were women.

I am not arguing that women should not want to pursue plea-sure, to 'get to the top' and be successful. Nor am I suggesting that men should now surrender all their power over to women. Turning the axis of power upside down is not the answer. The vague notion of 'girl power' (touted by pop bands such as the Spice Girls) and ad-verts that sneer at men's uselessness seem to do just this. This is not only unhelpful but may even be likened to the behaviour of a bully who was herself once bullied. What needs to be debated is whether the burlesque performer offers up a strategy of resistance that opens up more comprehensive communication. Does she challenge the ex-clusive uncompromising individualism forwarded by post-feminists such as Paglia and Wolf? As has been enunciated in some depth throughout this book, the burlesque star frequently wants power, fame, fortune and publicity. She wants to dazzle, to charm. She wants to *be* someone. Is she therefore *encouraging* selfishness, greed, neurosis and unhappiness? There is a thin line between the self who controls an image and selfishness itself.

Historical burlesque merged the chaos, dangers and pleasures of the city with a growing politicized revolt. The late nineteenth century and 1930s female performers' witty asides, sexy decadence, exuberant costume and political commentary combined a confident drive for success and pleasure with a knowing address that acknowledged the questionable stigma that came with her high visibility. What is interesting is how at particular points in history this politicized address crossed boundaries of class and culture.

Women from different classes were finding common ground and a collective language for their dissatisfaction. They were also finding a similar admiration for the burlesque performer's self-realized 'awarishness'. At the same time, well-meaning women's rights activists were pigeon-holing and sexually strait-jacketing women into genteel yet prestigious public roles, or, as was the case for working-class women, telling them how to clean up their act. Their feminism did not appeal to all. The burlesque performer catered to this discrepancy. Perhaps the current burlesque boom fills a similar role.

With traditional burlesque, the pleasures and politics of female resistance found an outlet. Taking her cue from 'the undutiful pleasure-seeking [immigrant] daughter',[63] the burlesque 'star' combined the 'Americanized' concept of the 'self-made' man and the immigrant tradition of the tightly knit family or community with its East European Jewish and Italian socialist and anarchist ideas. This synthesis challenged stereotypes of the working-class woman as victim, as downtrodden, as sluttish, as ignorant and as incapable of knowing what was good for her. Christine Stansell argues in *City of Women* (1987) that Lithuanian anarchist Emma Goldman, 'Red Emma' (who grew up in a *petit-bourgeois* Jewish family), arrived in New York in 1886 to turn this growing working-class feminism 'into a political vision of women's freedom'.[64] Interestingly she was admired and adopted as an iconic 'rebel woman' by first wave feminists.

Jacqueline Dowd Hall, in her essay on the Elizabethton rayon plant strike of 1929 in the Appalachian South, argues that the working-class female strikers similarly challenged stereotypes usually attributed to being young, working class and out in the public space. Their combination of 'fierceness with flirtation',[65] their use of laughter, their use of language, dress and gesture, pointed to a particularly inventive protest style that had an erotic charge. One flamboyant gesture was to wear a wide-brimmed hat made from an American Flag. They were affirming their rights to be treated equally and fairly as both citizens of America and as members of the female community.

What is intriguing about this piece of militant theatre is that it gained a wide network of support and attention. The young women's provocative, intelligent and audacious courtroom style enraptured the courtroom spectators, enlisted the support of the rest of the female community and attracted the admiration of middle-class activists who came to Elizabethton to offer their organizational skills and support. It also enraged and embarrassed officialdom. The more sexually lewd and disorderly of the women were charged and the others were let off because they came from 'good families'. However, the protest was exemplary in that it knitted together cross-gendered, cross-cultural, cross-class strategies with empowering effects, procuring solidarity amongst women who would not usually have deigned to be associated with each other, as well as securing a deepened sense of individual power. It left its mark.

This idea of highlighting and harnessing what is 'cross-culturally desirable'[66] is what Leila Ahmed claims Muslim and Western feminists must now do. They must critique Western feminism for its strengths and weaknesses, not to lambaste in competitive one-upmanship but to learn in order for women to move forward in realizing their capabilities and potential for growth. In the Muslim world Western feminism is linked to capitalism in that they both represent what Fatima Mernissi claims is 'the most dreaded danger to Islam as a group psychology: individualism'.[67]

In Chapter 4 (*see* Veiling and Nakedness) I referred to the two major Muslim concepts of *qaid* and *hijab*. To recap, *qaid* is a term for the uncontrollable rebellion of woman that was seen to represent a lawlessness of earthly pleasures that could wreak havoc on the community. *Hijab* is linked to keeping this rebellion in check. Some

Muslims are therefore keen to repress this self-affirming rebellious woman because of the lawlessness and disorder that she would bring to the Muslim community.

This tension between *qaid* and *hijab* also ironically snakes its way through the history of Western feminism. The overt display of 'feminine' sexuality is threatening to feminism since it is seen to bring shame on the female community. It is a disruptive force and a show of passion rather than reason, a demonstration of the physical 'low' rather than the spiritual 'high'. In the Muslim world, *qaid* relates to women's sexual power and their ability to offer their body to men other than their husbands. This becomes women's feared power, not necessarily acted upon, but a real seductive force that can be acted upon if the woman chooses to do so. The very real threat that emanates from this 'dishonest woman' was equally seen to undermine the 'respectability' and 'seriousness' of the feminist community. Feminists saw feminine allure, women's fixation on their feminine powers of attraction, as the reason for women's subordinate position in society. This kept women down.

Tussles over prettiness wind their knotty way through nineteenth, twentieth and into twenty-first century feminism. Feminists have not wanted their reputations besmirched by being associated with the kind of woman whose social success and power is attained by way of her sexual allure – her pampered and flirty 'prettiness' – rather than by way of her intellect. Also 'prettiness' introduces 'competition' between women as well as by definition excluding older, disabled or 'ugly' women as valid. Feminists have protected their own group's interests, their own community and their own rules of play. How do women therefore create solidarity when there is backbiting, suspicion, competitiveness, jealousy, anxiety, protectiveness and wariness, and where there remains a desire, for many, not to mix with 'those kinds of women' – the ones who perhaps 'might steal your husband'? (As if husbands have no minds of their own!)

Angela McRobbie and Jenny Garber's essay on girls and subcultures can perhaps help to explore further this problematic question of female 'competition' and exclusion. McRobbie and Garber argue that by way of 'a whole alternative network of responses and activities' girls negotiate their own space within or outside of male-dominated cultures. What is absolutely vital to my discussion is how girls have their own way of keeping boys (and the wrong kind of girls) out:

> Yeh – there's one up the club, I'm not saying her name but she's a proper one; she walks past and says, 'alright Tina'? – But she's one person I wouldn't go around with 'cause you'd get a name for yourself.[68]

In youth subcultures, girls' group behaviour is partly a resistance to their sexually subordinate position. Their behaviour, whether a defensive giggling retreat into cliquishness or an aggressive use of their sexuality to embarrass or undermine authority is, McRobbie and Garber claim, a direct reaction 'against a situation where masculine definitions (and sexual labelling...) are in dominance'.[69] Boys' groups therefore tend to be larger, for reasons of solidarity. For girls, the smaller the number the better, the purpose being 'to shut out other girls'.[70] This, I would add, is not only to protect their reputation but also, perhaps, to protect their boyfriend – to make sure his eyes do not roam! Yet these observations could also apply to grown women. Heterosexual (and probably also lesbian) women are, I would suggest, very wary of other women.

Burlesque's beauty lies, perhaps, with its ability to speak to and inspire a wide assortment of women. This was why it was seen as a danger to the status quo – a disease – for it challenged a male-defined cultural message with all its hierarchical sexual labelling that has persistently provoked much hostility and ostracism amongst women themselves. Much (though obviously not all) of the hostility that women feel towards each other is based on a sense of self-preservation. Young men's self-preservation comes from having many loyal friends who will not do the dirty on them and will not flirt with or sleep with their girl. For young women, it seems, only a select one or two can be trusted to be in their clique, to be their loyal friend; towards other women there remains suspicion, jealousy and insecurity.

Mainstream feminists react defensively to male sexual labelling by adding their consensus. Burlesque performers do not react defensively but parody this labelling ... and challenge it by disseminating different modes of femininity as a rebellious alternative retort. Part of what burlesque achieves is to create a female-defined space of self-realization, fantasy, sexuality and success.

A question that I posed at the beginning of the book (and again in this chapter) but have consciously left hanging until now, must finally be addressed. Can this network of female solidarity be achieved equally by a performer such as Dita Von Teese, who does not seem to be informed by politicized debate?

There is no denying that Von Teese is a 'success story'. She is financially independent, an accomplished ballet, swing and Argentine tango dancer, and rich. She also has an astute sense of business, building up from scratch her own business empire. Von Teese herself humbly attributes this success to those 'strippers' and burlesque 'stars' who have come before her. She undoubtedly respects, admires and emulates female performers like Gypsy Rose Lee and Sally Rand, crediting these women for making her line of business more easily accessible and acceptable. Von Teese also consistently demonstrates and comments how she exemplifies how a 'plain' girl can reinvent herself by way of costume, self-pride and confidence, and how a working-class girl can as a result find fame and fortune. I would argue, however, that even though Dita Von Teese's alternative style, 'prettiness', celebrity status and success inspires many young women, she still remains resolutely unfeminist and resolutely individualist.

I am not arguing though that Von Teese is claiming to be a feminist or particularly political. What needs to be drawn to a conclusion is what this admiration for artistes such as Von Teese may suggest about young women's present aspirations, pleasures, values and politics.

The experience that initiated my debates for this book were my feelings of both empowerment and vulnerability when watching Ursula Martinez strip. This performance mixed forms, it fused the 'low' with the 'high', art with non-art, and the artist with the artiste, thus challenging my class and cultural expectations, prejudices and judgments. Burlesque consciously highlights this shifting boundary and in doing this radically acts as a mediator, bridging forms, bridging viewer and performer, theatre and society, the self and the other, safety and danger, and by doing so highlights hypocrisy, contradiction, shame, sin and transgression. New burlesque acts in this mediatory fashion and as such straddles that ground where oppositional values clash, and where contradiction is thrashed out.

The delightful Dita takes centre stage in this transgressive arena, activating unresolved personal and political debates concerning pleasure, power, money, desire, sexual display and image-making that are exuberantly expressed and experienced through the explicit female body. It is intriguing again how 'prettiness' still remains a sticking point at the border control between feminism and non-feminism.

Burlesque performance questions feminism; it questions my politics. It permits the expression of a tantalizing, female-centred erotic that is playful and pleasurable, a female erotic that is executed with utter panache yet where absolute success is built upon 'feminine submission' and 'helplessness'. This therefore opens up exciting, yet raw and exposing debates between antagonistic foes.

In this head-on collision between two systems, burlesque allows the female viewer to question the point where solidarity breaks down. Young women need to be fully aware of the consequences of their display, yet they must not be cut off from their own bodies and the knowledge and personal strength that comes from experiencing and imaging their erotic pleasure. Feminism therefore needs to be equivocally poised between pleasure and politics, and female display must be complimented with a direct address to acknowledge this perceived contradiction. Burlesque performers offer up a powerful position for young women – but in order for there to be pizzazz there must also be a wink, a nudge and a 'knowing' smile.

Conclusion: Showdown

FEMINIST FLUIDITY

s our contemporary burlesque stripper happy? Is she a vital, healthy expression of a new, confident, 'knowing' generation of young women?

In the introduction I discussed the now murky and confused concepts of postfeminism and post-feminism, and pointed to the importance of bracketing the hyphen. One of the key intentions I set out to achieve in this book was to highlight a clear contradiction that has threaded its way through the history of feminism. This sore point of contention – the issue of 'prettiness' – has been the spanner in the works. There has always existed a large fraction of women who have just not seen eye to eye with 'traditional' feminists over this very point. Why can't we be sexually attractive? What is wrong with wanting to appeal to the opposite sex? Why do I have to conform to a 'masculine' way of acting, dressing and behaving, in order to earn my right to a public life? Why can't I mix pleasure with politics, or make pleasure my politics?

By bracketing the hyphen I want to show clearly that this debacle within feminism is precisely what drives it along. One-sided debate makes for very limited discussion. I am neither saying that we should now be condemning feminists as puritanical, pleasure-less man haters nor that heterosexual women should be able to flirt, bare their breasts and strip their clothes off when they like, if they like, because that is their right. What I am saying is that this is a veritable minefield with no clear-cut answer. This is a tricky issue.

Trying to force the ideology of 'feminism' into a stern rejection of the 'sexualized body' or a frivolous adoption of sexual display is not going to solve anything. Sexualized imagery is neither wholly positive nor wholly negative. The system both empowers and exploits. To look at the situation from only one intolerant perspective is not giving the whole picture.

Picking and dissecting this hyphen further, we plainly see that its use is to link the 'post' (what comes afterwards) with 'feminism' (what came before). Postfeminism was the discrediting of 'feminism', the desire to move forward without the shackles of what was seen as a very middle-class, masculinized, de-sexualized perspective on womanhood. Post-feminism, on the other hand, reflects the acceptance of feminism. The aims, it was argued, were the same – self-realization, equal opportunities, the freedom to earn a living – but the strategy was more inclusive. However, post-feminist politics in retrospect contained the same pitfalls as the 'traditional' feminism it was critiquing. These glamorous ladettes gave out the message that girls needed to behave like boys, and be brashly sluttish, to succeed in life. My conscious decision to make a distinction between postfeminism and post-feminism was to clear the water before then being able to understand and identify a dynamic trend of nagging resistance that crosses class, race and sexual lines.

I began my introduction with a description of my experience of going to see Ursula Martinez in *Show Off*. As a stripper who is a lesbian, she clearly represents that faction of gay theory that has contributed a powerful new way of seeing the sex–gender–sexuality axis. My book has consciously not concentrated on lesbianism and femininity; this is already a prolifically well-researched area and was not the angle I wanted to take. *Show Off* (in my way of seeing) was not purely about Ursula's lesbian politics. It was about the power and 'low', vulnerable status of women's 'feminine' sexual public display.

At the start of her show, Martinez is enveloped in the 'protective wall'[1] of her sexuality. At the end of her show she strips again but this time she loses this protective shield and is left incredibly vulnerable and exposed. These stripteases are in effect 'the show', as Martinez informs us, to my disgruntlement, after the initial striptease. These opposing stripteases sit on either side of a 'post-show discussion' spoof where the issues generated by Martinez's 'exposure' are played out through banter, film, controlled audience participation and humour. Sitting in the auditorium watching such naked display my emotions and thoughts are polarized and pulsate between admiration and anger, discomfort and pleasurable camaraderie. I was standing on unstable, incomprehensible and theoretically dislocated ground.

Bracketing the hyphen between feminism and anti(-)feminism or post(-)feminism helps to locate this discomfort. The hyphen puts an emphasis on a more fluid interchange between 'feminism' and its seeming antithesis of 'non-feminism', a constant shifting between positions, a communication, a tension, a repulsion even, between 'correct' and 'incorrect' politics, between 'femininity' and 'feminism'.

The 'stars' of burlesque made tangible this symbiotic hot-headed antagonism. Their acts both reflected and represented the overt sexuality that was being paraded by young women, an 'awarishness', or sexual awareness that was an appropriation of the direct searching gaze, unveiled face, and bright, attractive and stylish clothing and self-sufficiency of the 'common prostitute' or *fille publique*. But the burlesque performer also synthesized this desiring and desirable 'femininity' with the political rhetoric and theatrical guerrilla spectacle of the mid-nineteenth-century 'traditional' feminists – the dare-devil antics that carved the way for the eventual suffrage for all women. This synthesis points to an ambivalent desire both to want to be part of the system, to enjoy the pleasures of the city, of fashion, of earning money, of make-up, of flirting, of enjoying one's body and the attention of others, whilst also acknowledging a resistance to and a wariness of this very same system.

This anxious process I have named 'feminist fluidity'. This is not another 'wishy-washy', all-encapsulating term. It defines that ambivalent area of pleasure and displeasure where you are pulled between your 'weak' need for attention and love – for someone to want to open a door for you, to be looked at in an appreciative way, to want to be 'pretty', to look 'nice', to shave your legs and dye your hair – and your need for a public recognition of your abilities, talents, skills and intelligence. Can you not be sexy, be feminine, want a nice face and a nice backside and be a 'strong' feminist? Does wearing no make-up and growing your armpit hair really place you on the moral high ground? There is still an evident tension and divisiveness between women who blatantly want to realize and perhaps even exploit their desirability and their sexiness, such as Paris Hilton and Christina Aguilera, and contemporary feminists like Ariel Levy, Angela Phillips and Deborah L. Tolman who question the actual benefits for young women of this commodified pert and pouting display.

Why do women have to appear constantly poised for sex, constantly in desperate need of attention and validation for their physical worthiness? Levy comments that even professional women at the top of the scale in terms of money and responsibilities have to 'dabble in exhibitionism' and titillate in order to feel like they have 'really made it'.[2]

Testifying to this point is the genuinely disturbing image that was placed on the front page of *Vanity Fair*'s 2006 Hollywood special issue. This photograph, taken by Annie Leibovitz, was of new rising starlets Keira Knightley and Scarlett Johansson posing naked, with Tom Ford sitting just behind them in a suit. What was alarming about this photograph was that Scarlett Johansson's pose was such that her legs were slightly open and something about it became pornographic rather than merely erotic. I wondered if Johansson realized the significance of this pose with its 'ready' and 'willing' message that her 'fuckability' was her 'saleability'.

Contemporary feminist writers such as Levy, Tolman and Phillips passionately and persuasively argue how this appearance of lust, as opposed to real sexual pleasure, allure or connection leads to a sense of disconnection from our bodies and the knowledge that this gives us about who we are. As Tolman argues: 'Feeling desire in response to another person is a route to knowing, to being, oneself through the process of relationship.'[3] Without sexual subjectivity, without an erotic voice, young women become easier to manipulate and exploit.

These writers are wary of a sexuality that is only known in terms of being wanted, that is only tasted through being desired. Where are young women's desires ... where are their pleasures? This book has sought to demonstrate, however, that for many women sexual display can be a complicitous and reciprocal pleasure. Being desired (as opposed to desiring) does not necessarily have to be passive. Burlesque performers willingly indulge in this controlled compliancy, in wanting to be appreciated and adored. They want to dress up, be 'feminine', be sexual, be sexy ... They want to be sensational.

Burlesque performers therefore use a controlled manipulation of how they are represented by way of sexual 'feminine' stereotypes. They reinvent and reinvigorate their public identity by way of more unconventional styles and therefore widen the pallet of erotic imagery. They inject quirkiness into predictability and ooze charisma and confidence through unconventional skin and flesh. This desire to be desired, this insistence that they can be desired, both disruptively and disobediently plays up to narrowly defined 'ideals' *and* parodies 'fuckability'. It is an act of derision as well as an act of self-pride.

These artistes/artists excessively camp up 'femininity' by way of exaggerated and sometimes even ridiculous pastiche. The World Famous *BOB* with her Marilyn Monroe impersonation or Dirty Martini with her fan dance and strategically placed popping balloons are decadent and theatrical creations of 'womanliness' that express both a desire for play and a pooh-poohing of mainstream cultural messages which inform them at every turn that their body is not 'pretty'.

Many of these acts give vent to the sense of anger and exasperation that many women feel at constantly being made to feel insufficient. This sense of frustration is confidently and acerbically expressed by female popstar Lily Allen in the lyrics for her song 'Everything's Just Wonderful':

> I wanna be able to eat spaghetti bolognaise,
> and not feel bad about it for days and days and days.
> In the magazines they talk about weight loss,
> If I buy those jeans I can look like Kate Moss,
> Oh no it's not the life I chose,
> But I guess that's the way that things go,

Burlesque performers express that growing indignation at the chasm that divides being sexy from being sexual, that sexiness seems to have nothing yet obviously should have everything to do with women's erotic sensations, pleasure, bodies and thoughts. Public displays of 'feminine' sexual flesh were and are still pulled between the woman's desire for sexual agency and the 'masculinized' imagery and stereotypes that pin her into pornographic one-dimensionality.

By hijacking 'femininity' the burlesque performer made and makes a spectacle out of what I would call 'erotic rebellion', a non-verbal female resistance. In the mid-nineteenth century the burlesque performer's revelation of leg was just magnifying the female trends that were already in circulation. Fashion moved towards the crinoline for both freedom of movement and erotic sensation. Likewise young girls were removing hats in order to be able to look and be seen. In the interwar years, Gypsy's act played on the appeal of the femme fatale with her sexually potent allure and prepossessed aloof ungovernable sexual power in order to assert a sense of her own sexual and intellectual self-determination. In the contemporary burlesque revival the retro look with its hat, long gloves and corset equally plays on the modern young women's choice in erotic femininity and self-attentiveness and a female-identified sensual awareness.

However, as the nude and pornographic traditions reveal, women's show of flesh and their sexual displays of 'femininity' have always reflected male fantasy, so using the very same language is playing a dangerous game. The use of make-up, fashion, plastic surgery, Botox or dieting sits precariously between playful self-invention and sensation – a desire to pleasurably fashion oneself by way of colour, fabric and role play – and utter insecurity and inadequacy. Looking good therefore takes precedence over feeling good. Seeming worthwhile takes precedence over being fulfilled. Being successful boils down to being 'pretty' and being 'feminine'. In fact, at present there is a whole rash of books and films on the market about being the perfect woman and doing 'femininity' well, about making it into an exquisite art form and wanting to fine-tune the artistic excellence of pleasing men (as we have seen with the popularity of the geisha and the courtesan).

However, when performers like Von Teese fit so perfectly into sexually 'submissive' stereotypes of the 'ideal' woman, how can there be room for subversion? Her imagery and persona skate on thin ice between consolidating mainstream values and creating new sensual erotic models. Like Lydia Thompson and Gypsy Rose Lee, modern burlesque performance is both a pastiche and a parody of the 'modern girl' with her 'fake lust' and seemingly ungovernable emotional detachment. New burlesque performers 'ham this up' with sensual gusto. They are exquisitely fake. Like Hannah Wilke's performance, however, Von Teese's imagery seems too close to the present representational system – it is purely pastiche rather than parody. For other acts, such as Dirty Martini, Miss Immodesty Blaize and indeed Ursula Martinez, humour and the smile become the way to fuse a feminist critical edge with pleasurable postfeminist flaunting. It becomes a means of communicating this 'knowing' luxuriating compliance to a system of representation that as yet offers up no other erotic forms of expression.

Throughout this book reference has been made to the pre-feminist 'cheesecake' smile of Bettie Page and the uncertain smile of Hannah Wilke as a 'knowing' means of acknowledging a fluidly feminist position. This smile neither operates as a temporary liberatory respite, like Jo Anna Issaak's strategic use of laughter[4] ... nor as 'simulated' pleasure.[5] I would like to forward this smile as a radically insightful and sophisticated tool that signals occupation and resistance: an unsettling and penetrating pleasure formed in oppositional displeasure. Lily Allen's infectious, angry, 'smiling', bitter-sweet acquiescence, her retro-fifties clothing and sexual allure perhaps take this feminist fluidity 'beyond burlesque', giving us a glimpse of how these new modes of female subjectivity have started to 'infect' the mainstream.

The first section of this conclusion has focused on burlesque's compliant and subversive use of femininity and the smile as a means of expressing a fluidly feminist position. The final section of this book will explore how the burlesque performer's 'viral' transgression of borders and sexual categories confuses and questions our own engrained cultural and personal definitions of shame, morality, self-respect and empowerment.

Virus

So, has burlesque been appropriated back into the system? The answer of course is that it has. When you see young groups of women thrusting and cavorting in quite a sanitized way on children's Saturday television, with young teenies and tweenies bopping along, you know that the sting may well have left the bite.

However, I would argue that the burlesque performer has left her mark: her image, her winking smile and her audacity ripples through our cultural psyche. As I have consistently stressed throughout this book, burlesque's ability to cross forms, genders, class, culture and ethnicity, and its ability to break down boundaries between the audience and the performer, the theatrical space and society, is what makes burlesque a uniquely corrosive and therefore dangerously anarchic cultural force.

The affects felt by burlesque could be compared to that of a virus. This, I feel, is a powerfully appropriate metaphor for a form that creeps up on you, breaks down your defences and then overpowers your system. Or, to focus on the biological analogy, once a virus has breached your system it is there to stay, erupting when your defences are weak or when your body is run down. Even if barriers are erected, there is always a new mutation that slips through. It is constantly there and the system is constantly wary of its disruptive potential.

When burlesque first erupted into the cultural psyche it was welcomed, but it soon came to be described as a disease, as pollution. It had diseased the pure moral spiritual body of the nation and was, simply by its very presence, challenging and thus encouraging a questioning of the system as it stood. The burlesque performer was revealing a different way of seeing, living and behaving that was threatening to the status quo because she made transparent how power, pleasure, freedom of expression and wealth were usually distributed.

When I was surfing the Internet for the purpose of this book, I was inadvertently infiltrated by spyware. I felt completely helpless and out of control in its wake, knowing at that exact moment this pollutant was in my system ransacking my hard drive for useful information like credit card numbers or email addresses, which it could then send back to its sender. With a double click, it had entered my system and was now embedded deep inside by computer's body and memory, disruptively wreaking havoc. With that same curiosity that compels you to open an email or enter a website, the audience members flocked excitedly and adventurously to burlesque in a bid for pleasure and a desire to see what lies beyond the visible.

The term 'virus' is therefore a succinct way of elucidating the way in which the burlesque performer transgresses and renegotiates borders, transforming the way in which that 'body' (cultural, social, sexual/sexualized) normally operates. I have appropriated this term from an editorial in *Fuse Magazine*, a Canadian journal dedicated to art, media and politics. In this editorial Izida Zorde refers to a speech that was given at the Canadian Art Gallery Educator's conference by

Declan McGonagle (director of the City Art Centre in Dublin and internationally renowned writer and commentator on art). In relation to community arts, McGonagle argues for a participatory porous model of art whereby the artist can participate in the social space and the non-artist can participate in the art space. Zorde argues that what this means is 'a shift for the art audience from consumer to participant, a shift that would alter the art process from the *glacial to the viral*'[6] [my emphasis].

This argument can be conceptually adapted to generate a parallel discussion in relation to burlesque. By straddling the axis of performance artist/cabaret/strip joint artiste, the burlesque performer brings into focus several key issues. First, there are class-based divisions. By becoming this monstrous hybrid, she disrespects boundaries and labels and therefore questions the 'glacial' stand-off between them and the social motivations behind them. Australian's Lola the Vamp sees any differentiation between stripping and burlesque as the privileging of one above the other. This would, she asserts, 'make the performance a political project, privileging either a patriarchal or a feminist perspective'.[7] Burlesque 'toys intimately' with the performers' sexuality but it is, she argues, too easy to say that burlesque therefore is about woman's sexuality in today's culture. For Lola, burlesque is a form that 'expands' with every new body and with every new interpretation and aesthetic.

Burlesque *is* an expansive form that allows for complexity. Yet this is what in fact privileges this particular form; its elasticity has allowed women accessibility and therefore the freedom to reinvent stripping but within safer and more self-reflective boundaries. Lynda Nead, in relation to Miss Immodesty Blaize's 'Reverse Strip', comments that she found it a beautiful 'gentle old form of eroticism', yet what she found fascinating about this form of erotic display was that it was difficult to call it either fully 'legitimate' art or entirely an 'underworld' pornography for the 'loud and aroused'.[8] In relation to whether burlesque as a form empowers or exploits women, though, she is adamant. If the images created by the 'benign' performances created by Immodesty could be read for what they actually were it would indeed be empowering but 'it is what other people do with this imagery that is the problem'.

This is what is provocative and important about the burlesque phenomenon. It is not easy to pin down, it is always in a process of becoming and it hovers over, yet somehow evades, clear patriarchal or feminist perspectives. The burlesque performer negotiates afresh the space between herself and the viewer by challenging the way in which she should be judged and perceived. Categories blur: the respectable with the disrespectable; 'hussy' and 'lady'; 'bad' girl and 'good' girl; flirt and feminist; nude and the pin-up; liberated and oppressed; exposed and veiled. In doing this she questions and disturbs habitual (monetary, moral, cultural) readings of these hierarchical dichotomies. The burlesque performer's body becomes that 'porous' midpoint of uncertainty, of cross-contamination and daring conjecture.

The spectacle of the female body also becomes a means by which we can gauge political, cultural and moral value systems. When Jack Straw suggested in October 2006 that the face veil was 'a visible statement of separation and of difference', he was admonishing the social and cultural inaccessibility of fully veiled female display. In response, Rajnaara Akhtar (chair of the international campaign group Protect Hijab) questioned what right Straw had 'to request that any women remove any item of clothing'.[9] At the other extreme, British 'topless' model Jodie Marsh spoke disarmingly in the *Guardian* about her hurt and anger at how she was received by the public, with people hurling abuse at her in the streets with such labels as 'slag', 'bitch', 'thick' and 'slapper'. She is actually quite damaged by these comments but equally angry at why this labelling still persists. She chooses to model as a living, since she finds it glamorous and empowering. It does not follow therefore, that she is promiscuous.[10]

These two 'extremes' of visibility and 'availability' bookend public debates over displays of 'femininity' and female sexuality that are seen to define and measure cultural definitions of morality, acceptability, respectability and social cohesion. Whether veiled or exposed, these marginalized extremes of the scopic (visual) system are nevertheless not clear-cut. As Rajnaara Akhtar argues: 'when less than five per cent of Muslim women observe the full veil ... it is not prudent to lay the blame of the lack of social cohesion at their feet'.[11] The 'unavailable' hyper-visibility of the full veil and the illusion of 'availability' created by the glamour model, challenge and confuse categorical readings of their body. To refer back to Izida Zorde's discussion of the 'viral', these margins problematize 'the main text'.[12] Their display offsets dominant values.

The public domain is still male territory and how women behave is still judged, determined and defined by 'masculinized' judgments and sexual labelling. Christine Stansell recounts the nineteenth-century tale of a young woman who was raped –'Choke the God-damned vagabond!'[13] – because, unlike young men, women who were out on their own were seen as easy game and were purely 'asking for it'. By being more public with their sexual display, when at that point the only women known to the street were prostitutes, women were opening themselves up to abuse, and murky and dangerous miscomprehension. It is interesting how the most recent police warnings to young women about binge-drinking carry the threat that 'if you get drunk, you'll get raped'. All of these accounts demonstrate the difficult line that women negotiate by attempting to reclaim back some control over their public image.

Burlesque performers participate from within this space of renegotiation by disrupting mainstream associations made between display and 'availability', and by confusing the 'moral' spectrum that slides from invisibility (veiled therefore unavailable) to visibility (exposed, available and therefore a 'whore'). The tease acknowledges both the powerlessness and control that earmarks veiling and nakedness and by wavering in that hazy halfway house intervenes knowingly in this process of revelation, the process of using and losing power.

This book argues that stripping, pornography and prostitution may well translate into real action at an economic level, but this sex work does not necessarily secure these women any actual subject power or action at an institutional level. Some young women may well choose to bare all and earn as much money as they can whilst they have an audience who will pay good money to see them naked. Does this make it right? Who is profiting? Hilary Evans states in her book *The Oldest Profession* (1979) that moralists who mocked at labels describing the 'common prostitute' as a 'woman of pleasure' and a 'fille de joie' were failing to understand how prostitution actually lifted many young women not just above the poverty line but well into a life of luxury that they would never have been able to achieve with their own background and 'low' status.[14]

However, 'well-to-do' women and men do not have to either sell their bodies to strangers or (in the case of boxing for working-class boys) get punched in the face in order to live a luxurious life. It is still an exploitation of the poor, especially in the case of prostitution, where the customers tend to be richer than the prostitutes. Similarly, the high-class courtesan (nouveau riche) whore used her 'profession' to elevate herself above her allotted station in life to achieve riches on a par with the most 'respectable' as well as allowing her to hobnob (and bed down) with princes. As courtesan Cora Pearl exclaimed: 'My independence was all my fortune, and I have known no other happiness; and it is still what attaches me to life.'[15] However, she was still a prostitute and would have been judged and dismissed as such. She still had to 'know her place'.

The burlesque performer refused to 'know her place'. Her beguiling powers of seduction and sex appeal meant that she had an audience gripped with anticipation; they were therefore putty in her hands. Men wanted her and women wanted to be like her. Categories, labels and boundaries that were there to divide and control were now haemorrhaging uncontrollably into each other. These 'low' women were mixing with the famous, the glitterati and other legitimate, talented 'stars', forming part of the social elite, and they were therefore beginning to have some actual clout.

This 'bad', 'low' stripper was now verging on 'respectable', creating an unthinkable hybrid who blurred boundaries between 'low' and 'high', respectable and disreputable, the 'haves' with the 'have nots', the popular and the cultural intellectual cream. She was suggesting a more equal distribution of power for she was challenging the 'masculinized' control of her image as well as the actual consistency of middle-class identity. The burlesque performer was wilfully, decadently, pleasurably and proudly asserting her visibility in defiance of those who insisted on her invisibility and silence.

For middle-class women the performer's promiscuous behaviour, sexy clothes, tantalizing revelation of leg and flash of torso were reassuringly counteracted by the performer's equally zealous protection of their reputation or their already passionate betrothal. This was a self-respecting, sexual body that emanated self-pride – not everyone will be getting their dirty hands on *this* body. By being 'low', sexual and asserting a certain morality and subject power these performers become uncategorizable and offered up to women female-centred, female-generated pleasures. The courtesan and femme fatale inspired an equal amount of hypnotic fascination but with the burlesque star, who tantalized in her very real personification of economic, sexual and intellectual power, this sense of power was not seen to be compromising morality. Burlesque stars upheld their self-respect and honour and unlike the femme fatale did not crumble at the finale.

By learning about the tales of Gypsy Rose Lee bathing in her diamonds or wearing a floor-length cape of real orchids to some opening night, women were coming across an exciting new 'femininity' that was daring to proudly mix a 'low', sexual, 'feminized' body with the 'respectable'. Women were therefore beginning to realize their deepening sense of subject power by asserting their own glamorous, appealing visual presence in the public domain and sexualizing a suppressed sense of the erotic through the luxury commodity. Self-made burlesque performers like Gypsy Rose Lee, Lydia Thompson and our present queen, Dita Von Teese – who are together trashy, 'low' and plain yet glamorous, rich and famous – give us very real ideas 'above our station'. They make us dream, yearn, want more out of life. They make you realize how dissatisfied you are with your own slog, toil and drudgery, your own grey, flat existence. They make you question your lot and want a bit of sparkle too.

There are obviously other 'stars' like David and Victoria Beckham, Jennifer Lopez or Jordan and Peter Andre, who are seen in many quarters as tacky, 'blingy' and coming from 'the streets', who have had more visibility and therefore more impact than the burlesque stars. What is different about the burlesque performer is that she confidently couples her 'sexual' display with a sharp wit, to acknowledge the imbalances of power in society that still need to be addressed.

This is what is utterly 'monstrous' and incomprehensible yet totally seductive and appealing about the burlesque performer. She is resolutely individualist, leading a life of luxury and celebrity by 'selling' her sexual body and therefore profiting unquestionably from the existing representational system. She is also, however, provocatively intervening in the creation of her own image as artist and subject. By collapsing the self that protects one's image with selfishness, the artist with the artiste and the self-determined subject with objecthood, the burlesque performer dynamically and confidently renegotiates alternative modes of sexual and erotic display and image-making. By way of the smile, the wink or the bitter-sweet patter, the burlesque performer is also admitting that she is still trapped within existing value systems and erotic forms. If she does not use these sharp, witty asides in her act, how does that matter of redress happen?

The ripples I felt after going to see Ursula Martinez's performance in *Show Off* still affect me; I experienced the dissolution of boundaries and a Cheshire Cat smile that just did not go away. It resounds in my memory, in my flesh … with the borders between humour and seriousness, the intellect and the sensual, power and vulnerability, desire and desirability, sexiness and shame, blurring and bleeding profusely. It continues to affect me and it continues to make me reflect. The show still goes on …

and the show must go on…

Notes

INTRODUCTION

1 Laura Mulvey, 'Visual pleasure and narrative cinema', *Screen* xvi (1975), p.30.

2 See *The Ministry of Burlesque* blurb used to describe 'rising star' Dolly Mae at *www.ministryofburlesque.com/community/what-is-burlesque.php* (accessed 27 July 2006).

3 Dirty Martini quoted in Michelle Baldwin, *Burlesque {and the New Bump-n-Grind}* (Denver, CO: Speck Press, 2004), p.31.

4 See 'International Women's Day 2006', at *www.womankind.org.uk/iwd-06.html* (accessed 10 July 2006), p.1.

5 Arifa Akbar, 'Only one British female in four calls herself a feminist', *Independent*, 8 March 2006, p.2.

6 Tracey Emin in *Observer Reader's Evening* (London: Saatchi Gallery, 2003), taken from a Ph.D. thesis by Remes Outi, 'The role of confession in late twentieth-century British art' (Reading: University of Reading, 2005).

7 Robert C. Allen, *Horrible Prettiness: Burlesque and American Culture* (Chapel Hill, NC, and London: University of North Carolina Press, 1991), p.81.

8 Taken from Colette's wonderfully decadent *The Pure and The Impure* (Harmondsworth: Penguin, 1980). This was originally published in French as *Ces Plaisirs* in 1932.

9   Betty Friedan, *The Feminine Mystique* (London: Penguin, 1982 [1963]), p.3.

10 Ibid., p.68.

11 Griselda Pollock, *Old Mistresses: Women, Art and Ideology* (London: Routledge and Kegan Paul, 1981), p.127.

12 Sarah Gamble (ed.), *The Routledge Companion to Feminism and Postfeminism* (London and New York: Routledge, 2001), p.44.

13 The 14th conference of the Women's History Network, entitled 'Women, Art and Culture: Historical Perspectives', Southampton, September 2005.

14 See Camille Paglia, *Sex, Art, and American Culture* (New York: Vintage Books, 1992); Rene Denfeld, *The New Victorians: A Young Woman's Challenge to the Old Feminist Order* (London: Simon and Schuster, 1995); Katie Roiphe, *The Morning After: Sex, Fear and Feminism* (Boston, MA: Little, Brown and Co., 1993); and Naomi Wolf, *The Beauty Myth* (London: Chatto and Windus, 1991).

15 See bell hooks, *Outlaw Culture: Resisting Representations* (New York: Routledge, 1994), p.102.

16 Lana Homeri in Akbar: 'Only one British female in four', p.1.

17 Bella Beretta in Baldwin: *Burlesque*, p.130.

18 Olive Logan, *Apropros of Women and Theatres* (New York: Carleton, 1869), p.152.

19 I thank Bryan Reynolds for directing me towards the first two of these writers. See Judith Lynne Hanna, 'Undressing the First Amendment and corsetting the striptease dancer', *The Drama Review* xlii/2 (T158) (1998), pp.38–69; Katherine Liepe-Levinson, *Strip Show: Performances of Gender and Desire* (London and New York: Routledge, 2002); Rachel Shteir, *Striptease: The Untold History of the Girlie Show* (Oxford and New York: Oxford University Press, 2004).

20 Examples include the touring Burly Q Review in the UK, the Tease-O-Rama burlesque convention in the USA, Ivan Kane's Forty Deuce in Los Angeles, The Slipper Room in New York City, Sidney, Australia's 34b and London's longest running burlesque night, the Whoopee! Club at The Cobden Club, to name but a few.

21 This line of thought is credited to Roger Cook who spoke about this sense of engagement in his opening speech at the conference 'Transversalities: Crossing Disciplines, Cultures and Identities', Reading University, September 2005.

22 Andrea Dworkin, *Woman Hating* (New York: E.P. Dutton, 1974), p.17.

CHAPTER 1

1   Allen, Robert C., *Horrible Prettiness: Burlesque and American Culture* (Chapel Hill, NC, and London: University of North Carolina Press, 1991), p.17.

2   Blessing, Jennifer, 'The art(ifice) of striptease: Gypsy Rose Lee and the masquerade of nudity', in Lisa Rado (ed.) *Modernism, Gender, and Culture: A Cultural Studies Approach* (New York: Garland, 1997), p.48.

3   Allen: *Horrible Prettiness*, p.178.

4   See the discussions in Sinclair, Andrew, *Prohibition: The Era of Excess* (London: Faber and Faber, 1962); Stansell, Christine, *City of Women: Sex and Class in New York 1789–1860* (Urbana and Chicago: University of Illinois Press, 1987); Smith-Rosenberg, Carroll, *Disorderly Conduct: Visions of Gender in Victorian America* (New York and Oxford: Oxford University Press, 1985); Peiss, Kathy, *Cheap Amusements: Working Women and Leisure in Turn-of-the-Century New York* (Philadelphia: Temple University Press, 1986); Saxton, Alexander, *The Rise and Fall of the White Republic: Class Politics and Mass Culture in Nineteenth-Century America* (London and New York: Verso, 1990); and Collier, James Lincoln, *The Rise of Selfishness in America* (New York and Oxford: Oxford University Press, 1991).

5   See Preminger, Erik Lee, *Gypsy and Me: At Home and On the Road with Gypsy Rose Lee* (London: André Deutsch, 1985), p.16, quoted in Blessing: 'The art(ifice) of striptease', pp.52–3.

6   Quoted in Blessing: 'The art(ifice) of striptease', p.53.

7   Corio, Ann, and Joseph DiMona, *This Was Burlesque* (New York: Grosset and Dunlap, 1968), p.86.

8   Minsky, Morton, and Milt Machlin, *Minsky's Burlesque: A Fast and Funny Look at America's Bawdiest Era* (New York: Arbor House, 1986) p.237.

9   Zeidman, Irving, *The American Burlesque Show* (New York: Hawthorn, 1967), p.149.

10 John Steinbeck in the blurb for Lee, Gypsy Rose, *Gypsy: Memoirs of America's Most Celebrated Stripper* (Berkeley, CA: Frog, 1957).

11 Headline from Bernard Sobel, *Burleycue: The Underground History of Burlesque Days* (New York: Farrar and Rinehart, 1931), p.19.

12 Quoted in Allen: *Horrible Prettiness*, p.20.

13 Sobel: *Burleycue*, p.19.

14 Curry, Ramona, '*Goin' to Town* and beyond: Mae West, film censorship and the comedy of *un*marriage', in Kristine Brunovska Karnick and Henry Jenkins, *Classical Hollywood Comedy* (New York and London: Routledge, 1995), p.232.

15 Green, William, 'Strippers and coochers – the quintessence of American burlesque', in Kenneth Richards and David Mayer (eds), *Western Popular Theatre* (London: Methuen, 1977), p.158.

16 Ibid.

17 Von Teese, Dita, with Bronwyn Garrity, *Burlesque and the Art of the Teese/Fetish and the Art of the Teese* (New York: Regan Books, 2006); Baldwin, Michelle, *Burlesque {and the New Bump-n-Grind}* (Denver: Speck Press, 2004); Shteir, Rachel, *Striptease: The Untold History of the Girlie Show* (Oxford and New York: Oxford University Press, 2004); and Bosse, Katharina, *New Burlesque* (New York: Distributed Art, 2003).

18 See Bradford DeLong, J., 'Slouching towards utopia? The economic history of the twentieth century: XIV, The Great Crash and the Great Slump' (Berkeley: University of California and National Bureau of Economic Research, February 1997) at *www.j-bradford-delong.net/TCEH/ Slouch_Crawsh14.html* (accessed 5 August 2006), pp.8, 12.

19 See Banks, James, Richard Blundell and James P. Smith, 'Financial wealth inequality in the United States and Great Britain' (academic paper for the Institute for Fiscal Studies and University College, London and RAND Corporation), 1 February 2001.

20 Zeidman, Irving, *The American Burlesque Show* (New York: Hawthorn, 1967), p.28.

21 Rothbard, Murray N., *America's Great Depression* (Kansas City, MO: Sheed and Ward, 1975), p.20.

22 Ibid., p.19.

23 Quoted in Allen: *Horrible Prettiness*, pp.11–12.

24 Ibid., p.12.

25 May, Erskine K., *Democracy in Europe* (London: Longmans, 1877), p.lxxi cited in Eric J. Hobsbawm, *The Age of Capital* (London: Weidenfeld and Nicolson, 1975), p.98.

26 Ibid.

27 Collier, James Lincoln, *The Rise of Selfishness in America* (New York and Oxford, Oxford University Press, 1991), p.31.

28 Ibid., p.27.

29 Ibid., p.33.

30 Saxton, Alexander, *The Rise and Fall of the White Republic: Class Politics and Mass Culture in Nineteenth-Century America* (London and New York: Verso, 1990), p.359.

31 Hobsbawm: *The Age of Capital*, p.1.

32   Weber, Max, *The Protestant Ethic and the Spirit of Capitalism* (London and New York: Routledge, 1992 [1904/5]), p.53.

33   Proverbs 22:29, *The Holy Bible*.

34   Weber: *The Protestant Ethic*, p.53.

35   Gilman, Charlotte Perkins, *Women and Economics: A Study of the Economic Relation Between Women and Men* (New York: Prometheus, 1994), p.113.

36   Ibid., p.108.

37   'A Stripteaser's Education', written by Broadway scriptwriter Edwin Gilbert, *Ziegfeld Follies of 1936*, Shubert Archive (Script Series 51).

38   Shteir: *Striptease*, p.185.

39   Von Teese with Garrity: *Fetish and the Art of the Teese*, p.10.

40   Ibid.

41   Paglia, Camille, 'Elizabeth Taylor: Hollywood's pagan queen', in Camille Paglia, *Sex, Art and American Culture* (New York: Vintage Books, 1992), p.17.

42   This expression is taken from the Mary Russo's essay 'Female grotesques', when she asks, 'In what sense can women really produce or make spectacles out of themselves?', in De Lauretis, Teresa (ed.), *Feminist Studies, Critical Studies* (Bloomington: Indiana University Press, 1986), p.217.

43   Zemon Davis, Natalie, *Society and Culture in Early Modern France* (London: Duckworth, 1975), pp.124–51.

44   Rowe, Kathleen, 'Roseanne: unruly woman as domestic goddess', *Screen* xxxi/4 (1990), p.411.

45   Allen: *Horrible Prettiness*, p.271.

46   Howells, William Dean, 'The new taste in theatricals', *Atlantic Monthly* (May, 1869), pp.642–3, in Allen: *Horrible Prettiness*, p.135.

47   White, Richard Grant, 'The Age of Burlesque', *Galaxy* (August, 1869), p.256, cited in Allen: *Horrible Prettiness*, p.137.

48   Howells, William Dean in *Appleton's Journal of Popular Literature, Science, and Art* (3 July, 1869), p.440, cited in Allen: *Horrible Prettiness*, p.136.

49   Greer, Germaine, *The Whole Woman* (London, New York, Toronto, Sydney and Auckland: Doubleday, 1999), pp.410–11.

50   Rowe, Dorothy, *Representing Berlin: Sexuality and the City in Imperial and Weimar Germany* (Aldershot: Ashgate, 2003), p.1.

51   Ibid., p.7.

52 Peiss, Kathy, *Hope in a Jar: The Making of America's Beauty Culture* (New York: Metropolitan Books, Henry Holt and Co., 1998), p.48.

53 Banner, Lois, *American Beauty* (New York: Knopf, 1983), p.119.

54 Curry, Ramona, 'Mae West as censored commodity: the case of Klondike Annie', *Cinema Journal* 31 (1991), pp.73, 65ff.

55 Allen: *Horrible Prettiness*, p.144, from Ruth Rosen, *The Lost Sisterhood: Prostitution in America, 1900–1918* (Baltimore, MD: John Hopkins University Press, 1982), pp.120–1.

56 Stuart, Andrea, *Showgirls* (London, Sydney, Auckland, Rosebank: Jonathan Cape, 1996), p.178.

57 Mary Shaw, Roy Maxwell and Debbie Lawlor, blurb for 'Cloudy concepts: estimating the number of teenage mothers in England', for the British Society for Population Studies annual conference in Bristol, 11 September 2003. Available at *www.lse.ac.uk/collections/BSPS/annualConference/2003/fertility11Sept9am.htm* (accessed 6 December 2005).

58 Linton, Elizabeth Lynn, *Modern Women and What is Said of Them* (New York: Redfield Publishers, 1868), p.28, cited in Maria-Elena Buszek, 'Representing "awarishness": burlesque, feminist transgression, and the 19th-century pin-up', *Drama Review* xliii/4 (T164) (1999), p.155.

59 Quoted in Allen: *Horrible Prettiness*, p.140.

60 Intriguingly, the *Collins Dictionary* discusses the sixteenth-century roots of the word 'garish' as coming from *gaure,* to stare. This is appropriate in this context as the clothing acted as the pretext for looking and being looked at.

CHAPTER 2

1 Clark, Kenneth, *The Nude: A Study of Ideal Art* (London: John Murray, 1956), p.1.

2 Ibid., p.6.

3 Nead, Lynda, *The Female Nude: Art, Obscenity and Sexuality* (London and New York: Routledge, 1992), p.6.

4 Ibid., p.14.

5 Tebbit's defence of Page Three girls is taken from Gamble, Sarah (ed.), *The Routledge Companion to Feminism and Postfeminism* (London and New York: Routledge, 2001), p.120.

6 Quoted in Gamble: *Routledge Companion*, p.297

7 'Cricket: let's have a ball', *Daily Star*, 10 September 2005, p.3.

8   This is a fascinating, well-documented area of study that includes: Lathers, Marie, *Bodies of Art: French Literary Realism and the Artist's Model* (Lincoln and London: University of Nebraska Press, 2001); Lipton, Eunice, *Alias Olympia: A Woman's Search for Manet's Notorious Model and Her Own Desire* (Ithaca and London: Cornell University Press, 1992); Borel, France, *The Seduction of Venus: Artists and Models* (New York: Rizzoli International, 1990); and Whitney, Chadwick and Isabelle de Courtivron, *Significant Others: Creativity and Intimate Partnerships* (London: Thames and Hudson, 1993).

9   Tickner, Lisa, 'The body politic: female sexuality and women artists since 1970', *Art History*, i/2 (June 1978), p.239, quoted in Nead: *The Female Nude*, pp.64–5.

10 Jones, Amelia, 'Interpreting feminist bodies', in Paul Duro (ed.), *The Rhetoric of the Frame* (Cambridge, New York and Melbourne: Cambridge University Press, 1996), p.235.

11 Quoted in Butler, Marilyn (ed.), *Burke, Paine, Godwin and the Revolution Controversy* (Cambridge, New York and Victoria: Cambridge University Press, 1984), p.76.

12 Patterson, Cynthia, and Bari J. Watkins, 'Rites and rights', in Helen Krich Chinoy and Linda Walsh Jenkins (eds), *Women in American Theatre* (New York: Theatre Communications Group, 1987), p.30.

13 Patterson and Watkins: 'Rites and rights', p.29.

14 Rowe, Kathleen, 'Roseanne: unruly woman as domestic goddess', *Screen* xxxi/4 (1990), p.411.

15 Quoted in Gamble: *Routledge Companion*, p.120.

16 Phillips, Melanie, *The Ascent of Women: A History of the Suffragette Movement and the Ideas Behind It* (London: Abacus, 2003), p.256.

17 Dworkin, Andrea, *Pornography: Men Possessing Women* (London: Women's Press, 1981), p.200.

18 The name Samois is taken from the name of the fictional estate of the lesbian dominatrix character, Ann-Marie, in Pauline Réage, *Story of O* (Paris: Jean-Jacques Pauvert, 1954).

19 Vance, Carol S. (ed.), *Pleasure and Danger: Exploring Female Sexuality* (Boston, MA: London: Routledge, 1984), pp.6–7.

20 Paglia, Camille, *Sex, Art, and American Culture* (New York: Vintage Books, 1992), p.11.

21 Ibid.

22 Ibid., p.10.

23 Forte, Jeanie, 'Women's performance art: feminism and postmodernism', in Sue-Ellen Case (ed.), *Performing Feminisms: Feminist Critical*

Theory and Theatre (Baltimore, MD, and London: John Hopkins University Press, 1990), p.251.

24   Ibid., p.254.

25   Schneider, Rebecca, *The Explicit Body in Performance* (London and New York: Routledge, 1997), p.17.

26   Cixous, Hélène, 'The laugh of the Medusa', in Elaine Marks and Isabelle de Courtivron (eds), *New French Feminisms* (New York: Schocken Books, 1981), p.266.

27   Boston Women's Health Book Collective, *Our Bodies, Ourselves: A Book by and for Women* (New York: Simon and Schuster, 1973), p.25.

28   Ibid.

29   In *The Dinner Party* (1974–9), Chicago installed a large triangular table laid for 39 female guests including Sappho, Hildegard of Bingen, Mary Wollstonecraft and Virgina Woolf. The controversy came from the fact that each place setting not only named that woman's artwork but also featured a flower-like sculpture representing the woman's vulva. See Kubitza, Annette, *Sexual Politics: Judy Chicago's* Dinner Party *in Feminist Art History* (Berkeley, Los Angeles and London: University of California Press, 1996).

30   Riley, Denise, *'Am I That Name?' Feminism and the Category of 'Women' in History* (Houndmills, Basingstoke and London: Macmillan, 1988).

31   Williams, Linda, *Hard Core: Power, Pleasure and the 'Frenzy of the Visible'* (Berkeley, Los Angeles and London: University of California Press, 1996), p.363.

32   Mulvey, Laura, 'Visual pleasure and narrative cinema', *Screen* 16 (autumn 1975), p.30.

33   Fuchs, Elinor, 'Staging the obscene body', *Drama Review* 33 (1989), p.33.

34   Jones, Amelia, *Body Art/Performing the Subject* (Minneapolis and London: University of Minnesota Press, 1998), p.199.

35   Dolan, Jill, *The Feminist Spectator as Critic* (London and Ann Arbor: UMI Research Press, 1988), p.81.

36   Tickner, Lisa, 'The body politic: female sexuality and women artists since 1970', *Art History*, i/2 (June 1978), p.239, in Rosemary Betterton (ed.), *Looking On: Images of Femininity in the Visual Arts and Media* (London, Boston, Sydney and Wellington: Pandora, 1987), p.248.

37   Krauss, Rosalind, 'Round table: the reception of the sixties', in *October* 69 (summer 1994), p.10, in Carolee Schneemann, *Imaging Her Erotics* (Cambridge, MA, and London: MIT Press, 2003), p.320.

38 Jones, Amelia, 'Post feminism, feminist pleasures, and embodied theories of art', in Joanna Frueh, Cassandra L. Langer and Arlene Raven (eds), *New Feminist Criticism: Art, Identity, Action* (New York: Icon Editions, 1994), p.28.

39 See Garb, Tamar, *Sisters of the Brush: Women's Artistic Culture in Late Nineteenth Century Paris* (New Haven and London: Yale University Press, 1994), pp.131–2.

40 Mitchell, Claudine, 'Intellectuality and sexuality: Camille Claudel, the fin de siècle sculptress', *Art History*, xii/4 (December 1989), p.436, in Chadwick and de Courtivron: *Significant Others*, p.24.

41 Chadwick and de Courtivron: *Significant Others*.

42 Paglia: *Sex, Art and American Culture*, p.39.

43 Quoted in Elwes, Catherine, Rose Garrard and Sandy Nairne, *About Time: Video, Performance and Installation by 21 Women Artists* (London: ICA, 1980), p.446.

44 A 1968 quotation from Schneemann, Carolee, *Cézanne: She Was a Greater Painter* (New York: Tresspass Press, 1975), in Lucy R. Lippard, *From the Center: Feminist Essays on Women's Art* (Toronto and Vancouver: Clarke, Irwin and Company, 1976), p.126.

45 Paglia, Camille, 'The beautiful decadence of Robert Mapplethorpe: a response to Rochelle Gurstein', in *Sex, Art, and American Culture: Essays* (New York: Vintage Books, 1992), p.39.

46 Lathers: *Bodies of Art*, p.12.

47 Bernheimer, Charles, *Figures of Ill-Repute: Representing Prostitution in Nineteenth-Century France* (Cambridge, MA, and London: Harvard University Press, 1989), p.96.

48 Schneemann: *Imaging Her Erotics*, p.44.

49 Ibid., p.35.

50 Ibid., p.34.

51 Ibid., p.43.

52 A phrase Rebecca Schneider took from a 1971 flyer announcing a showing of *Fuses* in London (Schneemann archives) in Schneider: *The Explicit Body in Performance*, p.74.

53 Carolee Schneemann in interview in Scott MacDonald, *Critical Cinema: Interviews with Independent Film Makers* (Berkeley: University of California Press, 1988), pp.134–51, in Schneider: *The Explicit Body in Performance*, p.76.

54 Schneeman in interview with MacDonald: *Critical Cinema*, p.138.

55 Schneemann: *Imaging Her Erotics*, p.138.

56　Rubin, Gayle, 'Thinking sex: notes for a radical theory of the politics of sexuality', in Vance (ed.): *Pleasure and Danger*, p.270.

57　Frueh, Joanna, *Monster Beauty: Building the Body of Love* (Berkeley: University of California Press, 2001), p.31.

58　Schneemann: *Imaging Her Erotics*, p.55.

59　Gibson, Kevin, 'Rant: the benefits of feminism', in Fashion & Lifestyle at *www.askmen.com/fashion/austin_100/120_fashion_style.html* (accessed 25 June 2005).

60　*Artforum* xiii/4 (December 1974), p.9.

61　Collins, James, in review 'Hannah Wilke: Ronald Feldman Gallery', *Artforum* xxii/10 (June 1974), p.72.

62　Wilke, Hannah, cited in Frueh, Joanna, 'Feminism', in Thomas H. Kocheiser, *Hannah Wilke: A Retrospective* (Columbia: University of Missouri Press, 1989), in Hilary Robinson (ed.), *Feminism–Art–Theory: An Anthology 1968–2000* (Oxford: Blackwell, 2001), p.580.

63　Alta in Gornick, Vivian and Barbara R. Moran (eds), *Woman in Sexist Society* (New York and London: Basic Books, 1971), p.3.

64　Firestone, Shulamith, *The Dialectic of Sex: The Case for Feminist Revolution* (London: Women's Press, 1979), p.144.

65　Stannard, Una, in Gornick and Moran (eds.): *Woman in Sexist Society*, p.125.

66　Hannah Wilke in interview with Amelia Jones, 22 November 1992 in Jones: *Body Art*, p.153.

67　hook, bells, 'The oppositional gaze: black female spectators', in Amelia Jones (ed.), *The Feminism and Visual Culture Reader* (London and New York: Routledge, 2003), p.97.

68　Berger, John, 'Way of seeing', abstract quoted in Jones (ed.): *Feminism and Visual Culture Reader*, p.37.

69　Buszek, Maria, 'Of Varga Girls and Riot Girls: the Varga Girl and WWII in the pin-up's feminist history', in *Alberto Vargas: The Esquire Pinups*, Spencer Museum of Art, University of Kansas: exhibition curated by Maria-Elena Buszek and Stephen Goddard, 29 September to 30 December 2001. Essays available at *www.ku.edu/~sma/vargas/buszek.htm* (accessed 18 May 2006).

70　See Munford, Joanne, 'Wake up and smell the lipgloss', in Gillis Stacy, Gillian Howie and Rebecca Munford, *Third Wave Feminism: A Critical Exploration* (Houndsmill and Basingstoke: Palgrave Macmillan, 2004).

71　Spence, Jo, *Putting Myself in the Picture: A Political, Personal and Photographic Autobiography* (London: Camden Press, 1986), pp.86–9.

CHAPTER 3

1 Kwolek-Folland, Angel, *Incorporating Women: A History of Women and Business in the United States* (New York: Palgrave, 1998), p.96.

2 Walsh, Margaret, 'Gendered endeavours: women and the reshaping of business culture', in *Women's History Review* xiv/2 (2005), pp.181–201.

3 Lee, Gyspy Rose, *Gypsy: Memoirs of America's Most Celebrated Stripper* (Berkeley, CA: Frog, 1999 [originally published by Harper in 1957]), p.284.

4 Ibid.

5 Walsh: 'Gendered endeavours', p.194.

6 This cult of sensibility began in the eighteenth century based on the discovery of the nervous system. It was concluded that women had more fragile, emotional and sensitive systems. This in turn justified calls for women to be more delicate and desexualized. These claims were perhaps originally intended to keep women firmly in the private domain but had the opposite effect of galvanizing feminists into very public humanitarian action.

7 Sorisio, Carolyn, 'A tale of two feminisms: power and victimization in contemporary feminist debate', in Leslie Heywood and Jennifer Drake (eds) *Third Wave Agenda: Being Feminist, Doing Feminism* (Minneapolis and London: University of Minnesota Press, 1997), p.145.

8 Stansell, Christine, *City of Women: Sex and Class in New York 1789–1860* (Urbana and Chicago: University of Illinois Press, 1987), p.100.

9 Walsh: 'Gendered endeavours', p.186.

10 Butler, Judith, *Gender Trouble: Feminism and the Subversion of Identity* (New York and London: Routledge, 1999), p.66.

11 Phillips, Melanie, *The Ascent of Woman: A History of the Suffragette Movement and the Ideas Behind It* (London: Abacas), p.4.

12 Taken from a quote in *The Little Upstart* v (November 1916), p.1, Equitable Life Assurance Society Archives (ELASA), New York, a newsletter for a woman's agency. 'We rather glory in our sauciness and impudence and pride ourselves upon the jewel of our inconsistency, and we snap our fingers at precedent and tradition. We want to have a sweetish number [or the newsletter] bubbling over with sentiment and have deliberately planned it', in Kwolek-Folland, Angel, *Engendering Business: Men and Women in the Corporate Office, 1870–1930* (Baltimore and London: John Hopkins University Press, 1994), p.174.

13 Kwolek-Folland: *Engendering Business*, p.174.

14 Ibid.

15 Ehrenreich, Barbara and Arlie Russell Hochschild (eds), *Global Woman: Nannies, Maids and Sex Workers in the New Economy* (London: Granta Books, 2003), p.11.

16 Bunting, Madeleine, 'The hidden toll we all pay: society is more efficient than ever, yet our needs for leisure and relationships never feature on the balance sheet', *Guardian*, 21 June 2004, p.15.

17 Scott, Kirsty, 'This isn't what we really, really want', *The Herald* (Glasgow), 18 April 1997, p.23.

18 Enloe, Cynthia, *Making Feminist Sense of International Politics: Bananas, Beaches and Bases* (London, Sydney and Wellington: Pandora, 1989), p.100.

19 Wilson, Graeme, 'Labour anger at £7,700 for Cherie's election hairdos', *Daily Telegraph*, 21 April 2006, p.2.

20 Kwolek-Folland: *Engendering Business*, p.175.

21 Glasscock, Jessica, *Striptease: From Gaslight to Spotlight* (New York: Abrams Books, 2003), p.39.

22 Straayer, Chris, 'The she-man: postmodern bi-sexed performance in film and video', in *Screen* xxxi/3 (1990), p.277.

23 Paglia, Camille, *Sex, Art, and American Culture* (New York: Vintage Books, 1992), p.5.

24 Ibid., p.4.

25 Ibid., p.10.

26 Sobel, Bernard, *Burleycue: The Underground History of Burlesque Days* (New York: Farrar and Rinehart, 1931), p.20.

27 Shteir, Rachel, 'Stormy weather: how a climate of rebellion, in theatre and society, wrought the death of burlesque in 1969', in *American Theatre* xx/4 (April 2003), p.28.

28 Yeager, Mary. A, *Women in Business*, Vol. 1 (Cheltenham and Northampton, MA: Elgar Reference Collection, 1999), p.xvii.

29 Kwolek-Folland: *Incorporating Women*, p.163.

30 Quoted in Corio, Ann, and DiMona, Joseph, *This Was Burlesque* (New York: Grosset and Dunlap, 1968), p.20.

31 Quoted in Zeidman, Irving, *The American Burlesque Show* (New York: Hawthorn Books, 1967), p.149.

32 Minsky, Morton and Milt Machlin, *Minsky's Burlesque: A Fast and Funny Look at America's Bawdiest Era* (New York: Arbor House, 1986), p.150.

33 Davis, Tracy C., *Actresses as Working Women: Their Social Identity in Victorian Culture* (London and New York: Routledge, 1991), p.139.

34 Ibid.

35 Quoted at *http.//en.wikipedia.org/wiki/Mary_Cunningham* (accessed 5 August 2006).

36 Lee, Susan, 'Goodness had everything to do with it', *New York Times*, 27 May 1984, at *www.query.nytimes.com/gst/fullpage.html* (accessed 6 August 2006).

37 Ibid.

38 Ibid.

39 Sellers, Patricia, 'Women, sex, and power', *Fortune*, 5 August 1996, p.44, cited in Kwolek-Folland: *Incorporating Women*, p.202.

40 Turner, Janice, 'Dirty young men', *Guardian Weekend*, 22 October 2005, p.32.

41 Phillips, Angela, 'The rise and fall of silent girly-girls in G-strings', *Times Higher*, 14 July 2006, p.17.

42 *The Economist* (1998) p.23, cited in Maggie O'Neill, *Prostitution and Feminism: Towards a Politics of Feeling* (Cambridge and Oxford: Polity Press, 2001) p.150.

43 O'Neill: *Prostitution and Feminism*, pp.150–1.

44 Browne, Junius Henri, *The Great Metropolis: A Mirror of New York* (San Francisco: American Publishing Company, 1869), pp.330–1.

45 Hanna, Judith Lynne, 'Undressing the First Amendment and corsetting the striptease dancer', *Drama Review* xlii/2 (T158) (summer 1998), p.57.

46 Liepe-Levinson, Katherine, *Strip Show: Performances of Gender and Desire* (London and New York: Routledge, 2002), p.151.

47 Adams, Parveen with Mark Cousins, 'The truth on assault', in Parveen Adams, *The Emptiness of the Image: Psychoanalysis and Sexual Differences* (London and New York: Routledge, 1996).

48 MacKinnon, Catherine, *Only Words* (Cambridge, MA: Harvard University Press, 1993), p.21, cited in Adams with Cousins: 'The truth on assault', p.59.

49 Ford, Richard, 'Mother wins fight for new law against violent porn on the net', *The Times*, 31 August 2006, p.6.

50 Allen, Robert C., *Horrible Prettiness: Burlesque and American Culture* (Chapel Hill and London: University of North Carolina Press, 1991), p.257.

51 Schneider, Rebecca, *The Explicit Body in Performance* (London and New York: Routledge, 1997), p.72, reworked by Katherine Liepe-Levinson in *Strip Show: Performances of Gender and Desire* (London and New York: Routledge, 2002), p.141.

52 Bebel, August, *Die Frau und der Sozialismus [Women under Socialism]* (1879 [1964 edition]), in Dorothy Rowe, *Representing Berlin: Sexuality and the City in Imperial and Weimar Germany* (Aldershot: Ashgate, 2003) p.83.

53 See Rosenthal, Margaret, F., *The Honest Courtesan: Veronica Franco, Citizen and Writer in Sixteenth-Century Venice* (Chicago: University of Chicago Press, 1992); Davidson, James, *Courtesans and Fishcakes: The Consuming Passions of Classical Athens* (London: Fontana Press, 1998); and Hickman, Katie, *Courtesans* (London: Harper Collins, 2003).

54 Recounted in Turner: 'Dirty young men', p.28.

55 Ibid., p.31.

56 Ibid., p.32.

57 Stansell: *City of Women*, pp.98–9.

58 Hickman, Katie, *Courtesans: Money, Sex and Fame in the Nineteenth Century* (London: Harper Collins, 2003), p.216.

59 From 'Aristocracy of harlotry' taken from Evans, Hilary, *The Oldest Profession: An Illustrated History of Prostitution* (Newton Abbot and London: David and Charles, 1979), p.146.

60 Davidson, James, *Courtesans and Fishcakes: The Consuming Passions of Classical Athens* (London: Fontana Press, 1998), p.125.

61 Rosenthal: *The Honest Courtesan*, p.68

62 Quoted in Evans: *The Oldest Profession*, p.151.

63 Von Teese, Dita, *Burlesque and the Art of the Teese* (New York: Regan Books, 2006), p.10.

CHAPTER 4

1 Logan, Olive, *Apropos of Women and Theatres* (New York and London: Carleton, 1869), p.152.

2 Beauvoir, Simone de, *The Second Sex* (London, Australia, New Zealand, South Africa: Vintage, 1997 [originally published by Gallimard in 1949]), p.549.

3 Peiss, Kathy, *Hope in a Jar: The Making of America's Beauty Culture* (New York: Metropolitan Books, Henry Holt & Company, 1998), p.38.

4 Peiss, Kathy, *Hope in a Jar: The Making of America's Beauty Culture* (New York: Metropolitan Books, Henry Holt & Co., 1998).

5 Crandall, C.H., 'What men think of women's dress', *North American Review* 161 (August 1895), p.253, in Peiss: *Hope in a Jar*, p.39.

6 Lowthorpe, Rebecca, 'Dita goes couture', *Elle* (UK edition, November, 2005), p.231.

7   Ibid.

8   Hickman, Katie, *Courtesans: Money, Sex and Fame in the Nineteenth Century* (London: Harper Collins, 2003), p.244.

9   Quoted in Lowthorpe: 'Dita goes couture', p.231.

10 Ibid., p.229.

11 'The Judgment of Paris', in *Greece and Rome: Myths and Legends* (London: Senate, 1994), p.274.

12 Banet-Weiser, Sarah, *The Most Beautiful Girl in the World: Beauty Pageants and National Identity* (Berkeley and Los Angeles: University of California Press, 1999), p.64.

13 Ibid., p.74.

14 Ibid., p.64.

15 Beauvoir: *The Second Sex*, p.550.

16 Ibid.

17 See Mintel, 'Britain's £1 billion extreme make-over', at *www.marketresearchworld.net/index.php?option* (posted 24 August 2007; accessed 25 August 2007). This Mintel research was compiled in conjunction with the British Association of Aesthetic Plastic Surgeons (BAAPS) and the Harley Medical Group.

18 See American Society for Aesthetic Plastic Surgery (ASAPS), '2006 ASAPS USA Cosmetic Surgery Statistics', at *www.consultingroom.com/Statistics/Display.asp?* (accessed 25 August 2007).

19 Quoted in Mackenzie, Suzie, 'Under the skin', *Guardian Weekend*, 22 October 2005, p.45.

20 Walker, Sharon, 'Confessions of a Botox junkie', *Harpers & Queen* (January, 2006), p.109.

21 Cook, Roger, opening speech at the conference 'Transversalities: crossing disciplines, cultures and identities', University of Reading, 16–18 September 2005.

22 Glasscock, Jessica, *Striptease: From Gaslight to Spotlight* (New York: Harry N. Abrams, 2003), p.27.

23 Hanks, Patrick (ed.), *Collins Dictionary of the English Language*, second edn (London and Glasgow: Collins, 1989).

24 Allen, Woody, 'The Purple Rose of Cairo', at *http://en.wikipedia.org/wiki/The_Purple_Rose_of_Cairo* (last modified 19 December 2005; accessed 2 January 2006).

25 Felski, Rita, *The Gender of Modernity* (Cambridge, MA, and London: Harvard University Press, 1995), p.76.

26 Dolan, Jill, 'Images of women and sexuality in burlesque comedy', *Journal of Popular Culture* xviii (1984), p.40.

27 Ibid.

28 Ibid., p.39.

29 Ibid., p.42.

30 Minsky, Morton, and Milt Machlin, *Minsky's Burlesque: A Fast and Funny Look at America's Bawdiest Era* (New York: Arbor House, 1986), p.40.

31 Miller, Daniel, *A Theory of Shopping* (New York: Cornell University Press, 1998), p.47.

32 Ibid., pp.47–8.

33 Marilyn Monroe, 'Diamonds are a girl's best friend' from *Gentlemen Prefer Blondes*. Lyrics by Leo Rubi, music by Jules Styne.

34 Monroe: 'Diamonds are a girl's best friend'.

35 Bassey, Shirley, 'Diamonds are forever', soundtrack for the James Bond film *Diamonds Are Forever* (1971). Lyrics by Don Black, music by John Barry.

36 Quoted in Nixon, Laura, 'Suicide girls', at *http://suicidegirls.com/words/Dita+von+Teese+by+Laura+Nixon/* (accessed 23 June 2005), p.2.

37 Laura Herbert, quoted in Sandra Nygaard, 'Bawdy beautiful: new burlesque shakes up San Francisco', at *http://sfgate.com/cgi-bin/article.cgi?file=/g /archive/2003/11 /07/ burlesquesf.DTL* (posted 7 November 2003; accessed 27 July 2006).

38 Ibid.

39 Manchester No Borders Group, *Hate Mail, Immigration Special 2005*, March 2005, p.9.

40 Dite Von Teese, quoted in Kara Mae Harris, 'Daring Dita and the art of the tease', at *www.atomicmag.com/articles/2001/dita_von_teese.shtml* (accessed 14 November 2005).

41 Allen, Robert C., *Horrible Prettiness: Burlesque and American Culture* (Chapel Hill and London: University of North Carolina Press, 1991), p.147.

42 Quoted in Wilson, Bruce, 'Muslim student wins scarf appeal', in *American Renaissance* at *www.amren.com/mtnews/archives/2005/03/muslim_student.php* (posted 3 March 2005; accessed 12 January 2006).

43 Shteir, Rachel, *Striptease: The Untold History of the Girlie Show* (Oxford and New York: Oxford University Press, 2004), pp.180–1.

44 Genesis 3:16, *The Holy Bible*.

45 Mernissi, Fatima, *Women's Rebellion and Islamic Memory* (London: Zed Books, 1996), p.56.

46 Baldwin, Michelle, *Burlesque {and the New Bump-n-Grind}* (Denver: Speck Press, 2004), p.60.

47 El Saadawi, Nawal, *The Nawal El Saadawi Reader* (London and New York: Zed Books, 1997), pp.138–40, cited in Haideh Moghissi, *Feminism and Islamic Fundamentalism: The Limits of Postmodern Analysis* (London and New York: Zed Books, 1999), p.46.

48 Ahmed, Leila, *Women and Gender in Islam: Historical Roots to a Modern Debate* (New Haven and London: Yale University Press, 1992), p.15.

49 Quoted in Hoodfar, Homa, 'The veil in their minds and on our heads: the persistence of colonial images of Muslim women', *Resources for Feminist Research*, xxii/3 & 4 (1993), cited in Moghissi: *Feminism and Islamic Fundamentalism:*, p.86.

50 Ahmed: *Women and Gender in Islam*, p.151.

51 Namakydoust, Azadeh, 'Covered in messages: the veil as a political tool', *The Iranian*, 8 May 2003, at *www.iranian.com/Women/2003/May/Veil/p.html*, (accessed 26 August 2006).

52 Moghissi: *Feminism and Islamic Fundamentalism*, p.5.

53 El Saadawi: *The Nawal El Saadawi Reader*, pp.138–40, cited in Moghissi: *Feminism and Islamic Fundamentalism*, p.46.

54 Hickman: *Courtesans*, p.268.

55 Quoted in Frueh, Joanna, 'Feminism', in Thomas H. Kocheiser (ed.), *Hannah Wilke: A Retrospective* (Columbia: University of Missouri Press, 1989), pp.41–9, cited in Hilary Robinson (ed.), *Feminism–Art–Theory: An Anthology 1968–2000* (Oxford and Maldon: Blackwell, 2001), p.580.

56 Weene, Seph, 'Venus', in *Heresies* iii/4 (1981), p.37, in Katherine Liepe-Levinson, *Strip Show: Performances of Gender and Desire* (London and New York: Routledge, 2002), p.171.

57 Kitten on the Keys, quoted in Sandra Nygaard, 'Bawdy beautiful: new burlesque shakes up San Francisco', at *http//sfgate.com/cgi-bin/article.cgi?file=/g/archive/2003 /11/07/burlesquesf.DTL* (posted 7 November 2003, accessed 27 July 2006).

58 Shteir: *Striptease*, p.181.

59 Baker, Roger, *Drag* (London: Cassell, 1994), p.156.

60 Frueh, Joanna: *Monster/Beauty: Building the Body of Love* (Berkeley and Los Angeles: University of California Press, 2001), p.2.

61 Ibid., p.74.

62 Liepe-Levinson: *Strip Show*, p.171.

63 Corio, Ann, and Joseph DiMona, *This Was Burlesque* (New York: Grosset and Dunlap, 1968), p.22.

64 'Striptease, its history and modern revival', *Woman's Hour*, Radio 4, 14 March 2006.

65 Quoted in Curtis, Nick, 'Blaize of glory', *Evening Standard* (London), 21 April 2005.

66 Ibid.

CHAPTER 5

1 Sacher-Masoch, Leopold von, *Venus in Furs* (New York, Toronto and London: Penguin Classics, 2000), p.38.

2 Deleuze, Gilles, 'Coldness and cruelty', in Gilles Deleuze, *Masochism* (New York: Zone Books, 1991) p.71.

3 Von Teese, Dita with Garrity, Bronwyn, *Burlesque and the Art of the Teese/Fetish and the Art of the Teese* (New York: Regan Books, 2006), p.101.

4 Josie Natorie, quoted in Frank DeCaro, 'Out from Under', *New York Newsday*, 7 April 1994, p.B43.

5 DuCann, Charlotte, 'Love and death on the London catwalk', *Guardian*, 15 October 1990, p.36, cited in Valerie Steele, *Fetish: Fashion, Sex and Power* (New York and Oxford: Oxford University Press, 1996), p.138.

6 Gamble, Sarah, *The Routledge Companion to Feminism and Postfeminism* (London and New York: Routledge, 2001), p.268.

7 Gamble: *Routledge Companion*, pp.229, 268.

8 Lola the Vamp, 'Burlesque: a short history of burlesque by Lola the Vamp', at *www.lolathevamp.net/burlesque.htm* (accessed 9 February 2007).

9 Lola the Vamp: 'Burlesque', at *www.lolathevamp.net/about.htm* (accessed 9 February 2007).

10 Stewart, Susan, *On Longing: Narratives of the Miniature, the Gigantic, the Souvenir, the Collection* (Durham: Dukes University Press, 1993), p.23, cited in Marilyn Ivy, *Discourses of the Vanishing: Modernity, Phantasm, Japan* (Chicago and London: University of Chicago Press, 1995), p.10.

11 Lola the Vamp: 'Burlesque', at *www.lolathevamp.net/about.htm* (accessed 9 February 2007).

12 Agamben, Giorgio, *Potentialities: Collected Essays in Philosophy* (Stanford, CA: Stanford University Press, 1999), p.196.

13 Ibid., p.195.

14 Ibid., p.203.

15 Davidson, James, *Courtesans and Fishcakes: The Consuming Passions of Classical Athens* (London: Fontana Press, 1998), p.129.

16 Ibid.

17 Ibid., p.134.

18 Ibid., p.133.

19 Levy, Ariel, *Female Chauvinist Pigs: Women and the Rise of Raunch Culture* (London: Pocket Books, 2006), p.31.

20 Ibid.

21 Ibid.

22 Baldwin, Michelle, *Burlesque {and the New Bump-n-Grind}* (Denver: Speck Press, 2004), p.131.

23 Ibid., p.28.

24 Logan, Olive, *Apropros of Women and Theatres* (New York: Carleton, 1869), p.127.

25 Ibid.

26 Corio, Ann, and Joseph DiMona, *This Was Burlesque* (New York: Grosset and Dunlap, 1968), p.94.

27 Ibid.

28 Green, William, 'Strippers and coochers – the quintessence of American burlesque', in David Mayer and Kenneth Richards (eds), *Western Popular Theatre* (London: Methuen, 1977), p.160.

29 See 'Coney Island circus sideshow' and 'Burlesque at the beach', at *www.coneyisland.com/burlesque.shtml* (accessed 27 July 2006).

30 Ibid.

31 See 'Midnight's carnival', at *www.glastonburyfestivals.co.uk/performance/index.asp?id=247* (accessed 27 July 2006).

32 Sinclair, Andrew, *Prohibition: The Era of Excess* (London: Faber and Faber, 1962), p.252.

33 Ruth Tutti-Frutti in 'Midnight's carnival', at *www.glastonburyfestivals.co.uk/performance/index.asp?id=247* (accessed 27 July 2006).

34 Green, Martin, and John Swan, *The Triumph of Pierrot: The Commedia dell'Arte and the Modern Imagination* (Pennsylvania: Pennsylvania State University Press, 1993), p.4.

35 Ibid., p.xiv.

36 Ibid.

37 Ibid., p.xii.

38 Immodesty Blaize in Curtis, Nick, 'Blaize of glory', *Evening Standard* (London), 21 April 2005.

39 Quoted in Stuart, Andrea, *Showgirls* (London, Sydney, Auckland and Rosebank: Jonathan Cape, 1996), p.24.

40 Von Teese with Garrity: *Burlesque and the Art of the Teese*, p.10.

41 Lippard, Lucy R., *Get the Message? A Decade of Art for Social Change* (New York: E.P. Dutton, 1984), p.118.

42 Ibid., p.117.

43 Rowe, Kathleen, 'Roseanne: unruly woman as domestic goddess', *Screen* xxxi/4 (winter 1990), p.411.

44 As depicted in *Noah and the Flood*, one of the English medieval mystery plays based around biblical tales.

45 Shteir, Rachel, *Striptease: The Untold History of the Girlie Show* (Oxford and New York: Oxford University Press, 2004), p.28.

46 Haddon, Archibald, *The Story of Music Hall: From Cave of Harmony to Cabaret* (London: Fleetway Press, 1935), p.20.

47 Stuart, Andrea, *Showgirls* (London: Jonathan Cape, 1996), p.25.

48 Ibid., p.26.

49 Bloomer, Amelia, in 'Editorial', *The Lily* iv/8 (August 1852), p.71, cited in Elizabeth Reitz Mullenix, 'Private women/public acts: petticoat government and the performance of resistance', *Drama Review* xlvi/1 (T173), (New York University and the Massachusetts Institute of Technology, spring 2002), p.107.

50 Bloomer: 'Editorial', p.71.

51 Quoted in Minsky, Morton, and Milt Machlin, *Minsky's Burlesque: A Fast and Funny Look at America's Bawdiest Era* (New York: Arbor House, 1986), p.150.

52 Allen, Robert C., *Horrible Prettiness: Burlesque and American Culture* (Chapel Hill and London: University of North Carolina Press, 1991), p.18.

53 Dita Von Teese, quoted in Laura Nixon, 'Suicide girls', at *http://suicidegirls.com/words/Dita+von+Teese+by+Laura+Nixon/* (accessed 23 June 2005), p.2.

54 Allen: *Horrible Prettiness*, p.271.

55 Reed, Jennifer, 'Roseanne: a "killer bitch" for Generation X', in Leslie Heywood and Jennifer Drake (eds), *Third Wave Agenda: Being Feminist, Doing Feminism* (Minneapolis and London: University of Minnesota Press, 1997), p.126.

56 Fox-Genovese, Elizabeth, *Feminism Without Illusions: A Critique of Individualism* (Chapel Hill: University of North Carolina Press, 1991), pp.14, 31, 137, cited in Leila Ahmed, *Women and Gender in Islam: Historical Roots to a Modern Debate* (New Haven and London: Yale University Press, 1992), pp.247–8.

57 Buonfino, Alessandra, and Geoff Mulgan, 'Goodbye to all that', in *Society Guardian*, 18 January 2006, p.1.

58 Fox-Genovese: *Feminism Without Illusions*, pp.14, 31, 137.

59 Buonfino and Mulgan: 'Goodbye to all that', p.1.

60 Sorisio, Carolyn, 'A tale of two feminisms: power and victimization in contemporary feminist debate', in Leslie Heywood and Jennifer Drake (eds), *Third Wave Agenda: Being Feminist, Doing Feminism* (Minneapolis and London: University of Minnesota Press, 1997), p.146.

61 Ibid., p.147.

62 Wolf, Naomi, *The Beauty Myth* (London: Chatto and Windus, 1991), p.241.

63 Stansell, Christine, *City of Women: Sex and Class in New York 1789–1860* (Urbana and Chicago: University of Illinois Press, 1987), p.221.

64 Ibid.

65 Hall, Jacqueline Dowd, 'Disorderly women: gender and labor militancy in the Appalachian South', *Journal of American History* 73 (1986–7), p.375.

66 Madan, T.N., 'Anthropology as cultural reaffirmation', first of three papers delivered as the William Allan Neilson Lectures at Smith College, Northampton, MA, October, 1990, pp.5–6, cited in Leila Ahmed, *Women and Gender in Islam: Historical Roots to a Modern Debate* (New Haven and London: Yale University Press, 1992), p.248.

67 Mernissi, Fatima, *Women's Rebellion and Islamic Memory* (London and New Jersey: Zed Books, 1996), p.109.

68 Teenage girl quoted in Angela McRobbie and Jenny Garber, 'Girls and subcultures', in Stuart Hall and Tony Jefferson (eds), *Resistance Through Rituals* (London, Melbourne, Sidney and Auckland: Open University Hutchinson University Library, 1976), p.216.

69 McRobbie and Garber: 'Girls and subcultures', p.210.

70 Ibid., p.222.

CONCLUSION

1 Ursula Martinez, in interview with BBC News: Arts, 'Ursula Martinez's naked ambition', on *http://new.bbc.co.uk/1/hi/entertainment/art/1492345.stm* (posted 15 August 2001, accessed 8 March, 2003), p.3.

2 Levy, Ariel, *Female Chauvinist Pigs: Women and the Rise of Raunch Culture* (London: Pocket Books, 2005), p.32.

3 Tolman, Deborah L., *Dilemmas of Desire: Teenage Girls Talk about Sexuality* (Cambridge, MA, and London: Harvard University Press, 2002), p.21.

4   Isaak, Jo Anna, 'In praise of primary narcissism: the last laughs of Jo
     Spence and Hannah Wilke' in Sidonie Smith and Julie Watson (eds),
     Interfaces: Women Autobiography, Image, Performance (Ann Arbor: Uni-
     versity of Michigan Press, 2002), p. 54.

5   Raven, Arlene, in Joanna Frueh, Cassandra L. Langer and Arlene Raven
     (eds), *New Feminist Criticism: Art, Identity, Action* (New York: Icon Edi-
     tions, 1994), p.3.

6   Izida Zorde, 'Editorial: a third reading based in participation', in *Fuse
     Magazine: Coming Out of the Margins*, xxviii/2 (2005), p.6.

7   Lola the Vamp, 'Burlesque: a short history of burlesque by Lola the
     Vamp', at *www.lolathevamp.net/burlesque.htm* (accessed 9 February
     2007).

8   Quoted in 'Striptease, its history and modern revival', *Woman's Hour*,
     Radio 4, 14 March 2006.

9   Akhtar, Rajnaara, 'Blaming the veil is wrong', at *http://commentisfree.
     guardian.co.uk/rajnaara_akhtar/2006/10/jack_straw_misses_the_point.
     html* (posted 6 October 2006; accessed 19 October 2006).

10   Jodie Marsh in Laura Barton, 'I could've been a lawyer. But I've taken
     the easiest, quickest route to making as much money as I can', *Guardian*,
     G2 supplement, 25 January 2006.

11   Akhtar: 'Blaming the veil is wrong'.

12   Zorde: 'Editorial', p.6.

13   Stansell, Christine, *City of Women: Sex and Class in New York 1789–1860*
     (Urbana and Chicago: University of Illinois Press, 1987), p.97.

14   Evans, Hilary, *The Oldest Profession: An Illustrated History of Prostitution*
     (Newton Abbot and London: David and Charles, 1979), pp.23–4.

15   Cora Peal in Katie Hickman, *Courtesans* (London: Harper Collins, 2003),
     p.333.

Bibliography

Books

Agamben, Giorgio, *Potentialities: Collected Essays in Philosophy* (Stanford, CA: Stanford University Press, 1999).

Ahmed, Leila, *Women and Gender in Islam: Historical Roots to a Modern Debate* (New Haven and London: Yale University Press, 1992).

Allen, Robert C., *Horrible Prettiness: Burlesque and American Culture* (Chapel Hill, NC, and London: University of North Carolina Press, 1991).

Angier, Roswell, *'...A Kind of Life': Conversations in the Combat Zone* (Danbury, NH: Addison House, 1976).

Baker, Roger, *Drag* (London: Cassell, 1994).

Bakhtin, Mikhail, *Rabelais and His World* (Bloomington: Indiana University Press, 1984).

Baldwin, Michelle, *Burlesque {and the New Bump-n-Grind}* (Denver: Speck Press, 2004).

Banet-Weiser, Sarah, *The Most Beautiful Girl in the World: Beauty Pageants and National Identity* (Berkeley and Los Angeles: University of California Press, 1999).

Banner, Lois, *American Beauty* (New York: Knopf, 1983).

Bataille, Georges, *Eroticism* (London: Marion Boyars, 1987).

Beauvoir, Simone de, *The Second Sex* (London: Vintage, 1997 [originally published by Gallimard in 1949]).

Berger, John, *Ways of Seeing* (Harmondsworth: Penguin Books, 1972).

Bernheimer, Charles, *Figures of Ill-Repute: Representing Prostitution in Nineteenth-Century France* (Cambridge, MA, and London: Harvard University Press, 1989).

Betterton, Rosemary (ed.), *Looking On: Images of Femininity in the Visual Arts and Media* (London, Boston, Sydney and Wellington: Pandora Press, 1987).

Borel, France, *The Seduction of Venus: Artists and Models* (New York: Rizzoli International, 1990).

Bosse, Katharina, *New Burlesque* (New York: Distributed Art Publishers, 2003).

Boston Women's Health Book Collective, *Our Bodies, Ourselves: A Book by and for Women* (New York: Simon and Schuster, 1973).

Brown, Junius Henri, *The Great Metropolis: A Mirror of New York* (San Francisco: American Publishing Company, 1869).

Buonfino, Alessandra and Geoff Mulgan, *Porcupines in Winter: The Pleasures and Pains of Living Together in Modern Britain* (London: The Young Foundation, 2006).

Butler, Judith, *Gender Trouble: Feminism and the Subversion of Identity* (New York and London: Routledge, 1999).

Butler, Marilyn (ed.), *Burke, Paine, Godwin and the Revolution Controversy* (Cambridge, New York and Victoria: Cambridge University Press, 1984).

Chadwick, Whitney, and Isabelle De Courtivron, *Significant Others: Creativity and Intimate Partnership* (London: Thames and Hudson, 1993).

Chadwick, Whitney, and Tirza True Latimer (eds), *The Modern Woman Revisited: Paris Between the Wars* (New Brunswick, NJ, and London: Rutgers University Press, 2003).

Clark, Kenneth, *The Nude: A Study of Ideal Art* (London: John Murray, 1956).

Colette, Sidonie-Gabrielle, *The Pure and The Impure* (Harmondsworth: Penguin Books, 1980 [first published in French as *Ces Plaisirs* in 1932]).
Collier, James Lincoln, *The Rise of Selfishness in America* (New York and Oxford: Oxford University Press, 1991).

Corio, Ann, and Joseph DiMona, *This Was Burlesque* (New York: Grosset and Dunlap, 1968).

Davidson, James, *Courtesans and Fishcakes: The Consuming Passions of Classical Athens* (London: Fontana Press, 1998).

Davis, Tracy C., *Actresses as Working Women: Their Social Identity in Victorian Culture* (London and New York: Routledge, 1991).

Deleuze, Gilles, 'Coldness and cruelty', in *Masochism* (New York: Zone Books, 1991).

Denfeld, Rene, *The New Victorians: A Young Woman's Challenge to the Old Feminist Order* (London: Simon and Schuster, 1995).

Dolan, Jill, *The Feminist Spectator as Critic* (London and Ann Arbor: UMI Research Press, 1988).

Dworkin, Andrea, *Pornography: Men Possessing Women* (London: Women's Press, 1981).

Dworkin, Andrea, *Woman Hating* (New York: E.P. Dutton, 1974).

Ehrenreich, Barbara, and Arlie Russell Hochschild, *Global Woman: Nannies, Maids and Sex Workers in the New Economy* (London: Granta, 2003).

El Saadawi, Nawal, *The Nawal El Saadawi Reader* (London and New York: Zed Books, 1997).

Elwes, Catherine, Rose Garrard and Sandy Nairne, *About Time: Video, Performance and Installation by 21 Women Artists* (London: ICA, 1980).

Enloe, Cynthia, *Making Feminist Sense of International Politics: Bananas, Beaches and Bases* (London, Sydney and Wellington: Pandora, 1989).

Evans, Hilary, *The Oldest Profession: An Illustrated History of Prostitution* (Newton Abbot and London: David and Charles, 1979).

Evans, Mary, *Love: An Unromantic Discussion* (Cambridge: Polity Press, 2003).

Falk, Bernard, *The Naked Lady: A Biography of Adah Isaacs Menkin* (London: Hutchinson, 1953 [first published in 1934]).

Faludi, Susan, *Backlash: The Undeclared War Against Women* (New York: Crown, 1991).

Felski, Rita, *The Gender of Modernity* (Cambridge, MA, and London: Harvard University Press, 1995).

Firestone, Shulamith, *The Dialectic of Sex: The Case for Feminist Revolution* (London: Women's Press, 1979).

Friedan, Betty, *The Feminine Mystique* (London: Penguin, 1982 [1963]).

Frueh, Joanna, *Monster/Beauty: Building the Body of Love* (Berkeley and Los Angeles: University of California Press, 2001).

Frueh, Joanna, Cassandra L. Langer and Arlene Raven (eds), *New Feminist Criticism: Art, Identity, Action* (New York: Icon Editions, 1994).

Gamble, Sarah (ed.), *The Routledge Companion to Feminism and Postfeminism* (London and New York: Routledge, 2001).

Garb, Tamar, *Sisters of the Brush: Women's Artistic Culture in Late Nineteenth Century Paris* (New Haven and London: Yale University Press, 1994).

Gilman, Charlotte Perkins, *Women and Economics: A Study of the Economic Relation Between Women and Men* (New York: Prometheus Books, 1994).

Glasscock, Jessica, *Striptease: From Gaslight to Spotlight* (New York: Harry N. Abrams, 2003).

Gornick, Vivian, and Barbara R. Moran (eds), *Woman in Sexist Society* (New York and London: Basic Books, 1971).

Graham, Judith (ed.), *Current Biography Yearbook* (New York: H.W. Wilson Company, 1992).

Green, Martin, and John Swan, *The Triumph of Pierrot: The Commedia dell'Arte and the Modern Imagination* (Pennsylvania: Pennsylvania State University Press, 1993).

Greer, Germaine, *The Whole Woman* (London, New York, Toronto, Sydney and Auckland: Doubleday, 1999).

Grosenick, Uta (ed.), *Women Artists in the 20th and 21st Century* (Koln, London, Madrid, New York, Paris and Tokyo: Taschen, 2001).

Grosz, Elizabeth, and Elspeth Probyn (eds), *Sexy Bodies: The Strange Carnalities of Feminism* (London and New York: Routledge, 1995).

Haddon, Archibald, *The Story of Music Hall: From Cave of Harmony to Cabaret* (London: Fleetway Press, 1935).

Hebdige, Dick, *Subculture: The Meaning of Style* (London: Methuen, 1979).

Hickman, Katie, *Courtesans: Money, Sex and Fame in the Nineteenth Century* (London: Harper Collins, 2003).

Hobsbawm, Eric J., *The Age of Capital* (London: Weidenfeld and Nicolson, 1975).

hooks, bell, *Outlaw Culture: Resisting Representations* (New York: Routledge, 1994).

Ivy, Marilyn, *Discourses of the Vanishing: Modernity, Phantasm, Japan* (Chicago and London: University of Chicago Press, 1995).

Jenkins, Simon, and Ann Sloman, *With Respect, Ambassador: An Inquiry into the Foreign Office,* (London: British Broadcasting Corporation, 1985).

Jones, Amelia (ed.), *The Feminism and Visual Culture Reader* (London: Routledge, 2003).

Jones, Amelia, *Body Art/Performing the Subject* (Minneapolis and London: University of Minnesota Press, 1998).

Juno, Andre, and Vivian Vale, *Angry Women* (San Francisco: Re/Search Publications, 1991).

Kipnis, Laura, *Bound and Gagged: Pornography and the Politics of Fantasy in America* (Durham, NC: Duke University Press, 1999).

Kristeva, Julia, *Powers of Horror: An Essay on Abjection* (New York: Columbia University Press, 1982).

Kubitza, Annette, *Sexual Politics: Judy Chicago's* Dinner Party *in Feminist Art History* (Berkeley, Los Angeles and London: University Of California Press, 1996).

Kwolek-Folland, Angel, *Incorporating Women: A History of Women and Business in the United States* (New York: Palgrave, 1998).

Kwolek-Folland, Angel, *Engendering Business: Men and Women in the Corporate Office, 1870–1930* (Baltimore and London: John Hopkins University Press, 1994).

Lathers, Marie, *Bodies of Art: French Literary Realism and the Artist's Model* (Lincoln and London: University of Nebraska Press, 2001).

Lebas, Catherine, and Annie Jacques, *La Coiffure en France du moyen age à nos jours* (Paris: Delmas International, 1979).

Lee, Gypsy Rose, *Gypsy: Memoirs of America's Most Celebrated Stripper* (Berkeley: Frog, 1957).

Levy, Ariel, *Female Chauvinist Pigs: Women and the Rise of Raunch Culture* (London: Pocket Books, 2006).

Liepe-Levinson, Katherine, *Strip Show: Performances of Gender and Desire* (London and New York: Routledge, 2002).

Linton, Elizabeth Lynn, *Modern Women and What is Said of Them* (New York: Redfield Publishers, 1868).

Liotta, Matthew A., *The Unborn Child* (New York: Liotta, 1931).

Lippard, Lucy R., *Get the Message? A Decade of Art for Social Change* (New York: E.P. Dutton, 1984).

Lippard, Lucy R., *From the Center: Feminist Essays on Women's Art* (Toronto and Vancouver: Clarke, Irwin and Co., 1976).

Lipton, Eunice, *Alias Olympia: A Woman's Search for Manet's Notorious Model and Her Own Desire* (Ithaca and London: Cornell University Press, 1992).

Logan, Olive, *Apropros of Women and Theatres*, (New York: Carleton, 1869).

Luker, Kristin, *Abortion and the Politics of Motherhood* (Berkeley, Los Angeles and London: University of California Press, 1984).

MacKinnon, Catherine, *Only Words* (Cambridge, MA: Harvard University Press, 1993).

McDonald, Helen, *Erotic Ambiguities: The Female Nude in Art* (London and New York: Routledge, 2001).

Mernissi, Fatima, *Women's Rebellion and Islamic Memory* (London: Zed Books, 1996).

Miller, Daniel, *A Theory of Shopping* (New York: Cornell University Press, 1998).

Mills, C. Wright, *The Power Elite* (Oxford, London and New York: Oxford University Press, 1956).

Minh-Ha, Trinh T., *Woman, Native, Other: Writing Postcoloniality and Feminism* (Bloomington: Indiana University Press, 1989).

Minsky, Morton, and Milt Machlin, *Minsky's Burlesque: A Fast and Funny Look at America's Bawdiest Era* (New York: Arbor House, 1986).

Moghissi, Haideh, *Feminism and Islamic Fundamentalism: The Limits of Postmodern Analysis* (London and New York: Zed Books, 1999).

Nead, Lynda, *The Female Nude: Art, Obscenity and Sexuality* (London and New York: Routledge, 1992).

Nochlin, Linda, *The Politics of Vision: Essays on Nineteenth-Century Art and Society* (London: Thames and Hudson, 1991).

O'Neill, Maggie, *Prostitution and Feminism: Towards a Politics of Feeling* (Cambridge and Oxford: Polity, 2001).

Paglia, Camille, *Sex, Art, and American Culture* (New York: Vintage Books, 1992).

Peiss, Kathy, *Hope in a Jar: The Making of America's Beauty Culture* (New York: Metropolitan Books, Henry Holt and Co., 1998).

Peiss, Kathy, *Cheap Amusements: Working Women and Leisure in Turn-of-the-Century New York* (Philadelphia: Temple University Press 1986).

Phillips, Melanie, *The Ascent of Women: A History of the Suffragette Movement and the Ideas Behind It* (London: Abacus, 2003).

Pollock, Griselda, *Old Mistresses: Women, Art and Ideology* (London: Routledge and Kegan Paul, 1981).

Preminger, Erik Lee, *Gypsy and Me: At Home and On the Road with Gypsy Rose Lee* (London: André Deutsch, 1985).

Rand, Erica, *Barbie's Queen Accessories* (Durham and London: Duke University Press, 1995).

Réage, Pauline, *Story of O* (London: Corgi Books, 1972).

Riley, Denise, *'Am I That Name?' Feminism and the Category of 'Women' in History* (Houndmills and London: Macmillan, 1988).

Roiphe, Katie, *The Morning After: Sex, Fear and Feminism* (Boston: Little Brown & Co., 1993).

Rosen, Ruth, *The Lost Sisterhood: Prostitution in America, 1900–1918* (Baltimore: John Hopkins University Press, 1982).

Rosenthal, Margaret, F., *The Honest Courtesan: Veronica Franco, Citizen and Writer in Sixteenth-Century Venice* (Chicago: University of Chicago Press, 1992).

Roth, Moira, *The Amazing Decade: Women and Performance Art in America 1970–1980* (Los Angeles: Astro Artz, 1983).

Rothbard, Murray N. *America's Great Depression* (Kansas City, MO: Sheed and Ward, 1975).

Rowe, Dorothy, *Representing Berlin: Sexuality and the City in Imperial and Weimar Germany* (Aldershot: Ashgate, 2003).

Rubery, Jill (ed.), *Women and Recession* (London and New York: Routledge and Kegan Paul, 1988).

Sacher-Masoch, Leopold von, *Venus in Furs* (New York, Toronto and London: Penguin Classics, 2000).

SAMOIS, *Coming to Power: Writing and Graphics on Lesbian s/m* (Boston: Alyson Publication, 1987).

Saxton, Alexander, *The Rise and Fall of the White Republic: Class Politics and Mass Culture in Nineteenth-Century America* (London and New York: Verso, 1990).

Schneemann, Carolee, *Imaging Her Erotics* (Cambridge, MA, and London: MIT Press, 2003).

Schneemann, Carolee, *Cézanne She Was a Greater Painter* (New York: Tresspuss Press, 1975).

Schneider, Rebecca, *The Explicit Body in Performance* (London and New York: Routledge, 1997).

Shteir, Rachel, *Striptease: The Untold History of the Girlie Show* (Oxford and New York: Oxford University Press, 2004).

Sinclair, Andrew, *Prohibition: The Era of Excess* (London: Faber and Faber, 1962).

Smith, Sidonie, and Julia Watson (eds), *Interfaces: Women, Autobiography, Image, Performance* (Ann Arbor: University of Michigan Press, 2002).

Smith-Rosenberg, Carroll, *Disorderly Conduct: Visions of Gender in Victorian America* (New York and Oxford: Oxford University Press, 1985).

Sobel, Bernard, *Burleycue: The Underground History of Burlesque Days* (New York: Farrar and Rinehart, 1931).

Spence, Jo, *Putting Myself in the Picture: A Political, Personal and Photographic Autobiography* (London: Camden Press, 1986).

Stallybrass, Peter, and Allon White, *The Politics and Poetics of Transgression* (Ithaca: Cornell University Press, 1986).

Stansell, Christine, *City of Women: Sex and Class in New York 1789–1860* (Urbana and Chicago: University of Illinois Press, 1987).

Steele, Valerie, *Fetish: Fashion, Sex and Power* (New York and Oxford: Oxford University Press, 1996).

Stewart, Susan, *On Longing: Narratives of the Miniature, the Gigantic, the Souvenir, the Collection* (Durham: Dukes University Press, 1993).

Stuart, Andrea, *Showgirls* (London, Sydney, Auckland and Rosebank: Jonathan Cape, 1996).

Tolman, Deborah L., *Dilemmas of Desire: Teenage Girls Talk about Sexuality* (Cambridge and London: Harvard University Press, 2002).

Vance, Carole S. (ed.), *Pleasure and Danger: Exploring Female Sexuality* (Boston, MA, and London: Routledge and Kegan, 1984).

Von Teese, Dita, with Bronwyn Garrity, *Burlesque and the Art of the Teese/ Fetish and the Art of the Teese* (New York: Regan Books, 2006).

Weber, Max, *The Protestant Ethic and the Spirit of Capitalism* (London and New York: Routledge, 1992 [first published in 1904/5]).

Welldon, Estela V., *Mother, Madonna, Whore: The Idealization and Denigration of Motherhood* (London: Free Association Books, 1988).

Wilentz, Sean, *Chants Democratic: New York City and the Rise of the American Working Class, 1788–1850* (New York and London: Oxford University Press, 1984).

Williams, Linda, *Hard Core: Power, Pleasure and the 'Frenzy of the Visible'* (Berkeley, Los Angeles and London: University of California Press, 1996).

Wollstonecraft, Mary, *A Vindication of the Rights of Woman*, edited and with an introduction by Miriam Brody Kramnick (Harmondsworth: Penguin, 1982 [1792]).

Wolf, Naomi, *The Beauty Myth* (London: Vintage, 1991).

Yeager, Mary A., *Women in Business*, Vol. 1 (Cheltenham and Northampton, MA: Elgar Reference Collection, 1999).

Zeidman, Irving, *The American Burlesque Show* (New York: Hawthorn Books, 1967).

Zemon Davis, Natalie, *Society and Culture in Early Modern France* (London: Gerald Duckworth and Co., 1975).

Essays

Adams, Parveen, with Mark Cousins, 'The truth on assault', in Parveen Adams, *The Emptiness of the Image: Psychoanalysis and Sexual Differences* (London and New York: Routledge, 1996).

Beauvoir, Simone de, 'Must we burn Sade?', in Marquis De Sade, *The One Hundred and Twenty Days of Sodom* (London: Arrow Books, 1990 [1955]).

Blessing, Jennifer, 'The art(ifice) of striptease: Gypsy Rose Lee and the masquerade of nudity', in Lisa Rado (ed.), *Modernism, Gender, and Culture: A Cultural Studies Approach* (New York: Garland, 1997), pp.47–63.

Camart, Cécile, 'New burlesque or the veil of pretence', in Katharina Bosse, *New Burlesque* (New York: Distributed Art Publishers, 2003), pp.81–6.

Cixous, Hélène, 'The laugh of the Medusa', in Elaine Marks and Isabelle de Courtivron (eds), *New French Feminisms* (New York: Schocken Books, 1981).

Curry, Ramona, '*Goin' to Town* and beyond: Mae West, film censorship and the comedy of *un*marriage', in Kristine Brunovska Karnick and Henry Jenkins, *Classical Hollywood Comedy* (New York and London: Routledge, 1995).

Forte, Jeanie, 'Women's performance art: feminism and postmodernism', in Sue-Ellen Case (ed.), *Performing Feminisms: Feminist Critical Theory and Theatre* (Baltimore and London: John Hopkins University Press, 1990).

Fox-Genovese, Elizabeth, *Feminism Without Illusions: A Critique of Individualism* (Chapel Hill, NC: University of North Carolina Press, 1991).

Frueh, Joanna, 'Feminism', in Thomas H. Kocheiser (ed.), *Hannah Wilke: A Retrospective* (Columbia: University of Missouri Press, 1989), pp.41–9.

Green, William, 'Strippers and coochers – the quintessence of American burlesque', in David Mayer and Kenneth Richards (eds), *Western Popular Theatre* (London: Methuen and Co., 1977), pp.157–68.

hooks, bell, 'The oppositional gaze: black female spectators' in Jones, Amelia (ed.), *The Feminism and Visual Culture Reader* (London: Routledge, 2003), pp.94–105.

Humphries, Jane, 'Women's unemployment in restructuring America: The changing experience of women in three recessions', in Rubery, Jill (ed.), *Women and Recession* (London and New York: Routledge and Kegan Paul, 1988), pp.15–47.

Isaak, Jo Anna, 'In praise of primary narcissism: the last laughs of Jo Spence and Hannah Wilke' in Smith and Watson (eds): *Interfaces*, p.54.

Jones, Amelia, 'Interpreting feminist bodies', in Paul Duro, *The Rhetoric of the Frame* (Cambridge, New York and Melbourne: Cambridge University Press, 1996), pp.223–41.

Krzywinska, Tanya, 'Cicciolina and the dynamics of transgression and abjection in explicit sex films', in Michele Aaron, *The Body's Perilous Pleasures: Dangerous Desires and Contemporary Culture* (Edinburgh: Edinburgh University Press, 1999), pp.188–209.

Marx, Karl, 'From the Paris notebooks [self-estrangement]', in Joseph O' Malley with Richard A. Davis (ed. and trans.) *Early Political Writings* (Cambridge, New York and Melbourne: Cambridge University Press, 1994), pp.71–78.

McRobbie, Angela and Jenny Garber, 'Girls and subcultures', in Stuart Hall and Tony Jefferson (eds), *Resistance Through Rituals* (London, Melbourne, Sidney and Auckland: Open University Hutchinson University Library, 1976), pp.209–22.

Munford, Joanne, 'Wake up and smell the lipgloss', in Stacy Gillis, Gillian Howie and Rebecca Munford, *Third Wave Feminism: A Critical Exploration* (Houndsmill: Palgrave Macmillan, 2004), pp.142–53.

Paglia, Camille, 'The beautiful decadence of Robert Mapplethorpe: a response to Rochelle Gurstein', in Camille Paglia, *Sex, Art, and American Culture: Essays* (New York: Vintage Books, 1992).

Patterson, Cynthia, and Bari J. Watkins, 'Rites and rights', in Helen Krich Chinoy and Linda Walsh Jenkins (eds), *Women in American Theatre* (New York: Theatre Communications Group, 1987), pp.29–33.

Reed, Jennifer, 'Roseanne: a "killer bitch" for Generation X', in Leslie Heywood and Jennifer Drake (eds), *Third Wave Agenda: Being Feminist, Doing Feminism* (Minneapolis and London: University of Minnesota Press, 1997), pp.122–33.

Rubin, Gayle, 'Thinking sex: notes for a radical theory of the politics of sexuality', in Carole S. Vance (ed.), *Pleasure and Danger: Exploring Female Sexuality* (Boston, MA, and London: Routledge and Kegan, 1984), pp. 267–319.

Russo, Mary, 'Female grotesques', in Teresa De Lauretis (ed.), *Feminist Studies, Critical Studies* (Bloomington: Indiana University Press, 1986), pp.213–29.

Silverman, Kaja, 'Fragments of a fashionable discourse', in Shari Benstock and Suzanne Ferriss (eds), *On Fashion* (New Brunswick, NJ: Rutgers University Press, 1994), pp. 183–96.

Sorisio, Carolyn, 'A tale of two feminisms: power and victimization in contemporary feminist debate', in Leslie Heywood and Jennifer Drake (eds): *Third Wave Agenda*, pp.134–49.

Underdown, D.E., 'The taming of the scold: The enforcement of patriarchal authority in early modern Europe', in Anthony Fletcher and John Stevenson (eds) *Order and Disorder in Early Modern England* (London, New York, New Rochelle, Melbourne and Sydney: Cambridge University Press, 1985), pp. 116–17.

Waldby, Catherine, 'Destruction: boundary erotics and refigurations of the heterosexual male body', in Elizabeth Grosz and Elspeth Probyn (eds), *Sexy Bodies: The Strange Carnalities of Feminism* (London and New York: Routledge, 1995), pp.266–77.

Watson, Helen, 'Women and the veil: personal responses to global process', in Akbar Ahmed and Hastings Donnan (eds), *Islam, Globalization and Postmodernity* (London and New York: Routledge, 1994), pp.141–59.

Journals, magazines, newspapers

Akbar, Arifa, 'Only one British female in four calls herself a feminist', *The Independent*, 8 March 2006.

Bakewell, Joan, 'Where have all the feminists gone?', *Daily Mail*, 28 March 2006.

Barton, Laura, 'I could've been a lawyer. But I've taken the easiest, quickest route to making as much money as I can', *G2* supplement, *Guardian*, 25 January 2006.

Bloomer, Amelia, 'Editorial', *The Lily* iv/8 (August, 1852), p.71.

Buonfino, Alessandra, and Geoff Mulgan, 'Goodbye to all that', *Society Guardian*, 18 January 2006, pp.1–2.

Buszek, Maria-Elena, 'Representing "awarishness": burlesque, feminist transgression, and the 19th-century pin-up', *Drama Review* xliii/4 (T164) (winter 1999), pp.141–62.

Chaumont, Magdeleine, 'Les élégances: confidences', *Comoedia*, 17 June 1925.

Crandall, C.H., 'What men think of women's dress', *North American Review* 161 (August 1895), pp.251–4.

Curry, Ramona, 'Mae West as censored commodity: the case of Klondike Annie', *Cinema Journal* 31 (fall 1991), pp.211–37.

Curtis, Nick, 'Blaize of glory', *Evening Standard* (London), 21 April 2005.

Dolan, Jill, 'Images of women and sexuality in burlesque comedy', *Journal of Popular Culture* xviii (1984), pp. 37–47.

Ford, Richard, 'Mother wins fight for new law against violent porn on the net', *The Times*, 31 August 2006.

Fuchs, Elinor, 'Staging the obscene body', *Drama Review* xxxiii (1989), pp. 33–58.

Hall, Jacqueline Dowd, 'Disorderly women: gender and labor militancy in the Appalachian South', *Journal of American History* lxxiii (1986–7), pp.354–82.

Hanna, Judith Lynne, 'Undressing the First Amendment and corsetting the striptease dancer', *Drama Review* xlii/2 (T158) (summer 1998), pp. 38–69.

Lowthorpe, Rebecca, 'Dita goes couture', *Elle* (UK edition), November 2005, p. 226–33.

Mackenzie, Suzie, 'Under the skin', *Guardian Weekend*, 22 October 2005, pp. 38–45.

Manchester No Borders Group, *Hate Mail: Immigration Special 2005*, March 2005.

Mulvey, Laura, 'Visual pleasure and narrative cinema', *Screen* xvi (autumn 1975), p. 30.

Phillips, Angela, 'The rise and fall of silent girly-girls in G-strings', *Times Higher*, 14 July 2006.

Root, Jane, 'Distributing *A Question of Silence*', *Screen* xxvi/6 (1985), pp.58–64.

Rowe, Kathleen, 'Roseanne: unruly woman as domestic goddess', *Screen* xxxi/4 (winter 1990), pp. 408–19.

Shteir, Rachel, 'Stormy weather: how a climate of rebellion, in theatre and society, wrought the death of burlesque in 1969', *American Theatre*, xx/4 (April 2003), pp. 28–31.

Straayer, Chris, 'The she-man: postmodern bi-sexed performance in film and video', *Screen* xxxi/3 (autumn 1990), pp.262–80.

Tickner, Lisa, 'The body politic: female sexuality and women artists since 1970', *Art History* i/2 (June 1978), pp. 236–31.

Turner, Janice, 'Dirty young men', *Guardian Weekend*, 22 October 2005, pp. 28–35.

Walker, Sharon, 'Confessions of a Botox junkie', *Harpers & Queen*, January 2006.

Walsh, Margaret, 'Gendered endeavours: women and the reshaping of business culture', *Women's History Review* xiv/2 (2005), pp. 181–201.

Weene, Seph, 'Venus', *Heresies* iii/4 (1981), pp. 36–8.

Wilson, Graeme, 'Labour anger at £7,700 for Cherie's election hairdos', *Daily Telegraph*, 21 April 2006.

Unpublished papers

Banks, James Richard Blundell, and James P. Smith, 'Financial wealth inequality in the United States and Great Britain' (academic paper for Institute for Fiscal Studies and University College, London, RAND), 1 February 2001.

Cook, Roger, 'Transversalities: crossing disciplines, cultures and identities' presented at conference at Reading University, 16–18 September 2005.

Remes Outi, 'The role of confession in late twentieth-century British art', Ph.D. thesis (Reading: University of Reading 2005).

Bibliography

Vogt, Julie, 'The Queen Ann brand of burlesque', paper given on the 'Critical Displacements' panel at the Women and Theatre's 26th annual conference, sponsored by Columbia College Chicago Art and Design Department and the Institute for the Study of Women and Gender in the Arts and Media, 1–2 August 2006.

Websites

Akhtar, Rajnaara, 'Blaming the veil is wrong', at *http://commentisfree.guardian.co.uk/rajnaara_akhtar/2006/10/jack_straw_misses_the_point.html* (posted 6 October 2006; accessed 19 October 2006).

Allen, Woody, 'The Purple Rose of Cairo', at http://en.wikipedia.org/wiki/The_Purple_Rose_of_Cairo (last modified 19 December 2005; accessed 2 January 2006).

BBC News: Arts, 'Ursula Martinez's naked ambition', at http://new.bbc.co.uk/1/hi/entertainment/art/1492345.stm (posted 15 August 2001; accessed 8 March 2003).

Bradford DeLong, J., 'Slouching towards utopia? The economic history of the twentieth century: XIV, The great crash and the great slump', University of California at Berkeley and National Bureau of Economic Research, February 1997, at www.j-bradford-delong.net/TCEH/Slouch_Crawsh14.html (posted 2 March 1997; accessed 5 August 2006).

Brooke, Stephen, 'A new world for women? Abortion law reform in Britain during the 1930s', *American Historical Review* cvi/2 (April 2001), at *www.historcooperative.org/journals/ahr/106.2/ah000431.html* (accessed 14 November 2005).

Buszek, Maria, 'Of Varga Girls and Riot Girls: the Varga Girl and WWII in the pin-up's feminist history', in *Alberto Vargas: The Esquire Pinups*, Spencer Museum of Art, University of Kansas, exhibition curated by Maria-Elena Buszek and Stephen Goddard, 29 September–30 December 2001), at *www.ku.edu/~sma/vargas/buszek.htm* (accessed 18 May 2005).

'Coney Island Circus Sideshow', at *www.coneyisland.com/sideshow.shtml* (accessed 26 August 2006).

Edwards, Tanya L., 'Christina, Gwen Stefani, Dita Von Teese: help bring back burlesque', at *www.mtv.com/news/articles/1458472/20021104/story.jhtml* (posted 11 April 2002; accessed 14 November 2005).

Gibson, Kevin, 'Rant: the benefits of feminism', Fashion & Lifestyle, at *www.askmen.com/fashion/austin_100/120_fashion_style.html* (accessed 25 June 2005).

'International Women's Day 2006', at *www.womankind.org.uk/iwd-06.html* (accessed 10 July 2006).

King, Jo, at *www.danceworks.net/JoKing.asp* (accessed 30 July 2006).

Lee, Susan, 'Goodness had everything to do with it', *New York Times*, 27 May 1984, at *query.nytimes.com/gst/fullpage.html* (accessed 6 August 2006).

Lola the Vamp, 'Burlesque: a short history of burlesque by Lola the Vamp', at *www.lolathevamp.net/burlesque.htm* (accessed 9 February 2007).

'Lone parent benefit – the end of Blair's honeymoon', at *www.socialistaction. org.uk/archive/98womenlone.htm* (posted February 1998; accessed 18 August 2006).

'Midnight's Carnival', at *www.glastonburyfestivals.co.uk/performance/index. asp?id=247* (accessed 27 July 2006).

Ministry of Burlesque, at *www.ministryofburlesque.com/community/what-is-burlesque.php* (accessed 27 July 2006).

Namakydoust, Azadeh, 'Covered in messages: the veil as a political tool', *The Iranian*, 8 May 2003, at *www.iranian.com/Women/2003/May/Veil/p.html* (accessed 26 August 2006).

Nixon, Laura, 'Suicide girls', at *http://suicidegirls.com/words/Dita+von+Teese +by+Laura+Nixon/* (accessed 23 June 2005).

Nygaard, Sandra, 'Bawdy beautiful: new burlesque shakes up San Francisco', at *http:sfgate.com/cgi-bin/article.cgi?file=/g/archive/2003/11/07/burlesquesf. DTL* (posted 7 November 2003; accessed 27 July 2007).

Perkins, Anne, 'Labour's benefits revolts', at *http//politics.guardian.co.uk/ Westminster/story/0,,461947,00,html* (posted 11 December 1997; accessed 20 August 2006).

Plant, Sheryl, 'Grazia Magazine', at *www.thefword.org.uk/reviews/2005/06/ grazia_magazine* (posted 17 June 2005; accessed 30 December 2005).

'Pornography', at *www.bbc.co.uk/dna/h2g2/pda/A679016?s_id* (accessed 20 August 2006).

Shaw, Mary, Roy Maxwell and Debbie Lawlor, blurb for 'Cloudy concepts: estimating the number of teenage mothers in England', for the British Society for Population Studies Annual Conference in Bristol (11 September 2003), at *www.lse.ac.uk/collections/BSPS/annualConference/2003/fertility11Sept9am.htm* (accessed 20 December 2005).

Walter, Natasha, 'When the veil means freedom', *Guardian*, 20 January 2004, at *http://education.guardian.co.uk/schoolsworldwide/story/0,14062,1127014,00.html* (accessed 5 January 2006).

Wilson, Bruce, 'Muslim student wins scarf appeal', *American Renaissance*, at *www.amren.com/mtnews/archives/2005/03/muslim_student.php* (posted 3 March 2005; accessed 12 January 2006).

World Famous *BOB*, at *www.worldfamousbob.com/html/diary.htm* (accessed 28 July 2006).

Index

A

abortion, 42
Adams, Parveen
  with Mark Cousins in *The Emptiness of the Image* (1996), 98
Ahmed, Leila, 132, 168
Allen, Lily, 178, 180
Allen, Robert C.
  Horrible Prettiness (1991), 6
  'horrible prettiness', 12, 38
ambivalence, 15, 104, 117
artificiality, 39, 111, 156
  Dita Von Teese, 114, 118
  liberation, 112, 118
  performance of the self, 112, 146, 147
  'Prettiness', 76, 112, 113, 119
artiste, 50, 64, 65, 66
  artist–artiste, 50, 64, 66, 68, 172, 177, 182, 187
  Carolee Schneemann, 68
  Dita Von Teese, 2, 3, 18, 144, 171
  'low', the, 3, 36, 172
  new burlesque, 4, 5, 14, 18, 107, 145, 146, 177
  prostitution, 66, 91
  strippers, 2
  traditional burlesque, 34, 153
awarishness, 45, 167, 175

B

Baldwin, Michelle
  Burlesque [and the New Bump 'n' Grind] (2004), 4, 131
Barbie, 114
Barr, Roseanne, 164
Berger, John
  Ways of Seeing (1972), 74, 75
Blaize, Immodesty, 3, 15, 24, 146, 148, 156, 179
  Immodesty Blaize and Walter's Burlesque, 24
  'Reverse Strip', 182
boom and bust, 12, 19, 25, 79
  burlesque boom, 3, 5, 14, 19, 46, 120, 167
  dot.com boom, 25
  economic boom and burlesque, 20, 79
Bosse, Katharina
  New Burlesque (2003), 4, 107
Botox, 117, 118, 179

Bowery girls (gals), 54, 81, 102
British Blondes, 22, 38, 89, 90, 111, 113
   cultural phenomenon, 18, 20, 21, 24, 41, 111
   Ixion, The Forty Thieves and Sinbad, 27
   legs, 134, 153
   Lydia Thompson, 23, 88, 160
   morality, 88, 159, 160
   physical standard, 86
   public speaking, 157, 163
burqa, 129
Buzsek, Maria, 72

c

café concerts (*café conc*), 44, 159
capitalism, 30, 79, 83, 84, 165, 166
   boom and bust, 19
   consumer capitalism, 105
   feminism, 165, 168
   Max Weber's *The Protestant Ethic and the Spirit of Capitalism* (1904/5), 30
   metropolitan industrial capitalism, 30, 95, 100
   patriarchy, 42, 55
carnival, 26, 154, 155, 164
Chicago, Judy, *The Dinner Party* (1974–9), 54, 196
Christianity, 131
Cinderella, 114, 115
circus, 4, 153, 154, 155, 207
Clark, Kenneth, 49, 50
class, 132, 167, 168, 172, 174, 180, 182
   bourgeois, 30, 156, 159, 160, 165, 167
      'bourgeoisification', 19, 30; and excess, 26; feminism, 36; low crossing into high, 41; and perks of power, 27, 28, 38, 64, 80, 81, 100; and prostitution, 67; respectability, 66, 113, 134; transgressing bourgeois sexual behaviour, 43, 70, 129

consumer capitalism, 105
   middle-class, 5, 20, 28, 32, 33, 44, 74
      cult of celebrity, 41; and depression, 30, 38, 82; and femininity, 6, 7; and feminism, 6, 10, 75, 83, 160, 161, 163, 166, 168; and the 'low', 106; motherhood, 84, 93; and public domain, 67; and respectability, 34, 97, 155; shopping, 123; and theatre, 12, 25, 29, 95, 96; transgressive sexual conventions, 40, 43, 158, 159, 186
   nouveau riche, 14, 31, 185
   ruling class, 26, 33, 64, 107, 159
   undermining hierarchy, 6, 18, 21, 37, 70, 112, 131
   working-class, 39, 167, 171, 185
      brash speech, 128, 159; and the female body, 63; money, 82; and morality, 50; new arrivals, 6, 31; and the public domain, 81, 104; prostitution, 50, 67, 101; resistance, 134, 163; sexual behaviour, 40; sexual spectacle, 8; stigma, 43; theatres, 99; traditional burlesque, 32
Claudel, Camille, 64
clitoridectomy, 43
commedia dell'arte, 155, 156
competition, 169, 170
contradiction, 9, 11, 62, 76, 129, 130, 136, 172, 173
cosmetic surgery, 113
courtesan, 101, 106, 179
   Dita Von Teese, 108, 148, 157
   and fashion, 133
   new burlesque, 46
   nineteenth-century, 14, 67
   and sexual allure, 147, 186
   and wealth, 107, 185

D

Davis, Natalie Zemon, 38
De Beauvoir, Simone, *The Second Sex* (1949), 52, 111, 112, 116, 184
democracy, 14, 28, 126, 127, 129, 131
depression, 25, 120
    bingeing and repression, 12, 19, 151
    Black Thursday, 25
    cheap entertainment, 23, 26
    fractured masculinity, 89
    Great Depression (1929–36), 18, 19, 25, 42, 82, 120, 121
    Long Depression (1873 to mid 1890s), 18, 19, 25
    middle-class, 30
    money, 80, 100;
    uncontained female sexuality, 43, 96;
    Wall Street Crash, 25
desire, 74, 130, 177
    and containment, 8
    feminist re-imaging of female sexual desire, 54, 56, 65, 67, 68
    female sexual agency, 178
    heterosexuality, 47
    indecency, 64, 69
    new burlesque, 172, 187
    objects of desire, 5, 75, 115, 137, 138, 145, 146, 164
    pornography, 51
    and power, 51, 77, 143
    shopping, 123
    unruly woman, 38
Deville, Kitten, 35
diamonds, 34, 121, 123, 124, 140, 204
Dirty Martini, 95, 179
displeasure, 46, 47, 54, 76, 176, 180
Dworkin, Andrea, 54, 71, 98

E

Elizabethton rayon plant strike (1929), 167, 168
Emin, Tracey, 5

empowerment, 10, 180
    the burlesque body, 6
    feminism, 19, 14, 32, 84
    paradox, 12, 60, 76, 100, 117, 118
    sexual spectacle, 5, 171
    sexuality, 145
erotica, 130
erotic dance, 4. 97, 99, 138
essentialism, 57

F

Faludi, Susan, *The Undeclared War Against Feminism* (1991), 9
fashion
    1950s retro-look, 121,178
    bondage, 131, 153, 149
    Botox, 117, 179
    the bra, 135, 136, 144
    'cage-crinoline', 178
    celebrity, 3, 7, 34, 90, 96, 102
    the corset
        anti-corset campaigners, 134, 136; Dita Von Teese, 35, 114, 118, 135, 144; fetish, 145; the Gibson Girl, 32; 'Grecian bend', 41; self-determination, 178
    Goths, 156
    Gothic Lolitas, 33
    Grecian Bend, 41, 161
    the New Look, 121
    piercing, 33
    prostitution, 45
    punk, 33, 118, 144, 156
    tattoos, 33, 108, 150, 156
female body, the, 76, 183
    class, 50
    containment, 42
    feminism, 12, 57
    male gaze, 3
    new burlesque, 36
    the nude tradition, 51
    and performance art, 58, 61, 62, 63, 75, 138
    and prostitution, 64, 65, 67, 101

female body, the *(cont.)*
  and public display, 5
  and representation, 11, 56
  unruly sexuality, 66
femininity, 44, 63, 65, 77, 86, 88,
    136, 145, 175
  and beauty, 115, 139, 144
  and business, 88, 89, 91, 106
  ideal 'pure' womanhood, 6, 7,
    121, 134
  and masquerade, 82
  new burlesque,135, 138, 150,
    180
    camp, 177; Dita Von Teese,
    124, 148, 179; erotic rebellion,
    178; and glamour, 4, 107;
    Immodesty Blaize, 140; power
    and pleasure, 17, 37; retro
    femininity, 108; sexual
    agency, 124
  seductive powers, 12, 73, 74
  sexualized femininity, 39, 40, 137
  traditional burlesque, 13, 38, 41,
    119, 127, 160, 171, 186
  and veiling/unveiling, 133, 183
fetish, 35, 36, 96, 118, 144, 145,
    146, 147, 148
Finley, Karen, 59
Firestone, Shulamith, 74
freedom, 126, 151
  of expression, 129, 136, 134,
    136, 178, 181, 182
  public domain, 12, 31, 43, 65,
    161, 167, 174
  sexuality, 14, 35, 36, 39, 145,
    149, 178
  veiling/unveiling, 129, 131, 133
Friedan, Betty, *The Feminine
    Mystique* (1963), 7
Frueh, Joanna, 70, 138

G
gaze, 49
  contemporary feminism, 5, 11
  female gaze, 62, 77, 140
  female sexuality, 51, 70

fille publique, 45
  judgment, 74, 75, 150
  male gaze, 3, 56, 61, 62, 138,
    147, 148
  prostitution, 44, 45, 65–8, 175
  Ursula Martinez, 36, 37
gender, 19, 104, 131, 156
  burlesque body, 6
  and business, 77, 80, 82, 85, 86,
    87, 89, 91
  consumer culture, 7
  the female nude, 50
  feminism, 12
  gender ideals, 115, 116
  new burlesque, 36, 37, 138, 180
  nineteenth-century, 31, 64
  performance art, 60
  post-feminism, 83
  public domain, 103
  sexual allure, 8
  sexuality, 76, 136, 137, 174
  traditional burlesque, 18, 21, 23,
    27, 34, 39, 41, 105
'gifts', 101, 102, 104
Girl of the Period, 44
girl power, 9, 39, 52, 166
Giuliani, Rudolph (Mayor), 95, 96,
    99
Goldman, Emma ('Red Emma'), 167
greed, 20, 31, 94, 102, 122, 166
Greer, Germaine, 39, 163

H
Hanna, Judith Lynne, 11, 97
hijab, 14, 126, 131, 168, 169, 183
Hill, Jenny ('Vital Spark'), 159
Hilton, Paris, 149, 176
honky tonk, 19, 29, 30, 96, 154
'horrible prettiness', 12, 38
Howells, William Dean, 38, 39
humour
  beauty, 116
  British Blondes, 86, 127, 159
  feminism, 70, 72, 136, 163
  Gypsy Rose Lee, 32, 148
  honky tonk, 29

humour *(cont.)*
  Mae West, 23
  new burlesque, 37, 131, 140,
    146, 150, 175, 179, 187
  and the third wave, 9

I
immigration, 19, 20, 28, 29, 30, 38,
  80, 126, 167
individualism, 10, 83, 166, 168
industrialization, 20
intelligence, 3, 21, 32, 75, 87, 176

J
Jones, Amelia, 51, 60, 63

K
King, Jo, 4
knowingness, 140, 148
Kristeva, Julia
  Powers of Horror (1982), 59

L
lads' mags, 93, 101, 102, 105
Lee, Gypsy Rose, 4, 22, 80, 130,
    137, 157, 186
  'A Stripteaser's Education', 32
  business, 86, 90, 94
  courtesan, 106
  the depression, 96
  direct address, 21, 128
  Dita Von Teese, 34, 171
  feminism, 161
  humour, 148
  moving into the mainstream,
    18
  pastiche/parody, 179
  sexual allure, 178
  working-class, 33
'leg business', 18
  femininity, 77
  and the freak, 152
  morality, 96
  need for escape, 89
  publicity, 13
Levy, Ariel, 149, 176, 177

Liepe-Levinson, Katherine, 11, 138,
  190
Lippard, Lucy, 157, 158, 197
Lola the Vamp, 15, 145, 146, 147,
  148, 182

M
MacKinnon, Catharine, 54, 98
Madonna, 55, 87, 88, 94, 144, 145
Manet, Édouard
  Olympia (1863), 63, 65, 195
Mapplethorpe, Robert
  Man in Polyester Suit (1980), 66
Markham, Pauline, 8, 21, 91
Martinez, Ursula, 1, 2, 36, 37, 142,
  172, 174, 175, 179, 187
Menken, Adah Isaacs, 'The Naked
  Lady', 24, 41
Mernissi, Fatima, 131, 168
Merritt, Natacha, 60, 61, 62
Minsky Burlesque, 90, 99
Mistinguett, 157
money, 1, 13, 30, 69, 82
  celebrity, 35
  female independence, 30, 31, 80,
    106, 124, 176, 185
  new burlesque, 96, 172
  sex, 63, 94, 97
  sexual relationships, 122
  traditional burlesque, 27
motherhood, 6, 42, 58, 79, 93, 94,
  122
Mowlam, Mo, 163
Mulvey, Laura, 3, 59
music hall, 65, 108, 159
Muslim, 19, 129, 133
  feminism, 168
  Muslim community, 169
  Muslim traditions, 131
  veiling, 126, 132, 184
Muz, Julie Atlas, 3, 131
nakedness, 36, 37, 49, 50, 100, 129,
  131, 139, 168, 184
Nead, Lynda, 50, 139, 140
'New Woman', 161
Nude, the, 64, 65

Nude, the *(cont.)*
  containment, 47, 50, 59
  performance art, 61, 70, 73, 75, 138
  pornography, 51, 179
  objecthood, 61, 74, 77, 112, 144, 145, 147, 187

O
Olympia, Manet, 63, 65

P
Page, Bettie, 148, 149, 180
Paglia, Camille, 13, 36, 166
  Madonna, 87, 88, 94
  Olympia, 66
  pornography and prostitution, 55
  victimization, 83
  woman as sex object, 10
Paradox, 62, 64, 72, 82, 146
Phillips, Angela, 93, 176
Pin-up, 183
  Bettie Page, 148
  new burlesque, 17, 34, 35, 46, 124
  performance art, 72, 73, 75
  traditional burlesque, 45, 140
pleasure, 1, 2, 106, 155, 185
  and displeasure, 14, 46, 47, 54, 76, 117, 176
  the female body, 11
  female-generated pleasures, 186
  feminism, 83, 93, 174, 180
    and empowerment, 6; sexual agency, 13, 15; displeasure, 54; stereotypes, 75, male, 3; power, 10, 166; S/M, 55; and danger, 63, 122; shopping, 123; re-image erotic pleasure, 125; the tease, 139; lust, 177; traditional burlesque, 167
  resistance, 23
  parody, 46, 130
  performance art, 58, 59, 62, 65,

67, 69, 70, 73
  procreation and public policy, 42, 44
  new burlesque
    body-as-object, 107; Dita Von Teese, 171; erotic pleasures, 46, 172; femininity, 17, 138; forbidden fun, 135; Immodesty Blaize, 140; Lola the Vamp, 145, 146. 147; pleasure as revolt, 156, 181; sexualized display, 35; Ursula Martinez, 36, 37
  objecthood, 74
  and resistance, 178
  submissive pleasure, 148, 150
Pollock, Griselda, 7
pornography, 95, 98, 99, 104,184
  Andrea Dworkin, 54
  Camille Paglia, 55
  and erotica, 130, 182
  the nude, 51
post(-)feminism, 175
  postfeminism, 9, 11, 15, 56, 173, 174
  post-feminism, 6, 7, 8, 9, 53, 173, 174
  prefeminism, 17, 145
  pre-feminism, 7, 70, 121, 137, 180
power
  (*see also* empowerment)
  business, 82
  capital, 26
  class, 28
  desire, 51
  direct address, 158
  disempowerment, 2, 62, 104
  feminine, 108, 157
  'girl power', 9, 39
  humour, 148
  patriarchial–capitalist, 13, 15, 57, 81, 164, 167, 185, 187
  power dressing, 2, 86
  power play, 147
  publicity, 89, 90

power *(cont.)*
  sexual, 131, 139, 143, 178, 185
  sexual display, 5, 35, 38, 40, 52,
    96, 106
  spectacle, 53
  spectatorial, 37
  subject power, 186
  unruliness, 33
prettiness, 70, 73, 77, 87, 88, 121,
  125, 169, 172, 173
  'horrible prettiness', 12, 38
procreation, 44, 106
prostitution, 13, 43, 95, 130, 184,
  185
  Annie Sprinkle, 59
  artiste, 66
  femininity and business, 77, 89,
    91
  feminism, 55, 81
  power, 14
  public display, 64, 65, 104

Q
qaid, 131, 168, 169

R
representation, 3, 83
  collusion, 73, 74, 76, 179, 187
  dominant representational
    system, 3, 54, 56, 60, 61, 72
  female pleasures, 11
  feminism, 58, 100, 125
  pornography, 45, 50, 69, 98
respectability, 34, 36, 66, 97, 113,
  127, 153, 169, 183

S
sadomasochism (S/M), 55, 143
Saville, Jenny, 60, 117,
Schneemann, Carolee
  Interior Scroll (1975), 58
  Fuses (1964–7), 63, 68, 70
  Site [with Robert Morris] (1964),
    63–8
Schneider, Rebecca, 56, 100

second-wave feminism, 8, 9, 63, 69,
  121, 160
  'bra-burning feminist', 136
  consciousness-raising groups,
    57, 72, 162
  Shulamith Firestone, 74
  Vivian Gornick, and Barbara R.
    Moran, *Woman in Sexist Society*
    (1971), 73
  WITCH (Women's International
    Terrorist Conspiracy from
    Hell), 72
seduction, 35, 63, 102, 106, 138,
  139, 185
selfishness, 165
sex, 29, 68, 69
  and 'gifts', 101, 102, 104
  marriage, 43
  money, 105, 106, 121
  prostitution, 66, 95, 97, 98, 99,
    103, 130
  sex appeal, 2, 3, 61, 62
    business, 92, 94; and power,
    52, 167; traditional burlesque,
    89, 163, 185
  sex delinquent, 33
  sex object
    beauty ideals, 115; clichéd
    stereotypes, 46; cosmetic
    procedures, 113, 114,
    117; empowerment, 3; erotic
    parody; 140; femininity,
    139; feminism, 5, 15, 36;
    feminine submission, 144;
    the Nude, 51; objectification,
    52, 54; performance art,
    72, 73; sexual agency, 72, 137,
    146; sex symbols, 119;
    Western world, 14
  sexism, 74, 136, 145
  STDs, 44
  teenage pregnancy, 44
sexuality
  business, 86, 93
  and the female nude, 50

sexuality *(cont.)*
  female pleasure, 17, 43, 58, 65, 70, 75
  femininity, 37, 88, 107, 137, 169, 179, 183
  heterosexuality, 47, 49, 147, 164
  lesbianism, 2, 37, 55, 67, 136, 170, 174–5
  new burlesque, 34, 35, 38, 90, 146, 182
  paradox, 52
  sexual agency, 124, 125, 126, 131, 132, 148, 151, 165, 177, 178
  sexual labelling, 44, 150, 170, 171, 180
  sexual roles, 19, 31, 53, 71, 80, 123, 156
  the sexual spectacle
    the British Blondes, 17, 91, 159; erotic pleasure, 172; glamour, 40; 'greater sexuality', 87; performance art, 56, 63; sexual property, 100, 184; Ursula Martinez, 36, 175, 187
    traditional burlesque, 21, 24, 27, 32, 39, 41, 45
shopping, 122, 123
showgirl, 46, 107, 154, 159, 194
Shteir, Rachel, 11, 139, 140, 159
smile, 126
  Bettie Page, 180
  Betty Friedan, *The Feminine Mystique* (1963), 7
  new burlesque, 4, 36, 37, 38, 140, 163, 148, 172, 179, 187
  pleasure–displeasure, 76
  traditional burlesque, 8, 33
soubrettes, 12, 23, 87
speakeasy, 19, 154
Spence, Jo, 61, 74
Sprinkle, Annie, 59

Stansell, Christine, 31, 81, 103, 167, 184, 191
Stehli, Jemima, 61
stereotypes
  business, 91
  feminism, 75, 121
  immigrants, 28, 167
  new burlesque, 46, 105, 150, 177, 178, 179
  performance art, 57
  resistance, 14
striptease, 4, 138, 139
  feminism, 140
  new burlesque, 1, 24, 34, 36, 146, 152, 154, 175
  traditional burlesque, 18, 21, 32
subcultures, 118, 137, 170

T
terrorism
  7 July, 2005, 20
  9/11, 19, 20
  burqa, 129
  WITCH, 72
Thompson, Lydia, 4, 21, 27, 94, 105, 152, 160, 186
  'awarishness', 45
  dangers, 121
  'horrible prettiness', 38
  humour, 159, 179
  'leg business', 89
  liberating models of female agency, 8
  morality, 22, 88, 91, 158
  pazazz, 139
  respectability, 34, 41
  sex symbol, 119
  violating gender norms, 23, 85
Tolman, Deborah L., 176, 177
Tough Girls, 45, 102

U
'ugliness', 57, 137, 152, 163, 164, 169
unruly woman, 33, 37, 38

V

veiling, 14, 126
  Islam, 126–9, 131
  Patriotic Women's League, 132
  Shabina Begun, 128–9
  unveiling, 66, 108, 127, 128, 129
Von Teese, Dita, 2, 18, 35, 41, 105,
    108, 146, 171, 186
  artificiality, 114, 136
  Burlesque and The Art of the Teese
    (2006), 156
  business, 94, 95, 128, 148
  celebrity, 35, 90, 124
  fetish, 118, 135, 147
  masochism, 143, 144
  pin-up, 46, 124, 145

W

war
  Afghan, 126
  American Civil War (1861–5),
    19, 26, 28, 112
  boom and bust, 12, 13, 19, 89,
    151
  First World War, 32
West, Mae, 21, 23, 33, 40, 42, 45, 96
White, Richard Grant, 39
Wilke, Hannah, 13, 58, 63, 70, 71,
    136, 179
  I, Object: Memoirs of a Sugar-giver
    (1977–8), 62
  S.O.S. Starification Series
    (1974–5), 73
  *Portrait of the Artist with her
    Mother, Selma Butter* (1978–
    81), 76
Wolf, Naomi
  The Beauty Myth (1990), 10, 13,
    55, 83, 166
Wollstonecraft, Mary
  *Vindication of the Rights of
    Woman* (1792), 52, 196
Womankind Worldwide, 5, 10
women's rights movement
  Elizabeth Cady Stanton, 53

  Lucretia Mott, 53
  Mary Richardson, , 54
  Seneca Falls Conventions, 53
  suffragettes, 19, 43, 158
  Woman's Party, 53
World Famous *BOB*, The, 137, 177

Z

Ziegfeld, 99